The Complete
Instant Pot
Cookbook for Beginners

2000+ Days of Easy and Delicious Recipes for Breakfast, Lunch, Dinner, Desserts, and Snacks—Effortless Meals for Every Part of Your Day

George K. Moran

Copyright© 2025 By George K. Moran

All rights reserved worldwide.

No part of this book may be reproduced or transmitted in any form or by any means, electronic or mechanical, including photo- copying, recording or by any information storage and retrieval system, without written permission from the publisher, except for the inclusion of brief quotations in a review.

Warning-Disclaimer

The purpose of this book is to educate and entertain. The author or publisher does not guarantee that anyone following the techniques, suggestions, tips, ideas, or strategies will become successful. The author and publisher shall have neither liability or responsibility to anyone with respect to any loss or damage caused, or alleged to be caused, directly or indirectly by the information contained in this book.

Table of Contents

INTRODUCTION / 4

Chapter 1   Breakfasts / 6

Chapter 2   Beef, Pork, and Lamb / 17

Chapter 3   Poultry / 30

Chapter 4   Fish and Seafood / 42

Chapter 5   Snacks and Appetizers / 53

Chapter 6   Stews and Soups / 63

Chapter 7   Vegetables and Sides / 78

Chapter 8   Desserts / 88

Appendix 1   Instant Pot Cooking Timetable / 102

Appendix 2   INDEX / 103

INTRODUCTION

Revolutionizing Everyday Cooking with the Instant Pot

The modern kitchen is full of gadgets, but few have transformed home cooking as dramatically as the Instant Pot. This all-in-one, multi-functional appliance has captured the hearts of home cooks around the world, and for good reason. With its ability to sauté, pressure cook, slow cook, steam, and more, the Instant Pot brings convenience, speed, and versatility to meal preparation like never before.

This cookbook is designed to help you unlock the full potential of your Instant Pot, turning it into your most trusted kitchen companion. Whether you're new to Instant Pot cooking or have been using it for years, you'll find a wealth of recipes, tips, and tricks that will inspire you to cook creatively and efficiently. Let's dive into the magic of the Instant Pot and discover why it has become such a beloved tool in kitchens everywhere.

Why the Instant Pot Is a Game-Changer?

What makes the Instant Pot stand out in a sea of kitchen appliances? It's the combination of its speed, efficiency, and ability to produce consistently delicious results. At its core, the Instant Pot is a pressure cooker, which means it cooks food much faster than traditional methods by using high-pressure steam. This not only reduces cooking time but also helps retain the flavors and nutrients in your food, resulting in healthier, more flavorful dishes.

But the Instant Pot goes beyond just pressure cooking. Its multiple functions mean you can use it to sauté vegetables, slow-cook soups, steam fish, or even bake a cake, all with one appliance. It's the ultimate tool for busy individuals and families who want to enjoy home-cooked meals without spending hours in the kitchen. With the Instant Pot, you can whip up everything from a simple breakfast to an elaborate dinner party feast, all with minimal effort.

Cooking with Confidence

One of the greatest benefits of using an Instant Pot is the confidence it brings to home cooking. Many people find the idea of using a pressure cooker intimidating, but the Instant Pot is designed to be user-friendly, with safety features that make it accessible to cooks of all skill levels. Whether you're a seasoned chef or a beginner, the Instant Pot offers an easy, reliable way to prepare a wide range of dishes.

The recipes in this cookbook are crafted to help you build confidence in the kitchen. We start with the basics, walking you through simple, straightforward dishes that require minimal ingredients and preparation. As you become more comfortable with the appliance, you can move on to more complex recipes that showcase the full range of what the Instant Pot can do. By the end of this book, you'll be ready to tackle any recipe with ease.

The Benefits of Instant Pot Cooking

The Instant Pot is more than just a convenient appliance; it's also a healthier way to cook. Traditional cooking methods often involve high temperatures, which can break down nutrients in your food. The Instant Pot, on the other hand, uses steam and pressure to cook food quickly, preserving more of its natural vitamins and minerals. Additionally, because the Instant Pot requires less oil and liquid, it can help you create lighter, healthier dishes without sacrificing flavor.

Another key benefit of the Instant Pot is its ability to tenderize ingredients quickly. Whether you're cooking a tough cut of meat or hearty grains, the pressure cooker function can break down fibers in a fraction of the time required by conventional methods. This makes it perfect for preparing everything from fall-off-the-bone ribs to creamy risottos, all with minimal effort.

A Solution for Every Meal

With its versatility, the Instant Pot can handle just about any type of cooking. From breakfasts to desserts, from side dishes to full-course meals, there's almost no limit to what you can create. Here's a sneak peek into how you can make the most of this appliance:

1. Breakfasts Made Easy: Imagine waking up to a warm bowl of steel-cut oats, perfectly cooked overnight while you sleep, or starting your day with fluffy, homemade yogurt. The Instant Pot makes it all possible with just a few button presses.

2. Lunches on the Go: Preparing quick, healthy lunches has never been easier. Whip up a batch of vegetable soup, chili, or stew on the weekend and store portions for the week ahead. The Instant Pot's sauté function also allows you to brown meats or vegetables before pressure cooking, adding a depth of flavor to your meals.

3. Dinners in a Flash: From a comforting pot roast to a spicy chicken curry, the Instant Pot excels at creating rich, flavorful dinners without hours of prep work. You can also use it to make delicious side dishes like potatoes with parsley or steamed vegetables, all while your main course cooks.

4. Decadent Desserts: Yes, you can even make desserts in your Instant Pot! From creamy cheesecakes to decadent chocolate banana cakes, the Instant Pot's precision cooking ensures perfect results every time.

Why You'll Love This Cookbook?

This cookbook isn't just a collection of recipes; it's a guide to mastering the Instant Pot. Each recipe is designed to be clear, straightforward, and accessible, with tips and techniques to help you get the most out of your appliance. We'll cover everything from basic functions to advanced cooking techniques, ensuring that you feel confident and capable in the kitchen.

We've also included recipes that cater to a wide range of dietary preferences, from vegetarian and vegan options to gluten-free and low-carb dishes. This diversity means there's something for everyone, whether you're cooking for yourself, your family, or a special gathering.

The Instant Pot: A Tool for Every Lifestyle

No matter your lifestyle, the Instant Pot can adapt to meet your needs. For busy professionals, it offers a way to prepare healthy, home-cooked meals in a fraction of the time. For families, it provides a simple solution for preparing large, nutritious meals that everyone will love. For those who enjoy meal prepping, the Instant Pot makes it easy to cook in bulk and store meals for later use.

And if you're looking to experiment with new cuisines or cooking styles, the Instant Pot is the perfect tool. You can explore recipes from around the world, from Indian curries to Italian risottos, all with the confidence that your Instant Pot will deliver consistent, delicious results.

Embark on Your Instant Pot Journey

The Instant Pot is more than just an appliance; it's an invitation to explore, experiment, and enjoy the process of cooking. With this cookbook, you'll not only learn how to use your Instant Pot to its fullest potential but also discover new flavors, ingredients, and techniques that will transform the way you cook.

Whether you're preparing a simple meal for one or hosting a dinner party, the Instant Pot makes cooking enjoyable, efficient, and rewarding. So, let's get started on this culinary adventure together. Open your Instant Pot, turn to the first recipe, and prepare to be amazed by what you can create. Welcome to a new era of cooking — fast, easy, and full of flavor.

Chapter 1

Breakfasts

Crunchy Blueberry Almond Cereal

Prep time: 5 minutes | Cook time: 2 minutes | Serves 4

- ⅓ cup crushed roasted almonds
- ¼ cup almond flour
- ¼ cup unsalted butter, softened
- ¼ cup vanilla-flavored egg white protein powder
- 2 tablespoons Swerve
- 1 teaspoon blueberry extract
- 1 teaspoon ground cinnamon

1. Add all the ingredients to the Instant Pot and stir to combine. 2. Lock the lid, select the Manual mode and set the cooking time for 2 minutes on High Pressure. When the timer goes off, do a natural pressure release for 10 minutes, then release any remaining pressure. Open the lid. 3. Stir well and pour the mixture onto a sheet lined with parchment paper to cool. It will be crispy when completely cool. 4. Serve the cereal in bowls.

Southwest Avocado Frittata

Prep time: 5 minutes | Cook time: 20 minutes | Serves 4

- 2 tablespoons coconut oil
- ¼ cup diced onion
- ¼ cup diced green chilies
- ½ green bell pepper, diced
- 8 eggs
- 1 teaspoon salt
- ½ teaspoon chili powder
- ¼ teaspoon garlic powder
- ¼ teaspoon pepper
- ¼ cup heavy cream
- 4 tablespoons melted butter
- ½ cup shredded Cheddar cheese
- 1 cup water
- 2 avocados
- ¼ cup sour cream

1. Press the Sauté button and add coconut oil to Instant Pot. Add onion, chilies, and bell pepper. Sauté until onion is translucent and peppers begin to soften, approximately 3 minutes. While sautéing, whisk eggs, seasoning, heavy cream, and butter in large bowl. Pour into 7-inch round baking pan. 2. Press the Cancel button. Add onion and pepper mixture to egg mixture. Mix in Cheddar. Cover pan with aluminum foil. 3. Pour water into Instant Pot, and scrape bottom of pot if necessary to remove any stuck-on food. Place steam rack into pot and put in baking dish with eggs on top. Click lid closed. 4. Press the Manual button and set time for 25 minutes. 5. While food is cooking, cut avocados in half, remove pit, scoop out of shell and slice thinly. When timer beeps, quick-release the pressure. Serve with avocado slices and a spoonful of sour cream.

Nutty Cauliflower Porridge

Prep time: 40 minutes | Cook time: 5 minutes | Serves 4

- 2½ cups water, divided
- ½ cup raw cashews
- ½ cup almond slivers
- ¼ cup raw pumpkin seeds
- ¼ head cauliflower, chopped
- Sea salt, to taste
- ¼ cup heavy whipping cream
- Topping:
- ¼ cup hemp seeds
- ¼ cup chia seeds
- 1 tablespoon cinnamon

1. In a small bowl, add 2 cups of the water, the cashews, almonds and pumpkin seeds. Soak for 30 minutes. Drain the water and set aside. Reserve a few nuts and pumpkin seeds in a separate bowl to be used as garnish. 2. Pour the remaining ½ cup of the water into the Instant Pot and add the soaked nuts mixture, cauliflower and sea salt. 3. Lock the lid. Select the Manual mode and set the cooking time for 5 minutes at High Pressure. When the timer goes off, use a natural pressure release for 10 minutes, then release any remaining pressure. Carefully open the lid. 4. Transfer the cauliflower and nuts mixture to a food processor, add the heavy cream and pulse until smooth. 5. Season with a pinch of sea salt. Garnish with the reserved nuts, pumpkin seeds, hemp seeds and chia seeds and sprinkle with the cinnamon. Serve immediately.

Spicy Mexican Beef Morning Chili

Prep time: 5 minutes | Cook time: 45 minutes | Serves 4

- 2 tablespoons coconut oil
- 1 pound (454 g) ground grass-fed beef
- 1 (14-ounce / 397-g) can sugar-free or low-sugar diced tomatoes
- ½ cup shredded full-fat Cheddar cheese (optional)
- 1 teaspoon hot sauce
- ½ teaspoon chili powder
- ½ teaspoon crushed red pepper
- ½ teaspoon ground cumin
- ½ teaspoon kosher salt
- ½ teaspoon freshly ground black pepper

1. Set the Instant Pot to Sauté and melt the oil. 2. Pour in ½ cup of filtered water, then add the beef, tomatoes, cheese, hot sauce, chili powder, red pepper, cumin, salt, and black pepper to the Instant Pot, stirring thoroughly. 3. Close the lid, set the pressure release to Sealing, and hit Cancel to stop the current program. Select Manual, set the Instant Pot to 45 minutes on High Pressure and let cook. 4. Once cooked, let the pressure naturally disperse from the Instant Pot for about 10 minutes, then carefully switch the pressure release to Venting. 5. Open the Instant Pot, serve, and enjoy!

Classic Hard-boiled Eggs

Prep time: 2 minutes | Cook time: 2 minutes | Serves 9

- 9 large eggs

1. Pour 1 cup of water into the electric pressure cooker and insert an egg rack. Gently stand the eggs in the rack, fat ends down. If you don't have an egg rack, place the eggs in a steamer basket or on a wire rack. 2. Close and lock the lid of the pressure cooker. Set the valve to sealing. 3. Cook on high pressure for 2 minutes. 4. When the cooking is complete, hit Cancel and allow the pressure to release naturally. 5. Once the pin drops, unlock and remove the lid. 6. Using tongs, carefully remove the eggs from the pressure cooker. Peel or refrigerate the eggs when they are cool enough to handle.

Baked Eggs with Parmesan

Prep time: 5 minutes | Cook time: 10 minutes | Serves 1

- 1 tablespoon butter, cut into small pieces
- 2 tablespoons keto-friendly low-carb Marinara sauce
- 3 eggs
- 2 tablespoons grated Parmesan cheese
- ¼ teaspoon Italian seasoning
- 1 cup water

1. Place the butter pieces on the bottom of the oven-safe bowl. Spread the marinara sauce over the butter. Crack the eggs on top of the marinara sauce and top with the cheese and Italian seasoning. 2. Cover the bowl with aluminum foil. Pour the water and insert the trivet in the Instant Pot. Put the bowl on the trivet. 3. Set the lid in place. Select the Manual mode and set the cooking time for 10 minutes on Low Pressure. When the timer goes off, do a quick pressure release. Carefully open the lid. 4. Let the eggs cool for 5 minutes before serving.

Cranberry Almond Creamy Grits

Prep time: 10 minutes | Cook time: 10 minutes | Serves 5

- ¾ cup stone-ground grits or polenta (not instant)
- ½ cup unsweetened dried cranberries
- Pinch kosher salt
- 1 tablespoon unsalted butter or ghee (optional)
- 1 tablespoon half-and-half
- ¼ cup sliced almonds, toasted

1. In the electric pressure cooker, stir together the grits, cranberries, salt, and 3 cups of water. 2. Close and lock the lid. Set the valve to sealing. 3. Cook on high pressure for 10 minutes. 4. When the cooking is complete, hit Cancel and quick release the pressure. 5. Once the pin drops, unlock and remove the lid. 6. Add the butter (if using) and half-and-half. Stir until the mixture is creamy, adding more half-and-half if necessary. 7. Spoon into serving bowls and sprinkle with almonds.

Light and Fluffy Vanilla Pancakes

Prep time: 5 minutes | Cook time: 50 minutes | Serves 6

- 3 eggs, beaten
- ½ cup coconut flour
- ¼ cup heavy cream
- ¼ cup almond flour
- 3 tablespoons Swerve
- 1 teaspoon vanilla extract
- 1 teaspoon baking powder
- Cooking spray

1. In a bowl, stir together the eggs, coconut flour, heavy cream, almond flour, Swerve and vanilla extract. Whisk in the baking powder until smooth. 2. Spritz the bottom and sides of Instant Pot with cooking spray. Place the batter in the pot. 3. Set the lid in place. Select the Manual mode and set the cooking time for 50 minutes on Low Pressure. Once the timer goes off, perform a natural pressure release for 5 minutes, then release any remaining pressure. Carefully open the lid. 4. Let the pancake rest in the pot for 5 minutes before serving.

Pork Breakfast Patties

Prep time: 5 minutes | Cook time: 15 minutes | Serves 4

- 1 pound (454 g) 84% lean ground pork
- 1 teaspoon dried thyme
- ½ teaspoon dried sage
- ½ teaspoon garlic powder
- ½ teaspoon salt
- ¼ teaspoon pepper
- ¼ teaspoon red pepper flakes

1. Mix all ingredients in large bowl. Form into 4 patties based on preference. Press the Sauté button and press the Adjust button to lower heat to Less. 2. Place patties in Instant Pot and allow fat to render while patties begin browning. After 5 minutes, or when a few tablespoons of fat have rendered from meat, press the Cancel button. 3. Press the Sauté button and press the Adjust button to set heat to Normal. Sear each side of patties and allow them to cook fully until no pink remains in centers, approximately 10 additional minutes, depending on thickness.

Cheesy Vegetable Casserole

Prep time: 7 minutes | Cook time: 9 minutes | Serves 3

- 3 eggs, beaten
- ¼ cup coconut cream
- ¼ teaspoon salt
- 3 ounces (85 g) Brussel sprouts, chopped
- 2 ounces (57 g) tomato, chopped
- 3 ounces (85 g) provolone cheese, shredded
- 1 teaspoon butter
- 1 teaspoon smoked paprika

1. Grease the instant pot pan with the butter. 2. Put eggs in the bowl, add salt, and smoked paprika. Whisk the eggs well. 3. After this, add chopped Brussel sprouts and tomato. 4. Pour the mixture into the instant pot pan and sprinkle over with the shredded cheese. 5. Pour 1 cup of the water in the instant pot. Then place the pan with the egg mixture and close the lid. 6. Cook the meal on Manual (High Pressure) for 4 minutes. Then make naturally release for 5 minutes.

Classic Cinnamon Swirl Coffee Cake

Prep time: 10 minutes | Cook time: 45 minutes | Serves 8

- Cake:
- 2 cups almond flour
- 1 cup granulated erythritol
- 1 teaspoon baking powder
- Pinch of salt
- 2 eggs
- ½ cup sour cream
- 4 tablespoons butter, melted
- 2 teaspoons vanilla extract
- 2 tablespoons Swerve
- 1½ teaspoons ground cinnamon
- Cooking spray
- ½ cup water
- Icing:
- 2 ounces (56 g) cream cheese, softened
- 1 cup powdered erythritol
- 1 tablespoon heavy cream
- ½ teaspoon vanilla extract

1. In the bowl of a stand mixer, combine the almond flour, granulated erythritol, baking powder and salt. Mix until no lumps remain. Add the eggs, sour cream, butter and vanilla to the mixer bowl and mix until well combined. 2. In a separate bowl, mix together the Swerve and cinnamon. 3. Spritz the baking pan with cooking spray. Pour in the cake batter and use a knife to make sure it is level around the pan. Sprinkle the cinnamon mixture on top. Cover the pan tightly with aluminum foil. 4. Pour the water and insert the trivet in the Instant Pot. Put the pan on the trivet. 5. Set the lid in place. Select the Manual mode and set the cooking time for 45 minutes on High Pressure. When the timer goes off, do a quick pressure release. Carefully open the lid. 6. Remove the cake from the pot and remove the foil. Blot off any moisture on top of the cake with a paper towel, if necessary. Let rest in the pan for 5 minutes. 7. Meanwhile, make the icing: In a small bowl, use a mixer to whip the cream cheese until it is light and fluffy. Slowly fold in the powdered erythritol and mix until well combined. Add the heavy cream and vanilla extract and mix until thoroughly combined. 8. When the cake is cooled, transfer it to a platter and drizzle the icing all over.

Smoked Salmon Coddled Egg Toasts

Prep time: 5 minutes | Cook time: 10 minutes | Serves 4

- 2 teaspoons unsalted butter
- 4 large eggs
- 4 slices gluten-free or whole-grain rye bread
- ½ cup plain 2 percent Greek yogurt
- 4 ounces cold-smoked salmon, or 1 medium avocado, pitted, peeled, and sliced
- 2 radishes, thinly sliced
- 1 Persian cucumber, thinly sliced
- 1 tablespoon chopped fresh chives
- ¼ teaspoon freshly ground black pepper

1. Pour 1 cup water into the Instant Pot and place a long-handled silicone steam rack into the pot. (If you don't have the long-handled rack, use the wire metal steam rack and a homemade sling) 2. Coat each of four 4-ounce ramekins with ½ teaspoon butter. Crack an egg into each ramekin. Place the ramekins on the steam rack in the pot. 3. Secure the lid and set the Pressure Release to Sealing. Select the Steam setting and set the cooking time for 3 minutes at low pressure. (The pot will take about 5 minutes to come up to pressure before the cooking program begins.) 4. While eggs are cooking, toast the bread in a toaster until golden brown. Spread the yogurt onto the toasted slices, put the toasts onto plates, and then top each toast with the smoked salmon, radishes, and cucumber. 5. When the cooking program ends, let the pressure release naturally for 5 minutes, then move the Pressure Release to Venting to release any remaining steam. Open the pot and, wearing heat-resistant mitts, grasp the handles of the steam rack and lift it out of the pot. 6. Run a knife around the inside edge of each ramekin to loosen the egg and unmold one egg onto each toast. Sprinkle the chives and pepper on top and serve right away. 7. Note 8. The yolks of these eggs are fully cooked through. If you prefer the yolks slightly less solid, perform a quick pressure release rather than letting the pressure release naturally for 5 minutes.

Bacon-Wrapped Egg Cups

Prep time: 5 minutes | Cook time: 7 minutes | Serves 4

- 6 large eggs
- 2 strips cooked bacon, sliced in ¼-inch wide pieces
- ½ cup Cheddar cheese, divided
- ¼ teaspoon sea salt
- ¼ teaspoon black pepper
- 1 cup water
- 1 tablespoon chopped fresh flat leaf parsley

1. In a small bowl, beat the eggs. Stir in the cooked bacon, ¼ cup of the cheese, sea salt and pepper. Divide the egg mixture equally among four ramekins and loosely cover with aluminum foil. 2. Pour the water and place the trivet in the Instant Pot. Place two ramekins on the trivet and stack the other two on the top. 3. Lock the lid. Select the Manual mode and set the cooking time for 7 minutes at High Pressure. When the timer goes off, use a natural pressure release for 10 minutes, then release any remaining pressure. Carefully open the lid. 4. Top each ramekin with the remaining ¼ cup of the cheese. Lock the lid and melt the cheese for 2 minutes. Garnish with the chopped parsley and serve immediately.

Potato and Bacon Gratin

Prep time: 20 minutes | Cook time: 40 minutes | Serves 8

- 1 tablespoon olive oil
- 6 ounces bag fresh spinach
- 1 clove garlic, minced
- 4 large potatoes, peeled or unpeeled, divided
- 6 ounces Canadian bacon slices, divided
- 5 ounces reduced-fat grated Swiss cheddar, divided
- 1 cup lower-sodium, lower-fat chicken broth

1. Set the Instant Pot to Sauté and pour in the olive oil. Cook the spinach and garlic in olive oil just until spinach is wilted (5 minutes or less). Turn off the instant pot. 2. Cut potatoes into thin slices about ¼" thick. 3. In a springform pan that will fit into the inner pot of your Instant Pot, spray it with nonstick spray then layer ⅓ the potatoes, half the bacon, ⅓ the cheese, and half the wilted spinach. 4. Repeat layers ending with potatoes. Reserve ⅓ cheese for later. 5. Pour chicken broth over all. 6. Wipe the bottom of your Instant Pot to soak up any remaining oil, then add in 2 cups of water and the steaming rack. Place the springform pan on top. 7. Close the lid and secure to the locking position. Be sure the vent is turned to sealing. Set for 35 minutes on Manual at high pressure. 8. Perform a quick release. 9. Top with the remaining cheese, then allow to stand 10 minutes before removing from the Instant Pot, cutting and serving.

Bite-sized Chocolate Chip Muffins

Prep time: 5 minutes | Cook time: 20 minutes | Serves 7

- 1 cup blanched almond flour
- 2 eggs
- ¾ cup sugar-free chocolate chips
- 1 tablespoon vanilla extract
- ½ cup Swerve, or more to taste
- 2 tablespoons salted grass-fed butter, softened
- ½ teaspoon salt
- ¼ teaspoon baking soda

1. Pour 1 cup of filtered water into the inner pot of the Instant Pot, then insert the trivet. Using an electric mixer, combine flour, eggs, chocolate chips, vanilla, Swerve, butter, salt, and baking soda. Mix thoroughly. Transfer this mixture into a well-greased Instant Pot-friendly muffin (or egg bites) mold. 2. Using a sling if desired, place the pan onto the trivet and cover loosely with aluminum foil. Close the lid, set the pressure release to Sealing, and select Manual. Set the Instant Pot to 20 minutes on High Pressure and let cook. 3. Once cooked, let the pressure naturally disperse from the Instant Pot for about 10 minutes, then carefully switch the pressure release to Venting. 4. Open the Instant Pot and remove the pan. Let cool, serve, and enjoy!

Broccoli Cheddar Egg Muffins

Prep time: 10 minutes | Cook time: 10 minutes | Serves 7

- 5 eggs, beaten
- 3 tablespoons heavy cream
- ⅛ teaspoon salt
- ⅛ teaspoon black pepper
- 1 ounce (28 g) finely chopped broccoli
- 1 ounce (28 g) shredded Cheddar cheese
- ½ cup water

1. In a blender, combine the eggs, heavy cream, salt and pepper and pulse until smooth. 2. Divide the chopped broccoli among the egg cups equally. Pour the egg mixture on top of the broccoli, filling the cups about three-fourths of the way full. Sprinkle the Cheddar cheese on top of each cup. 3. Cover the egg cups tightly with aluminum foil. 4. Pour the water and insert the trivet in the Instant Pot. Put the egg cups on the trivet. 5. Lock the lid. Select the Manual mode and set the cooking time for 10 minutes on High Pressure. Once the timer goes off, perform a natural pressure release for 5 minutes, then release any remaining pressure. Carefully open the lid. 6. Serve immediately.

Strawberry Nut Millet Breakfast Bowl

Prep time: 0 minutes | Cook time: 30 minutes | Serves 8

- 2 tablespoons coconut oil or unsalted butter
- 1½ cups millet
- 2⅔ cups water
- ½ teaspoon fine sea salt
- 1 cup unsweetened almond milk or other nondairy milk
- 1 cup chopped toasted pecans, almonds, or peanuts
- 4 cups sliced strawberries

1. Select the Sauté setting on the Instant Pot and melt the oil. Add the millet and cook for 4 minutes, until aromatic. Stir in the water and salt, making sure all of the grains are submerged in the liquid. 2. Secure the lid and set the Pressure Release to Sealing. Press the Cancel button to reset the cooking program, then select the Porridge, Pressure Cook, or Manual setting and set the cooking time for 12 minutes at high pressure. (The pot will take about 10 minutes to come up to pressure before the cooking program begins.) 3. When the cooking program ends, let the pressure release naturally for 10 minutes, then move the Pressure Release to Venting to release any remaining steam. Open the pot and use a fork to fluff and stir the millet. 4. Spoon the millet into bowls and top each serving with 2 tablespoons of the almond milk, then sprinkle with the nuts and top with the strawberries. Serve warm.

Peppers, Kale, and Feta Greek Frittata

Prep time: 5 minutes | Cook time: 45 minutes | Serves 6

- 8 large eggs
- ½ cup plain 2 percent Greek yogurt
- Fine sea salt
- Freshly ground black pepper
- 2 cups firmly packed finely shredded kale or baby kale leaves
- One 12-ounce jar roasted red peppers, drained and cut into ¼ by 2-inch strips
- 2 green onions, white and green parts, thinly sliced
- 1 tablespoon chopped fresh dill
- ⅓ cup crumbled feta cheese
- 6 cups loosely packed mixed baby greens
- ¾ cup cherry or grape tomatoes, halved
- 2 tablespoons extra-virgin olive oil

1. Pour 1½ cups water into the Instant Pot. Lightly butter a 7-cup round heatproof glass dish or coat with nonstick cooking spray. 2. In a bowl, whisk together the eggs, yogurt, ¼ teaspoon salt, and ¼ teaspoon pepper until well blended, then stir in the kale, roasted peppers, green onions, dill, and feta cheese. 3. Pour the egg mixture into the prepared dish and cover tightly with aluminum foil. Place the dish on a long-handled silicone steam rack, then, holding the handles of the steam rack, lower it into the Instant Pot. (If you don't have the long-handled rack, use the wire metal steam rack and a homemade sling) 4. Secure the lid and set the Pressure Release to Sealing. Select the Pressure Cook or Manual setting and set the cooking time for 30 minutes at high pressure. (The pot will take about 15 minutes to come up to pressure before the cooking program begins.) 5. When the cooking program ends, let the pressure release naturally for 10 minutes, then move the Pressure Release to Venting to release any remaining steam. Open the pot and let the frittata sit for a minute or two, until it deflates and settles into its dish. Then, wearing heat-resistant mitts, grasp the handles of the steam rack and lift it out of the pot. Uncover the dish, taking care not to get burned by the steam or to drip condensation onto the frittata. Let the frittata sit for 10 minutes, giving it time to reabsorb any liquid and set up. 6. In a medium bowl, toss together the mixed greens, tomatoes, and olive oil. Taste and adjust the seasoning with salt and pepper, if needed. 7. Cut the frittata into six wedges and serve warm, with the salad alongside.

Chocolate Chip Fluffy Pancake

Prep time: 5 minutes | Cook time: 37 minutes | Serves 5 to 6

- 4 tablespoons salted grass-fed butter, softened
- 2 cups blanched almond flour
- ½ cup Swerve, or more to taste
- 1¼ cups full-fat coconut milk
- ¼ cup sugar-free chocolate chips
- ¼ cup organic coconut flour
- 2 eggs
- 1 tablespoon chopped walnuts
- ¼ teaspoon baking soda
- ½ teaspoon salt
- ½ cup dark berries, for serving (optional)

1. Grease the bottom and sides of your Instant Pot with the butter. Make sure you coat it very liberally. 2. In a large bowl, mix together the almond flour, Swerve, milk, chocolate chips, coconut flour, eggs, walnuts, baking soda, and salt. Add this mixture to the Instant Pot. Close the lid, set the pressure release to Sealing, and select Multigrain. Set the Instant Pot to 37 minutes on Low Pressure, and let cook. 3. Switch the pressure release to Venting and open the Instant Pot. Confirm your pancake is cooked, then carefully remove it using a spatula. Serve with the berries (if desired), and enjoy!

Breakfast Casserole with Sausage and Cauliflower

Prep time: 5 minutes | Cook time: 10 minutes | Serves 6

- 1 cup water
- ½ head cauliflower, chopped into bite-sized pieces
- 4 slices bacon
- 1 pound (454 g) breakfast sausage
- 4 tablespoons melted butter
- 10 eggs
- ⅓ cup heavy cream
- 2 teaspoons salt
- 1 teaspoon pepper
- 2 tablespoons hot sauce
- 2 stalks green onion
- 1 cup shredded sharp Cheddar cheese

1. Pour water into Instant Pot and place steamer basket in bottom. Add cauliflower. Click lid closed. 2. Press the Steam button and adjust time for 1 minute. When timer beeps, quick-release the pressure and place cauliflower to the side in medium bowl. 3. Drain water from Instant Pot, clean, and replace. Press the Sauté button. Press the Adjust button to set heat to Less. Cook bacon until crispy. Once fully cooked, set aside on paper towels. Add breakfast sausage to pot and brown (still using the Sauté function). 4. While sausage is cooking, whisk butter, eggs, heavy cream, salt, pepper, and hot sauce. 5. When sausage is fully cooked, pour egg mixture into Instant Pot. Gently stir using silicone spatula until eggs are completely cooked and fluffy. Press the Cancel button. Slice green onions. Sprinkle green onions, bacon, and cheese over mixture and let melt. Serve warm.

Nutty Slow-Cooked Granola

Prep time: 5 minutes | Cook time: 2 hours 30 minutes | Serves 10

- 1 cup raw almonds
- 1 cup pumpkin seeds
- 1 cup raw walnuts
- 1 cup raw cashews
- 1 tablespoon coconut oil
- ¼ cup unsweetened coconut chips
- 1 teaspoon sea salt
- 1 teaspoon cinnamon

1. In a large bowl, stir together the almonds, pumpkin seeds, walnuts, cashews and coconut oil. Make sure all the nuts are coated with the coconut oil. Place the nut mixture in the Instant Pot and cover the pot with a paper towel. 2. Lock the lid. Select the Slow Cook mode and set the cooking time for 1 hour on More. When the timer goes off, stir the nuts. Set the timer for another hour. 3. Again, when the timer goes off, stir the nut mixture and add the coconut chips. Set the timer for another 30 minutes. The cashews should become a nice golden color. 4. When the timer goes off, transfer the nut mixture to a baking pan to cool and sprinkle with the sea salt and cinnamon. Serve.

Avocado Super Green Power Bowl

Prep time: 10 minutes | Cook time: 10 minutes | Serves 1

- 1 cup water
- 2 eggs
- 1 tablespoon coconut oil
- 1 tablespoon butter
- 1 ounce (28 g) sliced almonds
- 1 cup fresh spinach, sliced into strips
- ½ cup kale, sliced into strips
- ½ clove garlic, minced
- ½ teaspoon salt
- ⅛ teaspoon pepper
- ½ avocado, sliced
- ⅛ teaspoon red pepper flakes

1. Pour water into Instant Pot and place steam rack on bottom. Place eggs on steam rack. Click lid closed. Press the Manual button and adjust time for 6 minutes. When timer beeps, quick-release the pressure. Set eggs aside. 2. Pour water out, clean pot, and replace. Press the Sauté button and add coconut oil, butter, and almonds. Sauté for 2 to 3 minutes until butter begins to turn golden and almonds soften. Add spinach, kale, garlic, salt, and pepper to Instant Pot. Sauté for 4 to 6 minutes until greens begin to wilt. Press the Cancel button. Place greens in bowl for serving. Peel eggs, cut in half, and add to bowl. Slice avocado and place in bowl. Sprinkle red pepper flakes over all. Serve warm.

Pecan Walnut Crunch Granola

Prep time: 10 minutes | Cook time: 2 minutes | Serves 12

- 2 cups chopped raw pecans
- 1¾ cups vanilla-flavored egg white protein powder
- 1¼ cups unsalted butter, softened
- 1 cup sunflower seeds
- ½ cup chopped raw walnuts
- ½ cup slivered almonds
- ½ cup sesame seeds
- ½ cup Swerve
- 1 teaspoon ground cinnamon
- ½ teaspoon sea salt

1. Add all the ingredients to the Instant Pot and stir to combine. 2. Lock the lid, select the Manual mode and set the cooking time for 2 minutes on High Pressure. When the timer goes off, do a natural pressure release for 10 minutes, then release any remaining pressure. Open the lid. 3. Stir well and pour the granola onto a sheet of parchment paper to cool. It will become crispy when completely cool. Serve the granola in bowls.

Shredded Pork Hash

Prep time: 10 minutes | Cook time: 15 minutes | Serves 4

- 4 eggs
- 10 ounces (283 g) pulled pork, shredded
- 1 teaspoon coconut oil
- 1 teaspoon red pepper
- 1 teaspoon chopped fresh cilantro
- 1 tomato, chopped
- ¼ cup water

1. Melt the coconut oil in the instant pot on Sauté mode. 2. Then add pulled pork, red pepper, cilantro, water, and chopped tomato. 3. Cook the ingredients for 5 minutes. 4. Then stir it well with the help of the spatula and crack the eggs over it. 5. Close the lid. 6. Cook the meal on Manual mode (High Pressure) for 7 minutes. Then make a quick pressure release.

Creamy Soft Scrambled Eggs

Prep time: 5 minutes | Cook time: 7 minutes | Serves 4

- 6 eggs
- 2 tablespoons heavy cream
- 1 teaspoon salt
- ¼ teaspoon pepper
- 2 tablespoons butter
- 2 ounces (57 g) cream cheese, softened

1. In large bowl, whisk eggs, heavy cream, salt, and pepper. Press the Sauté button and then press the Adjust button to set heat to Less. 2. Gently push eggs around pot with rubber spatula. When they begin to firm up, add butter and softened cream cheese. Continue stirring slowly in a figure-8 pattern until eggs are fully cooked, approximately 7 minutes total.

Mushroom and Bacon Quiche Lorraine

Prep time: 10 minutes | Cook time: 37 minutes | Serves 4

- 4 strips bacon, chopped
- 2 cups sliced button mushrooms
- ½ cup diced onions
- 8 large eggs
- 1½ cups shredded Swiss cheese
- 1 cup unsweetened almond milk
- ¼ cup sliced green onions
- ½ teaspoon sea salt
- ¼ teaspoon ground black pepper
- 2 tablespoons coconut flour

1. Press the Sauté button on the Instant Pot and add the bacon. Sauté for 4 minutes, or until crisp. Transfer the bacon to a plate lined with paper towel to drain, leaving the drippings in the pot. 2. Add the mushrooms and diced onions to the pot and sauté for 3 minutes, or until the onions are tender. Remove the mixture from the pot to a large bowl. Wipe the Instant Pot clean. 3. Set a trivet in the Instant Pot and pour in 1 cup water. 4. In a medium bowl, stir together the eggs, cheese, almond milk, green onions, salt and pepper. Pour the egg mixture into the bowl with the mushrooms and onions. Stir to combine. Fold in the coconut flour. Pour the mixture into a greased round casserole dish. Spread the cooked bacon on top. 5. Place the casserole dish onto the trivet in the Instant Pot. 6. Lock the lid, select the Manual mode and set the cooking time for 30 minutes on High Pressure. When the timer goes off, do a natural pressure release for 15 minutes, then release any remaining pressure. Open the lid. 7. Remove the casserole dish from the Instant Pot. 8. Let cool for 15 to 30 minutes before cutting into 4 pieces. Serve immediately.

Delicate Poached Eggs

Prep time: 5 minutes | Cook time: 5 minutes | Serves 4

- Nonstick cooking spray
- 4 large eggs

1. Lightly spray 4 cups of a 7-count silicone egg bite mold with nonstick cooking spray. Crack each egg into a sprayed cup. 2. Pour 1 cup of water into the electric pressure cooker. Place the egg bite mold on the wire rack and carefully lower it into the pot. 3. Close and lock the lid of the pressure cooker. Set the valve to sealing. 4. Cook on high pressure for 5 minutes. 5. When the cooking is complete, hit Cancel and quick release the pressure. 6. Once the pin drops, unlock and remove the lid. 7. Run a small rubber spatula or spoon around each egg and carefully remove it from the mold. The white should be cooked, but the yolk should be runny. 8. Serve immediately.

Vegetable and Cheese Frittata

Prep time: 10 minutes | Cook time: 10 minutes | Serves 4

- 4 eggs, beaten
- 2 ounces (57 g) Pecorino cheese, grated
- 3 ounces (85 g) okra, chopped
- 2 ounces (57 g) radish, chopped
- 1 tablespoon cream cheese
- 1 teaspoon sesame oil

1. Heat up sesame oil in the instant pot on Sauté mode. 2. Add chopped okra and radish and sauté the vegetables for 4 minutes. 3. Then stir them well and add cream cheese and beaten eggs. 4. Stir the mixture well and top with cheese. 5. Close the lid and cook the frittata on Sauté mode for 6 minutes more.

Smoked Salmon Asparagus Quiche Bites

Prep time: 15 minutes | Cook time: 15 minutes | Serves 2

- Nonstick cooking spray
- 4 asparagus spears, cut into ½-inch pieces
- 2 tablespoons finely chopped onion
- 3 ounces (85 g) smoked salmon (skinless and boneless), chopped
- 3 large eggs
- 2 tablespoons 2% milk
- ¼ teaspoon dried dill
- Pinch ground white pepper

1. Pour 1½ cups of water into the electric pressure cooker and insert a wire rack or trivet. 2. Lightly spray the bottom and sides of the ramekins with nonstick cooking spray. Divide the asparagus, onion, and salmon between the ramekins. 3. In a measuring cup with a spout, whisk together the eggs, milk, dill, and white pepper. Pour half of the egg mixture into each ramekin. Loosely cover the ramekins with aluminum foil. 4. Carefully place the ramekins inside the pot on the rack. 5. Close and lock the lid of the pressure cooker. Set the valve to sealing. 6. Cook on high pressure for 15 minutes. 7. When the cooking is complete, hit Cancel and quick release the pressure. 8. Once the pin drops, unlock and remove the lid. 9. Carefully remove the ramekins from the pot. Cool, covered, for 5 minutes. 10. Run a small silicone spatula or a knife around the edge of each ramekin. Invert each quiche onto a small plate and serve.

Potato Shredded Omelet

Prep time: 15 minutes | Cook time: 20 minutes | Serves 6

- 3 slices bacon, cooked and crumbled
- 2 cups shredded cooked potatoes
- ¼ cup minced onion
- ¼ cup minced green bell pepper
- 1 cup egg substitute
- ¼ cup fat-free milk
- ¼ teaspoon salt
- ⅛ teaspoon black pepper
- 1 cup 75%-less-fat shredded cheddar cheese
- 1 cup water

1. With nonstick cooking spray, spray the inside of a round baking dish that will fit in your Instant Pot inner pot. 2. Sprinkle the bacon, potatoes, onion, and bell pepper around the bottom of the baking dish. 3. Mix together the egg substitute, milk, salt, and pepper in mixing bowl. Pour over potato mixture. 4. Top with cheese. 5. Add water, place the steaming rack into the bottom of the inner pot and then place the round baking dish on top. 6. Close the lid and secure to the locking position. Be sure the vent is turned to sealing. Set for 20 minutes on Manual at high pressure. 7. Let the pressure release naturally. 8. Carefully remove the baking dish with the handles of the steaming rack and allow to stand 10 minutes before cutting and serving.

Morning Crunch Cereal

Prep time: 5 minutes | Cook time: 5 minutes | Serves 4

- 2 tablespoons coconut oil
- 1 cup full-fat coconut milk
- ½ cup chopped cashews
- ½ cup heavy whipping cream
- ½ cup chopped pecans
- ⅓ cup Swerve
- ¼ cup unsweetened coconut flakes
- 2 tablespoons flax seeds
- 2 tablespoons chopped hazelnuts
- 2 tablespoons chopped macadamia nuts
- ½ teaspoon ground cinnamon
- ½ teaspoon ground nutmeg
- ½ teaspoon ground turmeric

1. Set the Instant Pot to Sauté and melt the coconut oil. Pour in the coconut milk. 2. Add the cashews, whipping cream, pecans, Swerve, coconut flakes, flax seeds, hazelnuts, macadamia nuts, cinnamon, nutmeg, and turmeric to the Instant Pot. Stir thoroughly. 3. Close the lid, set the pressure release to Sealing, and hit Cancel to stop the current program. Select Manual, set the Instant Pot to 5 minutes on High Pressure, and let cook. 4. Once cooked, let the pressure naturally disperse from the Instant Pot for about 10 minutes, then carefully switch the pressure release to Venting. 5. Open the Instant Pot, serve, and enjoy!

Egg-Stuffed Bell Peppers

Prep time: 5 minutes | Cook time: 14 minutes | Serves 2

- 2 eggs, beaten
- 1 tablespoon coconut cream
- ¼ teaspoon dried oregano
- ¼ teaspoon salt
- 1 large bell pepper, cut into halves and deseeded
- 1 cup water

1. In a bowl, stir together the eggs, coconut cream, oregano and salt. 2. Pour the egg mixture in the pepper halves. 3. Pour the water and insert the trivet in the Instant Pot. Put the stuffed pepper halves on the trivet. 4. Set the lid in place. Select the Manual mode and set the cooking time for 14 minutes on High Pressure. When the timer goes off, do a quick pressure release. Carefully open the lid. 5. Serve warm.

Bacon Spinach Eggs

Prep time: 5 minutes | Cook time: 9 minutes | Serves 4

- 2 tablespoons unsalted butter, divided
- ½ cup diced bacon
- ⅓ cup finely diced shallots
- ⅓ cup chopped spinach, leaves only
- Pinch of sea salt
- Pinch of black pepper
- ½ cup water
- ¼ cup heavy whipping cream
- 8 large eggs
- 1 tablespoon chopped fresh chives, for garnish

1. Set the Instant Pot on the Sauté mode and melt 1 tablespoon of the butter. Add the bacon to the pot and sauté for about 4 minutes, or until crispy. Using a slotted spoon, transfer the bacon bits to a bowl and set aside. 2. Add the remaining 1 tablespoon of the butter and shallots to the pot and sauté for about 2 minutes, or until tender. Add the spinach leaves and sauté for 1 minute, or until wilted. Season with sea salt and black pepper and stir. Transfer the spinach to a separate bowl and set aside. 3. Drain the oil from the pot into a bowl. Pour in the water and put the trivet inside. 4. With a paper towel, coat four ramekins with the bacon grease. In each ramekin, place 1 tablespoon of the heavy whipping cream, reserved bacon bits and sautéed spinach. Crack two eggs without breaking the yolks in each ramekin. Cover the ramekins with aluminum foil. Place two ramekins on the trivet and stack the other two on top. 5. Lock the lid. Select the Manual mode and set the cooking time for 2 minutes at Low Pressure. When the timer goes off, use a natural pressure release for 5 minutes, then release any remaining pressure. Carefully open the lid. 6. Carefully take out the ramekins and serve garnished with the chives.

Ham and Baked Egg Delight

Prep time: 5 minutes | Cook time: 5 minutes | Serves 2

- 4 large eggs, beaten
- 4 slices ham, diced
- ½ cup shredded Cheddar cheese
- ½ cup heavy cream
- ½ teaspoon sea salt
- Pinch ground black pepper

1. Grease two ramekins. 2. In a large bowl, whisk together all the ingredients. Divide the egg mixture equally between the ramekins. 3. Set a trivet in the Instant Pot and pour in 1 cup water. Place the ramekins on the trivet. 4. Lock the lid. Select the Manual mode and set the cooking time for 5 minutes on High Pressure. When the timer goes off, perform a quick pressure release. Carefully open the lid. 5. Remove the ramekins from the Instant Pot. 6. Serve immediately.

Pumpkin Mini Mug Muffin

Prep time: 5 minutes | Cook time: 9 minutes | Serves 1

- ½ cup Swerve
- ½ cup blanched almond flour
- 2 tablespoons organic pumpkin purée
- 1 teaspoon sugar-free chocolate chips
- 1 tablespoon organic coconut flour
- 1 egg
- 1 tablespoon coconut oil
- ½ teaspoon pumpkin pie spice
- ½ teaspoon ground nutmeg
- ½ teaspoon ground cinnamon
- ⅛ teaspoon baking soda

1. Mix the Swerve, almond flour, pumpkin purée, chocolate chips, coconut flour, egg, coconut oil, pumpkin pie spice, nutmeg, cinnamon, and baking soda in a large bowl. Transfer this mixture into a well-greased, Instant Pot-friendly mug. 2. Pour 1 cup of filtered water into the inner pot of the Instant Pot, and insert the trivet. Cover the mug in foil and place on top of the trivet. 3. Close the lid, set the pressure release to Sealing, and select Manual. Set the Instant Pot to 9 minutes on High Pressure. 4. Once cooked, release the pressure immediately by switching the valve to Venting. Be sure your muffin is done by inserting a toothpick into the cake and making sure it comes out clean, as cook times may vary. 5. Remove mug and enjoy!

Pork Quill Egg Molds

Prep time: 15 minutes | Cook time: 15 minutes | Serves 4

- 10 ounces (283 g) ground pork
- 1 jalapeño pepper, chopped
- 1 tablespoon butter, softened
- 1 teaspoon dried dill
- ½ teaspoon salt
- 1 cup water
- 4 quill eggs

1. In a bowl, stir together all the ingredients, except for the quill eggs and water. Transfer the meat mixture to the silicone muffin molds and press the surface gently. 2. Pour the water and insert the trivet in the Instant Pot. Put the meat cups on the trivet. 3. Crack the eggs over the meat mixture. 4. Set the lid in place. Select the Manual mode and set the cooking time for 15 minutes on High Pressure. When the timer goes off, do a quick pressure release. Carefully open the lid. 5. Serve warm.

Blackberry Vanilla Delight Cake

Prep time: 10 minutes | Cook time: 25 minutes | Serves 8

- 1 cup almond flour
- 2 eggs
- ½ cup erythritol
- 2 teaspoons vanilla extract
- 1 cup blackberries
- 4 tablespoons melted butter
- ¼ cup heavy cream
- ½ teaspoon baking powder
- 1 cup water

1. In large bowl, mix all ingredients except water. Pour into 7-inch round cake pan or divide into two 4-inch pans, if needed. Cover with foil. 2. Pour water into Instant Pot and place steam rack in bottom. Place pan on steam rack and click lid closed. Press the Cake button and press the Adjust button to set heat to Less. Set time for 25 minutes. 3. When timer beeps, allow a 15-minute natural release then quick-release the remaining pressure. Let cool completely.

Triple Cheese Quiche

Prep time: 10 minutes | Cook time: 6 minutes | Serves 6

- 6 eggs, beaten
- 2 tablespoon cream cheese
- 1 teaspoon Italian seasoning
- ¼ cup shredded Cheddar cheese
- 3 ounces (85 g) Monterey Jack cheese, shredded
- 2 ounces (57 g) Mozzarella, shredded
- 1 cup water, for cooking

1. Pour water in the instant pot. 2. In the mixing bowl, mix up eggs cream cheese, Italian seasoning, and all types of cheese. 3. Pour the mixture in the baking cups (molds) and place them in the instant pot. 4. Close and seal the lid. 5. Cook the quiche cups for 6 minutes on Manual mode (High Pressure). 6. Make a quick pressure release.

Instant Pot Perfect Boiled Eggs

Prep time: 10 minutes | Cook time: 5 minutes | Serves 7

- 1 cup water
- 6 to 8 eggs

1. Pour the water into the inner pot. Place the eggs in a steamer basket or rack that came with pot. 2. Close the lid and secure to the locking position. Be sure the vent is turned to sealing. Set for 5 minutes on Manual at high pressure. (It takes about 5 minutes for pressure to build and then 5 minutes to cook.) 3. Let pressure naturally release for 5 minutes, then do quick pressure release. 4. Place hot eggs into cool water to halt cooking process. You can peel cooled eggs immediately or refrigerate unpeeled.

Creamy Kale Omelet

Prep time: 5 minutes | Cook time: 10 minutes | Serves 2

- 2 eggs
- 1 cup chopped kale
- 1 teaspoon heavy cream
- ⅔ teaspoon white pepper
- ½ teaspoon butter

1. Grease the instant pot pan with butter. 2. Beat the eggs in the separated bowl and whisk them well. 3. After this, add heavy cream and white pepper. Stir it gently. 4. Place the chopped kale in the greased pan and add the whisked eggs. 5. Pour 1 cup of water in the instant pot. 6. Place the trivet in the instant pot and transfer the egg mixture pan on the trivet. 7. Close the instant pot and set the Manual (High Pressure) program and cook the frittata for 5 minutes. Do a natural pressure release for 5 minutes.

Chapter 2
Beef, Pork, and Lamb

Chile Verde Pulled Pork with Tomatillos

Prep time: 15 minutes | Cook time: 1 hour 3 minutes | Serves 6

- 2 pounds (907 g) pork shoulder, cut into 6 equal-sized pieces
- 1 teaspoon sea salt
- ½ teaspoon ground black pepper
- 2 jalapeño peppers, deseeded and stemmed
- 1 pound (454 g) tomatillos, husks removed and quartered
- 3 garlic cloves
- 1 tablespoon lime juice
- 3 tablespoons fresh cilantro, chopped
- 1 medium white onion, chopped
- 1 teaspoon ground cumin
- ½ teaspoon dried oregano
- 1⅔ cups chicken broth
- 1½ tablespoons olive oil

1. Sprinkle salt and pepper evenly over the pork pieces, massaging the seasoning gently into the meat. Set aside for later use. 2. In a blender, combine the jalapeños, tomatillos, garlic cloves, lime juice, cilantro, onions, cumin, oregano, and chicken broth. Blend until the mixture is smooth and well-mixed. Set this sauce aside. 3. Activate Sauté mode and heat the olive oil in the pot. Once the oil is shimmering, place the pork pieces into the pot and sear them for about 4 minutes on each side until they are browned. 4. Pour the prepared jalapeño sauce over the pork and stir gently to ensure the pork is fully coated. 5. Secure the lid. Switch to Manual mode and program the cooking time to 55 minutes on High Pressure. 6. Once the cooking cycle is done, let the pressure release naturally for 10 minutes, then carefully release any remaining pressure. 7. Remove the lid, transfer the cooked pork to a cutting board, and shred it thoroughly using two forks. 8. Return the shredded pork to the pot and mix it well with the sauce. Serve immediately.

Beef Brisket with Cabbage

Prep time: 15 minutes | Cook time: 1 hour 7 minutes | Serves 8

- 3 pounds (1.4 kg) corned beef brisket
- 4 cups water
- 3 garlic cloves, minced
- 2 teaspoons yellow mustard seed
- 2 teaspoons black peppercorns
- 3 celery stalks, chopped
- ½ large white onion, chopped
- 1 green cabbage, cut into quarters

1. Place the brisket into the Instant Pot and pour the water over it. Add the garlic, mustard seeds, and black peppercorns to the pot. 2. Secure the lid tightly. Choose the Meat/Stew mode and set the cooking time to 50 minutes on High Pressure. 3. Once the cooking cycle ends, let the pressure release naturally for 20 minutes before carefully releasing any remaining pressure. Open the lid and remove only the brisket, transferring it to a serving platter. 4. Add the celery, onion, and cabbage to the pot. 5. Close the lid securely. Select the Soup mode and set the cooking time to 12 minutes on High Pressure. 6. When the cooking process is finished, use the quick-release function to release the pressure immediately. Open the lid, return the brisket to the pot, and allow it to warm in the liquid for about 5 minutes. 7. Remove the brisket from the pot, place it back on the platter, and slice it thinly. Arrange the cooked vegetables alongside the brisket and serve hot.

Chili Pork Loin

Prep time: 10 minutes | Cook time: 20 minutes | Serves 2

- 10 ounces (283 g) pork loin
- ¼ cup water
- 1 teaspoon chili paste
- ½ teaspoon ground black pepper
- ½ teaspoon salt

1. Cut the pork loin into medium-sized pieces. 2. Season the meat evenly with salt and ground black pepper. 3. Add chili paste to the pork pieces. 4. Use your hands to thoroughly mix the meat and chili paste together until evenly coated. 5. Pour water into the Instant Pot bowl and add the seasoned pork mixture. 6. Secure the lid and select the Meat/Stew mode. Set the cooking time to 25 minutes. 7. Once the cooking is complete, let the meat cool slightly until it is warm and ready to serve.

Moroccan Lamb Stew

Prep time: 5 minutes | Cook time: 50 minutes | Serves 3

- ½ cup coconut milk
- 1 teaspoon butter
- ½ teaspoon dried rosemary
- ¼ teaspoon salt
- ½ teaspoon ground coriander
- 13 ounces (369 g) lamb shoulder, chopped
- 1 teaspoon ground anise
- ¾ cup water

1. Slice the mushrooms and arrange them evenly in the Instant Pot bowl. 2. Add the remaining ingredients to the pot, ensuring everything is well combined. Secure the lid and seal it properly. 3. Select Manual mode and set the cooking time to 45 minutes. 4. Once the cooking cycle ends, allow the pressure to release naturally for 10 minutes before opening the lid.

French Dip Chuck Roast

Prep time: 5 minutes | Cook time: 70 minutes | Serves 6

- 2 tablespoons avocado oil
- 2 to 2½ pounds (907 g to 1.1 kg) chuck roast
- 2 cups beef broth
- 2 tablespoons dried rosemary
- 3 cloves garlic, minced
- 1 teaspoon salt
- ½ teaspoon black pepper
- ¼ teaspoon dried thyme
- ½ onion, quartered
- 2 bay leaves

1. Set the pot to Sauté mode and allow it to heat up. Once ready, pour in the avocado oil and add the roast. Sear the roast on all sides, turning as needed, for approximately 5 minutes. Press Cancel when searing is complete. 2. Pour the broth into the pot. 3. Sprinkle the rosemary, garlic, salt, pepper, and thyme over the roast. Place the onion and bay leaves around the roast in the pot. 4. Secure the lid and close the vent. Select High Pressure and set the cooking time to 50 minutes. Allow the pressure to release naturally for 15 minutes, then perform a manual release to let out any remaining steam. 5. Transfer the roast to a plate and shred it thoroughly using two forks. Strain the cooking liquid through a fine-mesh sieve to make jus. Serve the shredded roast with the jus on the side for dipping.

Pot Roast with Gravy and Vegetables

Prep time: 30 minutes | Cook time: 1 hour 15 minutes | Serves 6

- 1 tablespoon olive oil
- 3–4 pound bottom round, rump, or arm roast, trimmed of fat
- ¼ teaspoon salt
- 2–3 teaspoons pepper
- 2 tablespoons flour
- 1 cup cold water
- 1 teaspoon Kitchen Bouquet, or gravy browning seasoning sauce
- 1 garlic clove, minced
- 2 medium onions, cut in wedges
- 4 medium potatoes, cubed, unpeeled
- 2 carrots, quartered
- 1 green bell pepper, sliced

1. Select Sauté mode on the Instant Pot and add the oil, allowing it to heat. Season both sides of the roast with salt and pepper, then place it in the pot and sear for 5 minutes per side until browned. 2. Combine the flour, water, and Kitchen Bouquet in a small bowl, then spread the mixture evenly over the roast. 3. Add the garlic, onions, potatoes, carrots, and green pepper to the pot around the roast. 4. Close the lid securely and ensure the vent is set to sealing. Select Manual mode and program the cooking time for 1 hour and 15 minutes. 5. Once the cooking cycle is complete, allow the pressure to release naturally before opening the lid.

Mississippi Pork Butt Roast

Prep time: 10 minutes | Cook time: 6 hours | Serves 7

- 1 tablespoon ranch dressing mix
- 1½ pound (680 g) pork butt roast, chopped
- 1 cup butter
- 1 chili pepper, chopped
- ½ cup water

1. Add all the ingredients to the Instant Pot, ensuring they are evenly distributed. 2. Secure the lid and set the Instant Pot to cook on Low Pressure for 6 hours. 3. Once the cooking time is complete, carefully shred the meat and transfer it to a serving plate. Serve immediately.

Pork Chops in Creamy Mushroom Gravy

Prep time: 5 minutes | Cook time: 15 minutes | Serves 4

- 4 (5-ounce / 142-g) pork chops
- 1 teaspoon salt
- ½ teaspoon pepper
- 2 tablespoons avocado oil
- 1 cup chopped button mushrooms
- ½ medium onion, sliced
- 1 clove garlic, minced
- 1 cup chicken broth
- ¼ cup heavy cream
- 4 tablespoons butter
- ¼ teaspoon xanthan gum
- 1 tablespoon chopped fresh parsley

1. Season the pork chops with salt and pepper. Turn on the Instant Pot to Sauté mode and add the avocado oil and mushrooms. Cook the mushrooms for 3 to 5 minutes, stirring occasionally, until they start to soften. Add the onions and pork chops, and continue to sauté for another 3 minutes, browning the pork chops to a golden hue. 2. Stir in the garlic and pour in the broth. Secure the lid, ensuring it is properly closed, and select Manual mode, setting the cooking time to 15 minutes on High Pressure. When the timer finishes, allow the pressure to release naturally for 10 minutes, then carefully perform a quick release for any remaining pressure. 3. Open the lid and transfer the pork chops to a plate. Switch the Instant Pot back to Sauté mode and stir in the heavy cream, butter, and xanthan gum. Simmer the mixture for 5 to 10 minutes, or until the sauce thickens to your liking. Return the pork chops to the pot, coating them in the sauce. Serve warm, garnished with mushroom sauce and parsley.

Rosemary Lamb Chops

Prep time: 25 minutes | Cook time: 2 minutes | Serves 4

- 1½ pounds lamb chops (4 small chops)
- 1 teaspoon kosher salt
- Leaves from 1 (6-inch) rosemary sprig
- 2 tablespoons avocado oil
- 1 shallot, peeled and cut in quarters
- 1 tablespoon tomato paste
- 1 cup beef broth

1. Lay the lamb chops on a cutting board and press salt and rosemary leaves firmly onto both sides. Allow them to rest at room temperature for 15 to 30 minutes. 2. Turn the electric pressure cooker to the Sauté/More setting and heat the avocado oil until hot. 3. Sear the lamb chops for about 2 minutes on each side. If all the chops do not fit in a single layer, sear them in batches and set the browned chops aside on a plate. 4. In the same pot, add the shallot, tomato paste, and broth. Stir and cook for about 1 minute, scraping up the browned bits stuck to the bottom. Press Cancel to stop sautéing. 5. Return the lamb chops and any accumulated juices to the pot. 6. Secure the lid and lock it in place. Set the valve to sealing. 7. Cook the lamb chops on high pressure for 2 minutes. 8. When the timer ends, press Cancel and perform a quick pressure release. 9. Once the pin drops, unlock and remove the lid. 10. Plate the lamb chops immediately and serve hot.

Quick Steak Tacos

Prep time: 5 minutes | Cook time: 10 minutes | Serves 6

- 1 tablespoon olive oil
- 8 ounces sirloin steak
- 2 tablespoons steak seasoning
- 1 teaspoon Worcestershire sauce
- ½ red onion, halved and sliced
- 6 corn tortillas
- ¼ cup tomatoes
- ¾ cup reduced-fat Mexican cheese
- 2 tablespoons low-fat sour cream
- 6 tablespoons garden fresh salsa
- ¼ cup chopped fresh cilantro

1. Activate the Sauté function on the Instant Pot and wait until the display reads "hot," then pour in the olive oil. 2. Generously season the steak with steak seasoning, ensuring even coverage. 3. Place the steak into the pot and drizzle with Worcestershire sauce. 4. Sear the steak for 2–3 minutes on each side, cooking until it develops a rich brown color. 5. Remove the steak from the pot and slice it into thin strips. 6. Add the onion to the pot, along with any remaining olive oil and steak juices, and sauté until the onion becomes translucent. 7. Remove the cooked onions from the pot. 8. Warm the corn tortillas and layer each with steak, onions, tomatoes, cheese, sour cream, salsa, and cilantro before serving.

Cider-Herb Pork Tenderloin

Prep time: 15 minutes | Cook time: 18 minutes | Serves 4

- ¼ teaspoon ground cumin
- ½ teaspoon ground nutmeg
- ½ teaspoon dried thyme
- ½ teaspoon ground coriander
- 1 tablespoon sesame oil
- 1 pound (454 g) pork tenderloin
- 2 tablespoons apple cider vinegar
- 1 cup water

1. In a mixing bowl, combine ground cumin, ground nutmeg, thyme, ground coriander, and apple cider vinegar. Mix thoroughly to form a spice blend. 2. Rub the pork tenderloin evenly with the prepared spice mixture, ensuring it is well coated. 3. Set the Instant Pot to Sauté mode and heat the sesame oil for 2 minutes until hot. 4. Place the pork tenderloin into the pot and sear for 5 minutes on each side, or until the meat turns a light golden brown. 5. Pour water into the pot around the pork. 6. Secure the lid and seal it tightly. Select Manual mode (High Pressure) and set the cooking time to 5 minutes. 7. Once the cooking cycle is complete, allow the pressure to release naturally for 15 minutes before carefully opening the lid. Serve the tenderloin warm.

Creamy Pork Liver

Prep time: 5 minutes | Cook time: 7 minutes | Serves 3

- 14 ounces (397 g) pork liver, chopped
- 1 teaspoon salt
- 1 teaspoon butter
- ½ cup heavy cream
- 3 tablespoons scallions, chopped

1. Season the liver evenly with salt on a clean work surface, ensuring it is well coated. 2. Turn the Instant Pot to Sauté mode and add the butter, allowing it to melt completely. 3. Once the butter is melted, add the heavy cream, scallions, and liver to the pot, stirring gently to combine. 4. Secure the lid and set the Instant Pot to Manual mode, programming the cooking time for 12 minutes on High Pressure. 5. After the cooking cycle ends, let the pressure release naturally for 5 minutes before manually releasing any remaining pressure. Carefully open the lid. 6. Plate and serve the dish immediately while hot.

Beef and Sausage Medley

Prep time: 10 minutes | Cook time: 27 minutes | Serves 8

- 1 teaspoon butter
- 2 beef sausages, casing removed and sliced
- 2 pounds (907 g) beef steak, cubed
- 1 yellow onion, sliced
- 2 fresh ripe tomatoes, puréed
- 1 jalapeño pepper, chopped
- 1 red bell pepper, chopped
- 1½ cups roasted vegetable broth
- 2 cloves garlic, minced
- 1 teaspoon Old Bay seasoning
- 2 bay leaves
- 1 sprig thyme
- 1 sprig rosemary
- ½ teaspoon paprika
- Sea salt and ground black pepper, to taste

1. Select the Sauté function on the Instant Pot and allow it to heat. Add the butter and let it melt before cooking the sausage and steak for about 4 minutes, stirring occasionally. Once browned, remove and set aside. 2. Add the onion to the pot and sauté for 3 minutes, or until softened and translucent. Return the reserved sausage and steak to the pot along with the remaining ingredients, stirring to combine. 3. Secure the lid and set the vent to sealing. Select Manual mode and program the cooking time for 20 minutes on High Pressure. 4. When the cooking cycle ends, perform a quick pressure release. Carefully open the lid once the pressure has fully released. 5. Serve the dish immediately while hot.

Beef Ribs with Radishes

Prep time: 20 minutes | Cook time: 56 minutes | Serves 4

- ¼ teaspoon ground coriander
- ¼ teaspoon ground cumin
- 1 teaspoon kosher salt, plus more to taste
- ½ teaspoon smoked paprika
- Pinch of ground allspice (optional)
- 4 (8-ounce / 227-g) bone-in beef short ribs
- 2 tablespoons avocado oil
- 1 cup water
- 2 radishes, ends trimmed, leaves rinsed and roughly chopped
- Freshly ground black pepper, to taste

1. In a small bowl, combine the coriander, cumin, salt, paprika, and allspice. Thoroughly rub this spice blend over all sides of the short ribs. 2. Set the Instant Pot to Sauté mode and heat the oil. Place the short ribs in the pot, bone side up, and sear for about 4 minutes per side until browned. 3. Add the water to the pot, ensuring it surrounds the ribs. Secure the lid and select Manual mode, setting the cooking time to 45 minutes on High Pressure. 4. Once the cooking time ends, allow the pressure to release naturally for 10 minutes, then manually release any remaining pressure. Open the lid carefully. 5. Transfer the short ribs to a serving plate and set aside. 6. Add the radishes to the cooking liquid in the pot and position a metal steaming basket directly on top. Arrange the radish leaves inside the basket. 7. Close and secure the lid. Select Manual mode again, setting the cooking time to 3 minutes on High Pressure. 8. After cooking, perform a quick pressure release. Open the lid, remove the radish leaves, and transfer them to a serving bowl. Season the leaves lightly with salt and pepper. 9. Remove the radishes from the pot and place them over the seasoned leaves. Serve the dish hot alongside the short ribs.

Albóndigas Sinaloenses

Prep time: 15 minutes | Cook time: 10 minutes | Serves 6

- 1 pound (454 g) ground pork
- ½ pound (227 g) Italian sausage, crumbled
- 2 tablespoons yellow onion, finely chopped
- ½ teaspoon dried oregano
- 1 sprig fresh mint, finely minced
- ½ teaspoon ground cumin
- 2 garlic cloves, finely minced
- ¼ teaspoon fresh ginger, grated
- Seasoned salt and ground black pepper, to taste
- 1 tablespoon olive oil
- ½ cup yellow onions, finely chopped
- 2 chipotle chilies in adobo
- 2 tomatoes, puréed
- 2 tablespoons tomato passata
- 1 cup chicken broth

1. In a mixing bowl, combine the pork, sausage, 2 tablespoons of yellow onion, oregano, mint, cumin, garlic, ginger, salt, and black pepper. Mix thoroughly until well blended. 2. Shape the mixture into meatballs and set them aside. 3. Turn on the Instant Pot and select Sauté mode. Once hot, add the olive oil and cook the meatballs for about 4 minutes, stirring frequently to ensure even browning. 4. Add ½ cup of yellow onions, chilies in adobo, tomatoes passata, and broth to the pot. Gently stir to combine, then carefully return the reserved meatballs to the mixture. 5. Close and secure the lid, ensuring the vent is set to sealing. Select Manual mode and program the cooking time to 6 minutes on High Pressure. 6. When the cooking time ends, perform a quick pressure release. Open the lid cautiously once the pressure has been fully released. 7. Serve the meatballs immediately while hot.

Pork Meatballs with Thyme

Prep time: 15 minutes | Cook time: 16 minutes | Serves 8

- 2 cups ground pork
- 1 teaspoon dried thyme
- ½ teaspoon chili flakes
- ½ teaspoon garlic powder
- 1 tablespoon coconut oil
- ¼ teaspoon ground ginger
- 3 tablespoons almond flour
- ¼ cup water

1. In a mixing bowl, combine the ground pork, dried thyme, chili flakes, garlic powder, ground ginger, and almond flour. Mix thoroughly until the ingredients are well blended. 2. Shape the mixture into evenly sized meatballs and set them aside. 3. Turn on the Instant Pot to Sauté mode and melt the coconut oil. 4. Place the meatballs in a single layer in the Instant Pot and cook for about 3 minutes on each side, ensuring they are evenly browned. 5. Pour water into the pot, close the lid, and cook the meatballs for 10 minutes. Serve hot.

Beef Cheeseburger Pie

Prep time: 15 minutes | Cook time: 30 minutes | Serves 6

- 1 tablespoon olive oil
- 1 pound (454 g) ground beef
- 3 eggs (1 beaten)
- ½ cup unsweetened tomato purée
- 2 tablespoons golden flaxseed meal
- 1 garlic clove, minced
- ½ teaspoon Italian seasoning blend
- ½ teaspoon sea salt
- ½ teaspoon smoked paprika
- ½ teaspoon onion powder
- 2 tablespoons heavy cream
- ½ teaspoon ground mustard
- ¼ teaspoon ground black pepper
- 2 cups water
- ½ cup grated Cheddar cheese

1. Grease a round cake pan evenly with olive oil and set it aside. 2. Turn on the Instant Pot and select Sauté mode. Once hot, add the ground beef and cook for about 5 minutes, stirring occasionally, until browned. 3. Remove the beef from the pot and transfer it to a large mixing bowl. 4. To the bowl, add the beaten egg, tomato purée, flaxseed meal, garlic, Italian seasoning, sea salt, smoked paprika, and onion powder. Mix everything thoroughly until fully combined. 5. Spoon the meat mixture into the prepared cake pan, using a knife or spatula to spread it evenly. Set the pan aside. 6. In a separate medium bowl, whisk together the remaining eggs, heavy cream, ground mustard, and black pepper until smooth and combined. 7. Pour the egg mixture evenly over the meat mixture in the pan, then cover the pan tightly with aluminum foil. 8. Place the trivet into the Instant Pot and pour water into the pot's base. Carefully place the covered pan onto the trivet. 9. Secure the lid and set the vent to sealing. Select Manual mode and cook for 20 minutes on High Pressure. 10. Once cooking is done, let the pressure release naturally for 10 minutes, then release any remaining pressure manually. Allow the pie to rest in the pot for an additional 5 minutes. 11. Preheat your oven broiler to 450°F (235°C). 12. Open the Instant Pot, remove the pan, and carefully take off the foil. Sprinkle the shredded Cheddar cheese evenly over the top of the pie. 13. Place the pan under the broiler for about 2 minutes, or until the cheese is melted and golden brown. Cut the pie into six equal wedges and serve while hot.

Blade Pork with Sauerkraut

Prep time: 15 minutes | Cook time: 37 minutes | Serves 6

- 2 pounds (907 g) blade pork steaks
- Sea salt and ground black pepper, to taste
- ½ teaspoon cayenne pepper
- ½ teaspoon dried parsley flakes
- 1 tablespoon butter
- 1½ cups water
- 2 cloves garlic, thinly sliced
- 2 pork sausages, casing removed and sliced
- 4 cups sauerkraut

1. Season the blade pork steaks evenly with salt, black pepper, cayenne pepper, and dried parsley, ensuring all sides are coated. 2. Activate the Sauté mode on the Instant Pot and let it heat. Melt the butter in the pot, then sear the pork steaks for about 5 minutes, turning as needed to brown all sides. 3. Remove the steaks and clean the Instant Pot. Pour water into the pot and place a trivet at the bottom. 4. Position the blade pork steaks on the trivet. Using a knife, make small slits across the pork and insert garlic pieces into each slit. 5. Close and secure the lid. Select the Meat/Stew mode and set the cooking time to 30 minutes on High Pressure. 6. Once cooking is done, allow the pressure to release naturally for 15 minutes, then manually release any remaining pressure. Open the lid carefully. 7. Add the sausage and sauerkraut to the pot. Switch back to Sauté mode and cook for an additional 2 minutes, stirring until heated through. 8. Serve the pork steaks immediately while hot, along with the sausage and sauerkraut.

Carnitas Burrito Bowls

Prep time: 10 minutes | Cook time: 1 hour | Serves 6

- Carnitas
- 1 tablespoon chili powder
- ½ teaspoon garlic powder
- 1 teaspoon ground coriander
- 1 teaspoon fine sea salt
- ½ cup water
- ¼ cup fresh lime juice
- One 2-pound boneless pork shoulder butt roast, cut into 2-inch cubes
- Rice and Beans
- 1 cup Minute brand brown rice (see Note)
- 1½ cups drained cooked black beans, or one 15-ounce can black beans, rinsed and drained
- Pico de Gallo
- 8 ounces tomatoes (see Note), diced
- ½ small yellow onion, diced
- 1 jalapeño chile, seeded and finely diced
- 1 tablespoon chopped fresh cilantro
- 1 teaspoon fresh lime juice
- Pinch of fine sea salt
- ¼ cup sliced green onions, white and green parts
- 2 tablespoons chopped fresh cilantro
- 3 hearts romaine lettuce, cut into ¼-inch-wide ribbons
- 2 large avocados, pitted, peeled, and sliced
- Hot sauce (such as Cholula or Tapatío) for serving

1. Prepare the carnitas seasoning by combining chili powder, garlic powder, coriander, and salt in a small bowl. Mix well to ensure an even blend. 2. Add water and lime juice to the Instant Pot. Arrange the pork pieces in a single layer inside the pot and evenly sprinkle the chili powder mixture over the pork. 3. Secure the lid and set the Pressure Release to Sealing. Select the Meat/Stew setting and program the cooking time to 30 minutes on High Pressure. Allow about 10 minutes for the pot to build pressure before the cooking cycle begins. 4. Once the cooking program ends, let the pressure release naturally for at least 15 minutes. Then, move the Pressure Release to Venting to release any remaining steam. Carefully open the lid and transfer the pork to a plate or cutting board using tongs. 5. While the pressure is releasing, preheat your oven to 400°F. 6. Using heat-resistant mitts, remove the inner pot from the Instant Pot. Pour the cooking liquid into a fat separator and separate the fat. Alternatively, skim the fat from the surface using a ladle. Add water to the defatted liquid as needed to make a total of 1 cup. 7. To prepare the rice and beans, pour the 1 cup of cooking liquid back into the Instant Pot. Add the rice in an even layer. Insert a tall steam rack into the pot and place the black beans in a 1½-quart stainless-steel bowl on top of the rack, ensuring the bowl does not touch the lid once closed. 8. Secure the lid and set the Pressure Release to Sealing. Press Cancel to reset the cooking program, then select Pressure Cook or Manual mode and set the cooking time to 15 minutes on High Pressure. Allow about 5 minutes for the pot to build pressure. 9. While the rice and beans cook, use two forks to shred the pork into bite-size pieces. Spread the shredded pork evenly on a sheet pan and roast it in the preheated oven for 20 minutes, until crispy and browned. 10. To make the pico de gallo, combine the tomatoes, onion, jalapeño, cilantro, lime juice, and salt in a medium bowl. Mix well and set aside. 11. When the rice and beans finish cooking, allow the pressure to release naturally for 5 minutes, then move the Pressure Release to Venting to release any remaining steam. Open the pot carefully. Remove the bowl of beans and the steam rack, then lift out the inner pot. Fluff the rice with a fork, mixing in green onions and cilantro. 12. Assemble the bowls by dividing the rice, beans, carnitas, pico de gallo, lettuce, and avocados evenly among six bowls. Serve warm with hot sauce on the side.

Pork Steaks with Pico de Gallo

Prep time: 15 minutes | Cook time: 12 minutes | Serves 6

- 1 tablespoon butter
- 2 pounds (907 g) pork steaks
- 1 bell pepper, deseeded and sliced
- ½ cup shallots, chopped
- 2 garlic cloves, minced
- ¼ cup dry red wine
- 1 cup chicken bone broth
- ¼ cup water
- Salt, to taste
- ¼ teaspoon freshly ground black pepper, or more to taste
- Pico de Gallo:
- 1 tomato, chopped
- 1 chili pepper, seeded and minced
- ½ cup red onion, chopped
- 2 garlic cloves, minced
- 1 tablespoon fresh cilantro, finely chopped
- Sea salt, to taste

1. Activate the Sauté mode on the Instant Pot and allow it to heat up. Melt the butter in the pot, then sear the pork steaks for about 4 minutes, flipping to brown both sides evenly. 2. Add the bell pepper, shallot, garlic, wine, chicken bone broth, water, salt, and black pepper to the pot, stirring gently to combine. 3. Secure the lid and ensure it is properly sealed. Select Manual mode and set the cooking time to 8 minutes on High Pressure. 4. While the pork cooks, prepare the Pico de Gallo by combining all its ingredients in a small bowl. Cover and refrigerate until needed. 5. Once the cooking cycle is complete, perform a quick pressure release. Open the lid carefully to avoid steam. 6. Plate the pork steaks while warm and serve them with the chilled Pico de Gallo on the side.

Pork Taco Casserole

Prep time: 15 minutes | Cook time: 30 minutes | Serves 6

- ½ cup water
- 2 eggs
- 3 ounces (85 g) Cottage cheese, at room temperature
- ¼ cup heavy cream
- 1 teaspoon taco seasoning
- 6 ounces (170 g) Cotija cheese, crumbled
- ¾ pound (340 g) ground pork
- ½ cup tomatoes, puréed
- 1 tablespoon taco seasoning
- 3 ounces (85 g) chopped green chilies
- 6 ounces (170 g) Queso Manchego cheese, shredded

1. Pour water into the Instant Pot and place the trivet at the bottom. 2. In a mixing bowl, whisk together the eggs, cottage cheese, heavy cream, and taco seasoning until well combined. 3. Lightly grease a casserole dish and evenly spread the Cotija cheese across the bottom. Pour the egg mixture over the cheese, ensuring it is evenly distributed. 4. Carefully lower the casserole dish onto the trivet inside the Instant Pot. 5. Secure the lid and select Manual mode, setting the cooking time to 20 minutes on High Pressure. 6. When the cooking cycle finishes, perform a quick pressure release and open the lid cautiously. 7. Meanwhile, heat a skillet over medium-high heat. Add the ground pork and cook until browned, breaking it into crumbles with a fork. 8. Stir in the tomato purée, taco seasoning, and green chilies, mixing until well incorporated. Spread this mixture evenly over the cooked cheese crust. 9. Sprinkle the shredded Queso Manchego on top of the pork layer. 10. Close the lid and select Manual mode again, setting the cooking time to 10 minutes on High Pressure. 11. After cooking, perform a quick pressure release. Carefully open the lid and serve the casserole hot.

Filipino Pork Loin

Prep time: 10 minutes | Cook time: 40 minutes | Serves 4

- 1 pound (454 g) pork loin, chopped
- ½ cup apple cider vinegar
- 1 cup chicken broth
- 1 chili pepper, chopped
- 1 tablespoon coconut oil
- 1 teaspoon salt

1. Select Sauté mode on the Instant Pot and allow it to heat up. Melt the coconut oil in the pot. 2. Once the oil is hot, add the chili pepper and sauté for 2 minutes, stirring occasionally to release its flavor. 3. Add the chopped pork loin and sprinkle it with salt. Cook for 5 minutes, stirring to ensure the pork browns evenly. 4. Pour in the apple cider vinegar and chicken broth, stirring to combine the ingredients. 5. Secure the lid and seal it tightly. Select Manual mode and set the cooking time to 30 minutes on High Pressure. Once the cooking is complete, perform a quick pressure release. Open the lid carefully and serve.

BBQ Ribs and Broccoli Slaw

Prep time: 10 minutes | Cook time: 50 minutes | Serves 6

- BBQ Ribs
- 4 pounds baby back ribs
- 1 teaspoon fine sea salt
- 1 teaspoon freshly ground black pepper
- Broccoli Slaw
- ½ cup plain 2 percent Greek yogurt
- 1 tablespoon olive oil
- 1 tablespoon fresh lemon juice
- ½ teaspoon fine sea salt
- ¼ teaspoon freshly ground black pepper
- 1 pound broccoli florets (or florets from 2 large crowns), chopped
- 10 radishes, halved and thinly sliced
- 1 red bell pepper, seeded and cut lengthwise into narrow strips
- 1 large apple (such as Fuji, Jonagold, or Gala), thinly sliced
- ½ red onion, thinly sliced
- ¾ cup low-sugar or unsweetened barbecue sauce

1. Prepare the ribs by patting them dry with paper towels, then cutting the racks into six sections (3 to 5 ribs per section, depending on their size). Season the ribs generously on all sides with salt and pepper. 2. Pour 1 cup of water into the Instant Pot and insert the wire metal steam rack. Arrange the ribs on the rack, stacking them if necessary. 3. Secure the lid and set the Pressure Release to Sealing. Choose the Pressure Cook or Manual setting and set the cooking time to 20 minutes at high pressure. Note that the pot will take about 15 minutes to reach full pressure before cooking begins. 4. While the ribs cook, prepare the broccoli slaw. In a small bowl, whisk together the yogurt, oil, lemon juice, salt, and pepper until smooth. In a large bowl, combine the broccoli, radishes, bell pepper, apple, and onion. Pour the yogurt dressing over the vegetables and toss until well coated. 5. About 10 minutes before the ribs finish cooking, preheat your oven to 400°F and line a sheet pan with aluminum foil. 6. When the cooking cycle ends, perform a quick pressure release by moving the Pressure Release to Venting. Open the lid carefully and use tongs to transfer the ribs to the prepared sheet pan in a single layer. Brush both sides of the ribs with barbecue sauce, using about 2 tablespoons per section, then arrange them meaty-side up. Bake in the oven for 15 to 20 minutes, or until the ribs are lightly browned. 7. Serve the ribs warm with the broccoli slaw on the side.

Cilantro Pork

Prep time: 10 minutes | Cook time: 85 minutes | Serves 4

- 1 pound (454 g) boneless pork shoulder
- ¼ cup chopped fresh cilantro
- 1 cup water
- 1 teaspoon salt
- 1 teaspoon coconut oil
- ½ teaspoon mustard seeds

1. Add water to the Instant Pot, ensuring the base is covered. 2. Place the pork shoulder into the pot and add the fresh cilantro, salt, coconut oil, and mustard seeds on top. 3. Secure the lid and seal it tightly. Select Manual mode and set the cooking time to 85 minutes on High Pressure. 4. Once the cooking time is complete, perform a quick pressure release and carefully open the lid. 5. Serve the cooked pork shoulder hot, accompanied by the flavorful liquid from the Instant Pot.

Osso Buco with Gremolata

Prep time: 35 minutes | Cook time: 1 hour 2 minutes | Serves 6

- 4 bone-in beef shanks
- Sea salt, to taste
- 2 tablespoons avocado oil
- 1 small turnip, diced
- 1 medium onion, diced
- 1 medium stalk celery, diced
- 4 cloves garlic, smashed
- 1 tablespoon unsweetened tomato purée
- ½ cup dry white wine
- 1 cup chicken broth
- 1 sprig fresh rosemary
- 2 sprigs fresh thyme
- 3 Roma tomatoes, diced
- For the Gremolata:
- ½ cup loosely packed parsley leaves
- 1 clove garlic, crushed
- Grated zest of 2 lemons

1. On a clean work surface, evenly season the shanks on all sides with salt. 2. Turn the Instant Pot to Sauté mode and heat the oil until it shimmers. Add 2 shanks to the pot and sear them for about 4 minutes on each side until browned. Remove the shanks and set them aside in a bowl. Repeat the process with the remaining shanks. 3. Add the turnip, onion, and celery to the pot and sauté for 5 minutes, stirring occasionally, until the vegetables soften. 4. Stir in the garlic and unsweetened tomato purée, cooking for 1 more minute while stirring frequently. 5. Pour in the wine to deglaze the pot, using a wooden spoon to scrape up any browned bits stuck to the bottom. Bring the mixture to a boil. 6. Add the broth, rosemary, thyme, and seared shanks to the pot. Place the tomatoes on top of the shanks, ensuring they are evenly distributed. 7. Secure the lid tightly and select Manual mode. Set the cooking time to 40 minutes on High Pressure. 8. While the shanks are cooking, prepare the gremolata by combining parsley, garlic, and lemon zest in a small food processor. Pulse until the parsley is finely chopped, then refrigerate until ready to serve. 9. When the cooking cycle ends, let the pressure release naturally for 20 minutes before performing a manual release to remove any remaining pressure. Carefully open the lid. 10. To serve, transfer the shanks to a large shallow serving bowl, ladle the rich braising sauce over the top, and finish with a sprinkle of the fresh gremolata. Serve immediately.

Lamb Koobideh

Prep time: 15 minutes | Cook time: 30 minutes | Serves 4

- 1 pound (454 g) ground lamb
- 1 egg, beaten
- 1 tablespoon lemon juice
- 1 teaspoon ground turmeric
- ½ teaspoon garlic powder
- 1 teaspoon chives, chopped
- ½ teaspoon ground black pepper
- 1 cup water

1. In a mixing bowl, mix together all the ingredients except for water. 2. Form the mixture into meatballs and shape them into ellipse shapes. 3. Add water to the Instant Pot and place a trivet inside. 4. Arrange the prepared ellipse meatballs in a baking pan and place the pan on top of the trivet. 5. Close the lid and choose Manual mode, setting the cooking time to 30 minutes at High Pressure. 6. When the timer sounds, perform a quick pressure release and open the lid. 7. Serve the meatballs hot right away.

Turmeric Pork Loin

Prep time: 10 minutes | Cook time: 22 minutes | Serves 4

- 1 pound (454 g) pork loin
- 1 teaspoon ground turmeric
- 1 teaspoon coconut oil
- ½ teaspoon salt
- ½ cup organic almond milk

1. Slice the pork loin into strips and season evenly with salt and ground turmeric. 2. Activate Sauté mode on the Instant Pot and let it heat for 1 minute. Add the coconut oil and allow it to melt before adding the pork strips. 3. Cook the pork strips for about 6 minutes, stirring occasionally to ensure even browning. 4. Pour in the almond milk and close the lid securely. 5. Continue to sauté the pork for an additional 15 minutes, stirring occasionally for thorough cooking and a rich flavor.

Lamb Sirloin Masala

Prep time: 10 minutes | Cook time: 25 minutes | Serves 3

- 12 ounces (340 g) lamb sirloin, sliced
- 1 tablespoon garam masala
- 1 tablespoon lemon juice
- 1 tablespoon olive oil
- ¼ cup coconut cream

1. In a large bowl, combine the sliced lamb sirloin with garam masala, lemon juice, olive oil, and coconut cream. Toss thoroughly to ensure the lamb is evenly coated with the mixture. 2. Transfer the seasoned lamb to the Instant Pot and set it to Sauté mode. Cook for 25 minutes, flipping the lamb every 5 minutes to ensure even cooking on all sides. 3. Once the cooking is done, let the lamb rest in the pot for 10 minutes to cool slightly before serving. Serve warm.

Herbed Pork Roast with Asparagus

Prep time: 25 minutes | Cook time: 17 minutes | Serves 6

- 1 teaspoon dried thyme
- ½ teaspoon garlic powder
- ½ teaspoon onion powder
- ½ teaspoon dried oregano
- 1½ teaspoons smoked paprika
- ½ teaspoon ground black pepper
- 1 teaspoon sea salt
- 2 tablespoons olive oil, divided
- 2 pounds (907 g) boneless pork loin roast
- ½ medium white onion, chopped
- 2 garlic cloves, minced
- ⅔ cup chicken broth
- 2 tablespoons Worcestershire sauce
- 1 cup water
- 20 fresh asparagus spears, cut in half and woody ends removed

1. In a small bowl, whisk together thyme, garlic powder, onion powder, oregano, smoked paprika, black pepper, and sea salt until well mixed. Then, add 1½ tablespoons of olive oil and stir until fully incorporated. 2. Coat all sides of the pork roast with the oil and spice mixture. Place the roast in a covered dish and refrigerate for 30 minutes to marinate. 3. Turn on Sauté mode and brush the Instant Pot's bottom with the remaining olive oil. Once the oil is heated, add the pork roast and sear for about 5 minutes on each side or until it's nicely browned. Remove the roast and set it aside. 4. Add onions and garlic to the pot, sautéing for 2 minutes or until the onions are tender and the garlic is fragrant. 5. Pour in the chicken broth and Worcestershire sauce. 6. Secure the lid, select Manual mode, and set the cooking time to 15 minutes at High Pressure. 7. After cooking, let the pressure release naturally for 10 minutes, then quickly release any remaining pressure. 8. Open the lid, transfer the roast to a cutting board, cover with foil, and let it rest. Also, transfer the broth to a measuring cup and set aside. 9. Place a trivet in the Instant Pot and add water to the bottom. 10. Arrange the asparagus in an ovenproof bowl that fits into the Instant Pot, placing it on top of the trivet. 11. Lock the lid, choose Steam mode, and set a 2-minute cooking time. Once done, perform a quick pressure release. 12. Open the lid, transfer the asparagus to a serving platter, thinly slice the roast, and add it to the platter with the asparagus. Drizzle the reserved broth over everything and serve warm.

Basic Nutritional Values

Prep time: 20 minutes | Cook time: 2 hours | Serves 4 to 6

- 2 pounds beef roast, boneless
- ¼ teaspoon salt
- ¼ teaspoon pepper
- 1 tablespoon olive oil
- 2 stalks celery, chopped
- 4 tablespoons margarine
- 2 cups low-sodium tomato juice
- 2 cloves garlic, finely chopped, or 1 teaspoon garlic powder
- 1 teaspoon thyme
- 1 bay leaf
- 4 carrots, chopped
- 1 medium onion, chopped
- 4 medium potatoes, chopped

1. Pat the beef dry with paper towels and generously season all sides with salt and pepper. 2. Set the Instant Pot to Sauté mode and adjust the heat to "More." Heat the oil in the inner pot, then sear the beef for about 6 minutes, turning once, until browned on all sides. Transfer the beef to a plate. 3. Add the celery and margarine to the pot and cook for 2 minutes, stirring occasionally. Mix in the tomato juice, garlic, thyme, and bay leaf. Press Cancel to stop the Sauté function. 4. Return the beef to the pot, pressing it into the sauce to ensure it is well coated. Secure the lid and set the vent to sealing. Select Manual mode and cook on High Pressure for 1 hour and 15 minutes. 5. Once the cooking is complete, allow the pressure to release naturally. Transfer the beef to a cutting board and discard the bay leaf. 6. Skim off any excess fat from the surface of the sauce. Turn on Sauté mode again, adjust the heat to "More," and simmer the sauce for about 18 minutes, or until it reduces to approximately 2½ cups. Press Cancel to turn off Sauté mode. 7. Add the carrots, onion, and potatoes to the pot. Secure the lid, set the vent to sealing, and select Manual mode, cooking on High Pressure for 10 minutes. 8. When the timer finishes, perform a quick pressure release. Switch back to Sauté mode to keep the contents at a simmer. 9. Adjust seasoning with additional salt and pepper as needed before serving.

Korean Short Rib Lettuce Wraps

Prep time: 7 minutes | Cook time: 25 minutes | Serves 4

- ¼ cup coconut aminos, or 1 tablespoon wheat-free tamari
- 2 tablespoons coconut vinegar
- 2 tablespoons sesame oil
- 3 green onions, thinly sliced, plus more for garnish
- 2 teaspoons peeled and grated fresh ginger
- 2 teaspoons minced garlic
- ½ teaspoon fine sea salt
- ½ teaspoon red pepper flakes, plus more for garnish
- 1 pound (454 g) boneless beef short ribs, sliced ½ inch thick
- For Serving:
- 1 head radicchio, thinly sliced
- Butter lettuce leaves

1. Add the coconut aminos, vinegar, sesame oil, green onions, ginger, garlic, salt, and red pepper flakes to the Instant Pot. Stir well to combine, then add the short ribs, tossing to ensure they are evenly coated in the mixture. 2. Secure the lid and select Manual mode, setting the timer for 20 minutes on High Pressure. Once the cooking is complete, allow the pressure to release naturally. 3. Carefully remove the short ribs from the Instant Pot and transfer them to a warm plate, leaving the sauce in the pot. 4. Switch to Sauté mode and whisk the sauce continuously, cooking for about 5 minutes or until it thickens to your desired consistency. 5. Arrange the sliced radicchio on a serving platter, placing the short ribs on top. Drizzle the thickened sauce over the ribs and garnish with additional sliced green onions and red pepper flakes. Serve wrapped in lettuce leaves for a fresh and flavorful dish.

Cuban Pork Shoulder

Prep time: 20 minutes | Cook time: 35 minutes | Serves 3

- 9 ounces (255 g) pork shoulder, boneless, chopped
- 1 tablespoon avocado oil
- 1 teaspoon ground cumin
- ½ teaspoon ground black pepper
- ¼ cup apple cider vinegar
- 1 cup water

1. In a mixing bowl, combine the avocado oil, ground cumin, ground black pepper, and apple cider vinegar. Stir until well blended. 2. Add the pork shoulder to the spice mixture and mix thoroughly to ensure the meat is evenly coated. Place the seasoned pork onto a sheet of foil and wrap it tightly. 3. Pour water into the Instant Pot and insert the steamer rack into the base. 4. Place the wrapped pork shoulder onto the rack. Close the lid securely and ensure it is sealed. 5. Set the Instant Pot to cook the Cuban pork for 35 minutes on High Pressure. 6. Once the cooking cycle is complete, allow the pressure to release naturally for 10 minutes before carefully opening the lid. Serve as desired.

Easy Pot Roast and Vegetables

Prep time: 20 minutes | Cook time: 35 minutes | Serves 6

- 3–4 pound chuck roast, trimmed of fat and cut into serving-sized chunks
- 4 medium potatoes, cubed, unpeeled
- 4 medium carrots, sliced, or 1 pound baby carrots
- 2 celery ribs, sliced thin
- 1 envelope dry onion soup mix
- 3 cups water

1. Load the Instant Pot with chunks of pot roast and veggies, including potatoes, carrots, and celery. 2. Combine onion soup mix and water, then pour the mixture over everything in the pot. 3. Lock on the lid, ensuring the vent is in sealing position. Switch the Instant Pot to Manual mode and cook for 35 minutes. Once done, let the pressure release naturally.

Bone Broth Brisket with Tomatoes

Prep time: 5 minutes | Cook time: 75 minutes | Serves 4 to 5

- 2 tablespoons coconut oil
- ½ teaspoon garlic salt
- ½ teaspoon crushed red pepper
- ½ teaspoon dried basil
- ½ teaspoon kosher salt
- ½ teaspoon freshly ground black pepper
- 1 (14-ounce / 397-g) can sugar-free or low-sugar diced tomatoes
- 1 cup grass-fed bone broth
- 1 pound (454 g) beef brisket, chopped

1. Activate Sauté mode on the Instant Pot and melt the oil. In a medium bowl, combine the garlic salt, red pepper, basil, kosher salt, black pepper, and tomatoes, mixing well to create the sauce. 2. Pour the bone broth into the Instant Pot and place the brisket inside. Spoon the prepared sauce over the brisket, ensuring it is evenly covered. Cancel the Sauté program and secure the lid, setting the pressure release to Sealing. Select Manual mode and set the cooking time to 75 minutes on High Pressure. 3. When the cooking is complete, carefully switch the pressure release to Venting to release the steam. Open the lid, remove the brisket, and serve hot. If desired, pour the remaining sauce from the pot over the brisket for extra flavor.

Egg Meatloaf

Prep time: 20 minutes | Cook time: 25 minutes | Serves 6

- 1 tablespoon avocado oil
- 1½ cup ground pork
- 1 teaspoon chives
- 1 teaspoon salt
- ½ teaspoon ground black pepper
- 2 tablespoons coconut flour
- 3 eggs, hard-boiled, peeled
- 1 cup water

1. Coat a loaf pan with avocado oil. 2. In a mixing bowl, combine ground pork, chives, salt, ground black pepper, and coconut flour until well blended. 3. Pour the mixture into the loaf pan and smooth it out with a spatula. 4. Insert hard-boiled eggs into the meatloaf. 5. Add water to the Instant Pot and place a trivet inside. 6. Carefully position the loaf pan on top of the trivet. Close the Instant Pot lid. 7. Choose Manual mode and set the cooking time to 25 minutes at High Pressure. 8. When the timer goes off, allow a natural pressure release for 10 minutes, followed by a quick release for any remaining pressure. Open the lid. 9. Serve hot right away.

Bavarian Beef

Prep time: 35 minutes | Cook time: 1 hour 15 minutes | Serves 8

- 1 tablespoon canola oil
- 3-pound boneless beef chuck roast, trimmed of fat
- 3 cups sliced carrots
- 3 cups sliced onions
- 2 large kosher dill pickles, chopped
- 1 cup sliced celery
- ½ cup dry red wine or beef broth
- ⅓ cup German-style mustard
- 2 teaspoons coarsely ground black pepper
- 2 bay leaves
- ¼ teaspoon ground cloves
- 1 cup water
- ⅓ cup flour

1. Engage the Sauté function on the Instant Pot and pour in the oil. Brown the roast on both sides for approximately five minutes before pressing Cancel. 2. Add all the remaining ingredients, excluding the flour, into the Instant Pot. 3. Fasten the lid and ensure the vent is switched to sealing. Select Manual mode and adjust the cooking time to 1 hour and 15 minutes, allowing the pressure to release naturally afterwards. 4. Transfer the cooked meat and vegetables onto a large serving platter, covering them to retain warmth. 5. Extract a cup of liquid from the Instant Pot and blend it with the flour. Reactivate the Sauté mode, reintroduce the flour/broth mixture, and stir continuously until the broth achieves a smooth and thick consistency. 6. Serve the dish over noodles or spaetzle for an enjoyable meal.

Cheesesteak Stuffed Peppers

Prep time: 10 minutes | Cook time: 8 minutes | Serves 4

- 1 tablespoon butter
- 1 pound (454 g) shaved beef
- 4 ounces (113 g) mushrooms, coarsely chopped
- 2½ ounces (71 g) sliced onion
- 1 tablespoon Worcestershire sauce
- 1 teaspoon seasoned salt
- ¼ teaspoon salt
- ¼ teaspoon black pepper
- 4 large bell peppers (any color)
- ½ cup water
- 4 slices provolone cheese

1. Preheat the broiler. 2. Set the Instant Pot to Sauté mode and add the butter. Once melted, add the beef, mushrooms, and onion. Sauté for 2 to 3 minutes, stirring occasionally, until the vegetables soften. Mix in the Worcestershire sauce, seasoned salt, salt, and black pepper, stirring to combine evenly. Press Cancel to turn off Sauté mode. 3. Cut the tops off the bell peppers and remove the cores and seeds. Fill each pepper with approximately 4¼ ounces (120 g) of the meat mixture. Rinse out the Instant Pot to prepare for steaming. 4. Return the pot to the base and add the water along with the trivet. Arrange the stuffed peppers on top of the trivet. 5. Secure the lid and seal the vent. Select High Pressure and set the cooking time to 5 minutes. Once done, perform a quick pressure release. 6. Carefully remove the trivet from the pot and transfer the peppers to a baking sheet. Place a slice of provolone cheese on top of each pepper and broil for about 1 minute, or until the cheese is melted and bubbly. Serve immediately.

Garlic Butter Italian Sausages

Prep time: 15 minutes | Cook time: 20 minutes | Serves 4

- 1 teaspoon garlic powder
- 1 cup water
- 1 teaspoon butter
- 12 ounces (340 g) Italian sausages, chopped
- ½ teaspoon Italian seasoning

1. Toss the chopped Italian sausages with Italian seasoning and garlic powder, then place them in the instant pot. 2. Add butter and cook on Sauté for 10 minutes, stirring occasionally with the spatula. 3. Pour in water, close the lid, and switch to Manual mode (High Pressure). 4. Cook for 10 minutes, then let the natural pressure release for 10 minutes.

Golden Bacon Sticks

Prep time: 5 minutes | Cook time: 6 minutes | Serves 4

- 6 ounces (170 g) bacon, sliced
- 2 tablespoons almond flour
- 1 tablespoon water
- ¾ teaspoon chili pepper

1. Lay the sliced bacon on a clean surface and sprinkle it evenly with almond flour. Drizzle with water and top with the chili pepper, ensuring the bacon is well coated. 2. Place the prepared bacon into the Instant Pot. 3. Set the Instant Pot to Sauté mode and cook the bacon for 3 minutes on each side, turning carefully to ensure even cooking. Serve immediately while hot.

Shepherd's Pie with Cauliflower-Carrot Mash

Prep time: 10 minutes | Cook time: 35 minutes | Serves 6

- 1 tablespoon coconut oil
- 2 garlic cloves, minced
- 1 large yellow onion, diced
- 1 pound ground lamb
- 1 pound 95 percent lean ground beef
- ½ cup low-sodium vegetable broth
- 1 teaspoons dried thyme
- 1 teaspoon dried sage
- 1 teaspoon freshly ground black pepper
- 1¾ teaspoons fine sea salt
- 2 tablespoons Worcestershire sauce
- One 12-ounce bag frozen baby lima beans, green peas, or shelled edamame
- 3 tablespoons tomato paste
- 1 pound cauliflower florets
- 1 pound carrots, halved lengthwise and then crosswise (or quartered if very large)
- ¼ cup coconut milk or other nondairy milk
- ½ cup sliced green onions, white and green parts

1. Turn on the Sauté feature in the Instant Pot and warm up the oil with garlic for 2 minutes, or until the garlic is bubbling but still pale. Add onions and cook for 3 minutes, or until they start to become tender. Add lamb and beef, breaking up the meat with a wooden spoon or spatula as it cooks, for about 6 minutes, or until fully cooked with no pink remaining. 2. Stir in the broth, scraping up any browned bits from the bottom of the pot with your spoon or spatula. Add thyme, sage, pepper, ¾ teaspoon of salt, Worcestershire sauce, and lima beans, mixing well. Place a dollop of tomato paste on top without stirring it in. 3. Insert a tall steam rack into the pot, followed by placing cauliflower and carrots on top of the rack. 4. Lock the lid and set the Pressure Release to Sealing. Hit Cancel to reset the cooking program, then choose Pressure Cook or Manual mode and set a 4-minute cooking time at low pressure. (Note: The pot will take roughly 15 minutes to reach pressure before the cooking begins.) 5. Position an oven rack 4 to 6 inches beneath the heat source and preheat the broiler. 6. Upon completion of the cooking program, quickly release pressure by switching the Pressure Release to Venting. Open the pot and, using tongs, move the cauliflower and carrots to a bowl. Add coconut milk and the remaining 1 teaspoon of salt to the bowl. Using an immersion blender, puree the vegetables until smooth. 7. Wearing heat-resistant gloves, carefully remove the steam rack from the pot. Stir ½ cup of the mashed vegetables into the filling mixture in the pot, mixing in the tomato paste simultaneously. Take out the inner pot from the housing and transfer the mixture to a broiler-safe 9 by 13-inch baking dish, spreading it evenly. Top with the mashed vegetables and spread them out uniformly with a fork. Broil, checking frequently, for 5 to 8 minutes, or until the mashed vegetables are lightly golden. 8. Serve the shepherd's pie by spooning it onto plates, garnishing with green onions, and enjoy hot.

Chapter 3

Poultry

Whole Chicken with Herbs and Lemon

Prep time: 5 minutes | Cook time: 30 to 32 minutes | Serves 4

- 3 teaspoons garlic powder
- 3 teaspoons salt
- 2 teaspoons dried parsley
- 2 teaspoons dried rosemary
- 1 teaspoon pepper
- 1 (4-pound / 1.8-kg) whole chicken
- 2 tablespoons coconut oil
- 1 cup chicken broth
- 1 lemon, zested and quartered

1. Combine the garlic powder, salt, parsley, rosemary, and pepper in a small bowl. Rub this herb mix over the whole chicken. 2. Set your Instant Pot to Sauté and heat the coconut oil. 3. Add the chicken and brown for 5 to 7 minutes. Using tongs, transfer the chicken to a plate. 4. Pour the broth into the Instant Pot and scrape the bottom with a rubber spatula or wooden spoon until no seasoning is stuck to pot, then insert the trivet. 5. Scatter the lemon zest over chicken. Put the lemon quarters inside the chicken. Place the chicken on the trivet. 6. Secure the lid. Select the Meat/Stew mode and set the cooking time for 25 minutes at High Pressure. 7. Once cooking is complete, do a natural pressure release for 10 minutes, then release any remaining pressure. Carefully open the lid. 8. Shred the chicken and serve warm.

Texas-Style BBQ Chicken and Cabbage Slaw

Prep time: 5 minutes | Cook time: 20 minutes | Serves 6

- Chicken
- 1 cup water
- ¼ teaspoon fine sea salt
- 3 garlic cloves, peeled
- 2 bay leaves
- 2 pounds boneless, skinless chicken thighs (see Note)
- Cabbage Slaw
- ½ head red or green cabbage, thinly sliced
- 1 red bell pepper, seeded and thinly sliced
- 2 jalapeño chiles, seeded and cut into narrow strips
- 2 carrots, julienned
- 1 large Fuji or Gala apple, julienned
- ½ cup chopped fresh cilantro
- 3 tablespoons fresh lime juice
- 3 tablespoons extra-virgin olive oil
- ½ teaspoon ground cumin
- ¼ teaspoon fine sea salt
- ¾ cup low-sugar or unsweetened barbecue sauce
- Cornbread, for serving

1. To make the chicken: Combine the water, salt, garlic, bay leaves, and chicken thighs in the Instant Pot, arranging the chicken in a single layer. 2. Secure the lid and set the Pressure Release to Sealing. Select the Poultry, Pressure Cook, or Manual setting and set the cooking time for 10 minutes at high pressure. (The pot will take about 10 minutes to come up to pressure before the cooking program begins.) 3. To make the slaw: While the chicken is cooking, in a large bowl, combine the cabbage, bell pepper, jalapeños, carrots, apple, cilantro, lime juice, oil, cumin, and salt and toss together until the vegetables and apples are evenly coated. 4. When the cooking program ends, perform a quick pressure release by moving the Pressure Release to Venting, or let the pressure release naturally. Open the pot and, using tongs, transfer the chicken to a cutting board. Using two forks, shred the chicken into bite-size pieces. Wearing heat-resistant mitts, lift out the inner pot and discard the cooking liquid. Return the inner pot to the housing. 5. Return the chicken to the pot and stir in the barbecue sauce. You can serve it right away or heat it for a minute or two on the Sauté setting, then return the pot to its Keep Warm setting until ready to serve. 6. Divide the chicken and slaw evenly among six plates. Serve with wedges of cornbread on the side.

Creamy Coconut Chicken Curry

Prep time: 10 minutes | Cook time: 14 minutes | Serves 4 to 6

- 1 large onion, diced
- 6 cloves garlic, crushed
- ¼ cup coconut oil
- ½ teaspoon black pepper
- ½ teaspoon turmeric
- ½ teaspoon paprika
- ¼ teaspoon cinnamon
- ¼ teaspoon cloves
- ¼ teaspoon cumin
- ¼ teaspoon ginger
- ½ teaspoon salt
- 1 tablespoon curry powder (more if you like more flavor)
- ½ teaspoon chili powder
- 24-ounce can of low-sodium diced or crushed tomatoes
- 13½-ounce can of light coconut milk (I prefer a brand that has no unwanted ingredients, like guar gum or sugar)
- 4 pounds boneless skinless chicken breasts, cut into chunks

1. Sauté onion and garlic in the coconut oil, either with Sauté setting in the inner pot of the Instant Pot or on stove top, then add to pot. 2. Combine spices in a small bowl, then add to the inner pot. 3. Add tomatoes and coconut milk and stir. 4. Add chicken, and stir to coat the pieces with the sauce. 5. Secure the lid and make sure vent is at sealing. Set to Manual mode (or Pressure Cook on newer models) for 14 minutes. 6. Let pressure release naturally (if you're crunched for time, you can do a quick release). 7. Serve with your favorite sides, and enjoy!

Spiced Rub Whole Chicken

Prep time: 20 minutes | Cook time: 25 minutes | Serves 4

- 1½ pound (680 g) whole chicken
- 1 tablespoon poultry seasoning
- 2 tablespoons avocado oil
- 2 cups water

1. Pour water in the instant pot. 2. Then rub the chicken with poultry seasoning and avocado oil. 3. Put the chicken in the instant pot. Close and seal the lid. 4. Cook the meal in Manual mode for 25 minutes. When the time is finished, allow the natural pressure release for 10 minutes.

Tomato Paprika Chicken

Prep time: 10 minutes | Cook time: 20 minutes | Serves 2

- 8 ounces (227 g) chicken fillet, sliced
- 1 tomato, chopped
- 2 tablespoons mascarpone
- 1 teaspoon coconut oil
- 1 teaspoon ground paprika
- ½ teaspoon ground turmeric
- 1 tablespoon butter

1. Rub the chicken fillet with ground paprika, ground turmeric, and paprika. 2. Put the sliced chicken in the instant pot. 3. Add tomato, mascarpone, coconut oil, and butter. 4. Close the lid and cook the meal on Sauté mode for 20 minutes. 5. Stir it every 5 minutes to avoid burning.

Fried Cheese Shell Chicken Tacos

Prep time: 5 minutes | Cook time: 25 minutes | Serves 6

- Chicken:
- 4 (6-ounce / 170-g) boneless, skinless chicken breasts
- 1 cup chicken broth
- 1 teaspoon salt
- ¼ teaspoon pepper
- 1 tablespoon chili powder
- 2 teaspoons garlic powder
- 2 teaspoons cumin
- Cheese Shells:
- 1½ cups shredded whole-milk Mozzarella cheese

1. Combine all ingredients for the chicken in the Instant Pot. 2. Secure the lid. Select the Manual mode and set the cooking time for 20 minutes at High Pressure. 3. Once cooking is complete, do a quick pressure release. Carefully open the lid. 4. Shred the chicken and serve in bowls or cheese shells. 5. Make the cheese shells: Heat a nonstick skillet over medium heat. 6. Sprinkle ¼ cup of Mozzarella cheese in the skillet and fry until golden. Flip and turn off the heat. Allow the cheese to get brown. Fill with chicken and fold. The cheese will harden as it cools. Repeat with the remaining cheese and filling. 7. Serve warm.

Quinoa and Turkey with Unstuffed Bell Peppers

Prep time: 0 minutes | Cook time: 35 minutes | Serves 8

- 2 tablespoons extra-virgin olive oil
- 1 yellow onion, diced
- 2 celery stalks, diced
- 2 garlic cloves, chopped
- 2 pounds 93 percent lean ground turkey
- 2 teaspoons Cajun seasoning blend (plus 1 teaspoon fine sea salt if using a salt-free blend)
- ½ teaspoon freshly ground black pepper
- ¼ teaspoon cayenne pepper
- 1 cup quinoa, rinsed
- 1 cup low-sodium chicken broth
- One 14½-ounce can fire-roasted diced tomatoes and their liquid
- 3 red, orange, and/or yellow bell peppers, seeded and cut into 1-inch squares
- 1 green onion, white and green parts, thinly sliced
- 1½ tablespoons chopped fresh flat-leaf parsley
- Hot sauce (such as Crystal or Frank's RedHot) for serving

1. Select the Sauté setting on the Instant Pot and heat the oil for 2 minutes. Add the onion, celery, and garlic and sauté for about 4 minutes, until the onion begins to soften. Add the turkey, Cajun seasoning, black pepper, and cayenne and sauté, using a wooden spoon or spatula to break up the meat as it cooks, for about 6 minutes, until cooked through and no streaks of pink remain. 2. Sprinkle the quinoa over the turkey in an even layer. Pour the broth and the diced tomatoes and their liquid over the quinoa, spreading the tomatoes on top. Sprinkle the bell peppers over the top in an even layer. 3. Secure the lid and set the Pressure Release to Sealing. Press the Cancel button to reset the cooking program, then select the Pressure Cook or Manual setting and set the cooking time for 8 minutes at high pressure. (The pot will take about 15 minutes to come up to pressure before the cooking program begins.) 4. When the cooking program ends, let the pressure release naturally for at least 15 minutes, then move the Pressure Release to Venting to release any remaining steam. Open the pot and sprinkle the green onion and parsley over the top in an even layer. 5. Spoon the unstuffed peppers into bowls, making sure to dig down to the bottom of the pot so each person gets an equal amount of peppers, quinoa, and meat. Serve hot, with hot sauce on the side.

Traditional Chicken Salad

Prep time: 5 minutes | Cook time: 12 minutes | Serves 8

- 2 pounds (907 g) chicken breasts
- 1 cup vegetable broth
- 2 sprigs fresh thyme
- 1 teaspoon granulated garlic
- 1 teaspoon onion powder
- 1 bay leaf
- ½ teaspoon ground black pepper
- 1 cup mayonnaise
- 2 stalks celery, chopped
- 2 tablespoons chopped fresh chives
- 1 teaspoon fresh lemon juice
- 1 teaspoon Dijon mustard
- ½ teaspoon coarse sea salt

1. Combine the chicken, broth, thyme, garlic, onion powder, bay leaf, and black pepper in the Instant Pot. 2. Lock the lid. Select the Poultry mode and set the cooking time for 12 minutes at High Pressure. 3. When the timer beeps, perform a natural pressure release for 10 minutes, then release any remaining pressure. Carefully remove the lid. 4. Remove the chicken from the Instant Pot and let rest for a few minutes until cooled slightly. 5. Slice the chicken breasts into strips and place in a salad bowl. Add the remaining ingredients and gently stir until well combined. Serve immediately.

Bacon Lettuce and Tomato Chicken Salad

Prep time: 15 minutes | Cook time: 17 minutes | Serves 4

- 4 slices bacon
- 2 (6-ounce / 170-g) chicken breasts
- 1 teaspoon salt
- ½ teaspoon garlic powder
- ¼ teaspoon dried parsley
- ¼ teaspoon pepper
- ¼ teaspoon dried thyme
- 1 cup water
- 2 cups chopped romaine lettuce
- Sauce:
- ⅓ cup mayonnaise
- 1 ounce (28 g) chopped pecans
- ½ cup diced Roma tomatoes
- ½ avocado, diced
- 1 tablespoon lemon juice

1. Press the Sauté button to heat your Instant Pot. 2. Add the bacon and cook for about 7 minutes, flipping occasionally, until crisp. Remove and place on a paper towel to drain. When cool enough to handle, crumble the bacon and set aside. 3. Sprinkle the chicken with salt, garlic powder, parsley, pepper, and thyme. 4. Pour the water into the Instant Pot. Use a wooden spoon to ensure nothing is stuck to the bottom of the pot. Add the trivet to the pot and place the chicken on top of the trivet. 5. Secure the lid. Select the Manual mode and set the cooking time for 10 minutes at High Pressure. 6. Meanwhile, whisk together all the ingredients for the sauce in a large salad bowl. 7. Once cooking is complete, do a quick pressure release. Carefully open the lid. 8. Remove the chicken and let sit for 10 minutes. Cut the chicken into cubes and transfer to the salad bowl, along with the cooked bacon. Gently stir until the chicken is thoroughly coated. Mix in the lettuce right before serving.

Quick Speedy Chicken Cacciatore

Prep time: 5 minutes | Cook time: 30 minutes | Serves 6

- 2 pounds boneless, skinless chicken thighs
- 1½ teaspoons fine sea salt
- ½ teaspoon freshly ground black pepper
- 2 tablespoons extra-virgin olive oil
- 3 garlic cloves, chopped
- 2 large red bell peppers, seeded and cut into ¼ by 2-inch strips
- 2 large yellow onions, sliced
- ½ cup dry red wine
- 1½ teaspoons Italian seasoning
- ½ teaspoon red pepper flakes (optional)
- One 14½ ounces can diced tomatoes and their liquid
- 2 tablespoons tomato paste
- Cooked brown rice or whole-grain pasta for serving

1. Season the chicken thighs on both sides with 1 teaspoon of the salt and the black pepper. 2. Select the Sauté setting on the Instant Pot and heat the oil and garlic for 2 minutes, until the garlic is bubbling but not browned. Add the bell peppers, onions, and remaining ½ teaspoon salt and sauté for 3 minutes, until the onions begin to soften. Stir in the wine, Italian seasoning, and pepper flakes (if using). Using tongs, add the chicken to the pot, turning each piece to coat it in the wine and spices and nestling them in a single layer in the liquid. Pour the tomatoes and their liquid on top of the chicken and dollop the tomato paste on top. Do not stir them in. 3. Secure the lid and set the Pressure Release to Sealing. Press the Cancel button to reset the cooking program, then select the Poultry, Pressure Cook, or Manual setting and set the cooking time for 12 minutes at high pressure. (The pot will take about 15 minutes to come up to pressure before the cooking program begins.) 4. When the cooking program ends, perform a quick pressure release by moving the Pressure Release to Venting, or let the pressure release naturally. Open the pot and, using tongs, transfer the chicken and vegetables to a serving dish. 5. Spoon some of the sauce over the chicken and serve hot, with the rice on the side.

Mixed Greens Chicken Salad

Prep time: 5 minutes | Cook time: 20 minutes | Serves 4

- Chicken:
- 2 tablespoons avocado oil
- 1 pound (454 g) chicken breast, cubed
- ½ cup filtered water
- ½ teaspoon ground turmeric
- ½ teaspoon dried parsley
- ½ teaspoon dried basil
- ½ teaspoon kosher salt
- ½ teaspoon freshly ground black pepper
- Salad:
- 1 avocado, mashed
- 1 cup chopped arugula
- 1 cup chopped Swiss chard
- 1 cup chopped kale
- ½ cup chopped spinach
- 2 tablespoons pine nuts, toasted

1. Combine all the chicken ingredients in the Instant Pot. 2. Secure the lid. Select the Manual mode and set the cooking time for 20 minutes at High Pressure. 3. Meanwhile, toss all the salad ingredients in a large salad bowl. 4. Once cooking is complete, do a quick pressure release. Carefully open the lid. 5. Remove the chicken to the salad bowl and serve.

Chicken with Lemon, Fingerling Potatoes & Olives

Prep time: 20 minutes | Cook time: 21 minutes | Serves 4

- 4 (5- to 7-ounce / 142- to 198-g) bone-in chicken thighs, trimmed
- ½ teaspoon table salt
- ¼ teaspoon pepper
- 2 teaspoons extra-virgin olive oil, plus extra for drizzling
- 4 garlic cloves, peeled and smashed
- ½ cup chicken broth
- 1 small lemon, sliced thin
- 1½ pounds (680 g) fingerling potatoes, unpeeled
- ¼ cup pitted brine-cured green or black olives, halved
- 2 tablespoons coarsely chopped fresh parsley

1. Pat chicken dry with paper towels and sprinkle with salt and pepper. Using highest sauté function, heat oil in Instant Pot for 5 minutes (or until just smoking). Place chicken skin side down in pot and cook until well browned on first side, about 5 minutes; transfer to plate. 2. Add garlic to fat left in pot and cook, using highest sauté function, until golden and fragrant, about 2 minutes. Stir in broth and lemon, scraping up any browned bits. Return chicken skin side up to pot and add any accumulated juices. Arrange potatoes on top. Lock lid in place and close pressure release valve. Select high pressure cook function and cook for 9 minutes. 3. Turn off Instant Pot and quick-release pressure. Carefully remove lid, allowing steam to escape away from you. Transfer chicken to serving dish and discard skin, if desired. Stir olives and parsley into potatoes and season with salt and pepper to taste. Serve chicken with potatoes.

Spicy Kung Pao Chicken

Prep time: 5 minutes | Cook time: 17 minutes | Serves 5

- 2 tablespoons coconut oil
- 1 pound (454 g) boneless, skinless chicken breasts, cubed
- 1 cup cashews, chopped
- 6 tablespoons hot sauce
- ½ teaspoon chili powder
- ½ teaspoon finely grated ginger
- ½ teaspoon kosher salt
- ½ teaspoon freshly ground black pepper

1. Set the Instant Pot to Sauté and melt the coconut oil. 2. Add the remaining ingredients to the Instant Pot and mix well. 3. Secure the lid. Select the Manual mode and set the cooking time for 17 minutes at High Pressure. 4. Once cooking is complete, do a quick pressure release. Carefully open the lid. 5. Serve warm.

Casablanca-Style Chicken

Prep time: 20 minutes | Cook time: 12 minutes | Serves 8

- 2 large onions, sliced
- 1 teaspoon ground ginger
- 3 garlic cloves, minced
- 2 tablespoons canola oil, divided
- 3 pounds skinless chicken pieces
- 3 large carrots, diced
- 2 large potatoes, unpeeled, diced
- ½ teaspoon ground cumin
- ½ teaspoon salt
- ½ teaspoon pepper
- ¼ teaspoon cinnamon
- 2 tablespoons raisins
- 14½-ounce can chopped tomatoes
- 3 small zucchini, sliced
- 15-ounce can garbanzo beans, drained
- 2 tablespoons chopped parsley

1. Using the Sauté function of the Instant Pot, cook the onions, ginger, and garlic in 1 tablespoon of the oil for 5 minutes, stirring constantly. Remove onions, ginger, and garlic from pot and set aside. 2. Brown the chicken pieces with the remaining oil, then add the cooked onions, ginger and garlic back in as well as all of the remaining ingredients, except the parsley. 3. Secure the lid and make sure vent is in the sealing position. Cook on Manual mode for 12 minutes. 4. When cook time is up, let the pressure release naturally for 5 minutes and then release the rest of the pressure manually.

Escabèche-Style Chicken

Prep time: 5 minutes | Cook time: 15 minutes | Serves 4

- 1 cup filtered water
- 1 pound (454 g) chicken, mixed pieces
- 3 garlic cloves, smashed
- 2 bay leaves
- 1 onion, chopped
- ½ cup red wine vinegar
- ½ teaspoon coriander
- ½ teaspoon ground cumin
- ½ teaspoon mint, finely chopped
- ½ teaspoon kosher salt
- ½ teaspoon freshly ground black pepper

1. Pour the water into the Instant Pot and insert the trivet. 2. Thoroughly combine the chicken, garlic, bay leaves, onion, vinegar, coriander, cumin, mint, salt, and black pepper in a large bowl. 3. Put the bowl on the trivet and cover loosely with aluminum foil. 4. Secure the lid. Select the Manual mode and set the cooking time for 15 minutes at High Pressure. 5. Once cooking is complete, do a natural pressure release for 10 minutes, then release any remaining pressure. Carefully open the lid. 6. Remove the dish from the Instant Pot and cool for 5 to 10 minutes before serving.

Cheesy Mushroom Baked Chicken

Prep time: 5 minutes | Cook time: 15 minutes | Serves 4

- 1 tablespoon butter
- 2 cloves garlic, smashed
- ½ cup chopped yellow onion
- 1 pound (454 g) chicken breasts, cubed
- 10 ounces (283 g) button mushrooms, thinly sliced
- 1 cup chicken broth
- ½ teaspoon shallot powder
- ½ teaspoon turmeric
- ½ teaspoon dried basil
- ½ teaspoon dried sage
- ½ teaspoon cayenne pepper
- ⅓ teaspoon ground black pepper
- Kosher salt, to taste
- ½ cup heavy cream
- 1 cup shredded Colby cheese

1. Set your Instant Pot to Sauté and melt the butter. 2. Add the garlic, onion, chicken, and mushrooms and sauté for about 4 minutes, or until the vegetables are softened. 3. Add the remaining ingredients except the heavy cream and cheese to the Instant Pot and stir to incorporate. 4. Lock the lid. Select the Meat/Stew mode and set the cooking time for 6 minutes at High Pressure. 5. When the timer beeps, perform a natural pressure release for 10 minutes, then release any remaining pressure. Carefully remove the lid. 6. Stir in the heavy cream until heated through. Pour the mixture into a baking dish and scatter the cheese on top. 7. Bake in the preheated oven at 400ºF (205ºC) until the cheese bubbles. 8. Allow to cool for 5 minutes and serve.

Nutmeg-Infused Creamy Chicken

Prep time: 20 minutes | Cook time: 10 minutes | Serves 6

- 1 tablespoon canola oil
- 6 boneless chicken breast halves, skin and visible fat removed
- ¼ cup chopped onion
- ¼ cup minced parsley
- 2 (10¾-ounce) cans 98% fat-free, reduced-sodium cream of mushroom soup
- ½ cup fat-free sour cream
- ½ cup fat-free milk
- 1 tablespoon ground nutmeg
- ¼ teaspoon sage
- ¼ teaspoon dried thyme
- ¼ teaspoon crushed rosemary

1. Press the Sauté button on the Instant Pot and then add the canola oil. Place the chicken in the oil and brown chicken on both sides. Remove the chicken to a plate. 2. Sauté the onion and parsley in the remaining oil in the Instant Pot until the onions are tender. Press Cancel on the Instant Pot, then place the chicken back inside. 3. Mix together the remaining ingredients in a bowl then pour over the chicken. 4. Secure the lid and set the vent to sealing. Set on Manual mode for 10 minutes. 5. When cooking time is up, let the pressure release naturally.

Ann's Italian Hunter Chicken

Prep time: 25 minutes | Cook time: 3 to 9 minutes | Serves 8

- 1 large onion, thinly sliced
- 3 pound chicken, cut up, skin removed, trimmed of fat
- 2 6-ounce cans tomato paste
- 4-ounce can sliced mushrooms, drained
- 1 teaspoon salt
- ¼ cup dry white wine
- ¼ teaspoons pepper
- 1 to 2 garlic cloves, minced
- 1 to 2 teaspoons dried oregano
- ½ teaspoon dried basil
- ½ teaspoon celery seed, optional
- 1 bay leaf

1. In the inner pot of the Instant Pot, place the onion and chicken. 2. Combine remaining ingredients and pour over the chicken. 3. Secure the lid and make sure vent is at sealing. Cook on Slow Cook mode, low 7 to 9 hours, or high 3 to 4 hours.

Mexican-Style Chicken Carnitas

Prep time: 5 minutes | Cook time: 15 minutes | Serves 8

- 3 pounds (1.4 kg) whole chicken, cut into pieces
- ⅓ cup vegetable broth
- 3 cloves garlic, pressed
- 1 tablespoon avocado oil
- 1 guajillo chili, minced
- Sea salt, to taste
- ½ teaspoon paprika
- ⅓ teaspoon cayenne pepper
- ½ teaspoon ground bay leaf
- ⅓ teaspoon black pepper
- 2 tablespoons chopped fresh coriander, for garnish
- 1 cup crème fraiche, for serving

1. Combine all the ingredients except the coriander and crème fraiche in the Instant Pot. 2. Lock the lid. Select the Poultry mode and set the cooking time for 15 minutes at High Pressure. 3. When the timer beeps, perform a quick pressure release. Carefully remove the lid. 4. Shred the chicken with two forks and discard the bones. Garnish with the coriander and serve with a dollop of crème fraiche.

Moroccan-Spiced Chicken Tagine

Prep time: 15 minutes | Cook time: 11 minutes | Serves 4

- 2 (15-ounce / 425-g) cans chickpeas, rinsed, divided
- 1 tablespoon extra-virgin olive oil
- 5 garlic cloves, minced
- 1½ teaspoons paprika
- ½ teaspoon ground turmeric
- ½ teaspoon ground cumin
- ¼ teaspoon ground ginger
- ¼ teaspoon cayenne pepper
- 1 fennel bulb, 1 tablespoon fronds minced, stalks discarded, bulb halved and cut lengthwise into ½-inch-thick wedges
- 1 cup chicken broth
- 3 (2-inch) strips lemon zest, plus lemon wedges for serving
- 4 (5- to 7-ounce / 142- to 198-g) bone-in chicken thighs, skin removed, trimmed
- ½ teaspoon table salt
- ½ cup pitted large brine-cured green or black olives, halved
- ⅓ cup raisins
- 2 tablespoons chopped fresh parsley

1. Using potato masher, mash ½ cup chickpeas in bowl to paste. Using highest sauté function, cook oil, garlic, paprika, turmeric, cumin, ginger, and cayenne in Instant Pot until fragrant, about 1 minute. Turn off Instant Pot, then stir in remaining whole chickpeas, mashed chickpeas, fennel wedges, broth, and zest. 2. Sprinkle chicken with salt. Nestle chicken skinned side up into pot and spoon some of cooking liquid over top. Lock lid in place and close pressure release valve. Select high pressure cook function and cook for 10 minutes. 3. Turn off Instant Pot and quick-release pressure. Carefully remove lid, allowing steam to escape away from you. Discard lemon zest. Stir in olives, raisins, parsley, and fennel fronds. Season with salt and pepper to taste. Serve with lemon wedges.

BBQ Pulled Chicken

Prep time: 5 minutes | Cook time: 25 minutes | Serves 4

- 1 (5-pound / 2.2-kg) whole chicken
- 3 teaspoons salt
- 1 teaspoon pepper
- 1 teaspoon dried parsley
- 1 teaspoon garlic powder
- ½ medium onion, cut into 3 to 4 large pieces
- 1 cup water
- ½ cup sugar-free barbecue sauce, divided

1. Scatter the chicken with salt, pepper, parsley, and garlic powder. Put the onion pieces inside the chicken cavity. 2. Pour the water into the Instant Pot and insert the trivet. Place seasoned chicken on the trivet. Brush with half of the barbecue sauce. 3. Lock the lid. Select the Manual mode and set the cooking time for 25 minutes at High Pressure. 4. When the timer beeps, perform a natural pressure release for 10 minutes, then release any remaining pressure. Carefully remove the lid. 5. Using a clean brush, add the remaining half of the sauce to chicken. For crispy skin or thicker sauce, you can broil in the oven for 5 minutes until lightly browned. 6. Slice or shred the chicken and serve warm.

Greek-Style Chicken

Prep time: 25 minutes | Cook time: 20 minutes | Serves 6

- 4 potatoes, unpeeled, quartered
- 2 pounds chicken pieces, trimmed of skin and fat
- 2 large onions, quartered
- 1 whole bulb garlic, cloves minced
- 3 teaspoons dried oregano
- ¾ teaspoons salt
- ½ teaspoons pepper
- 1 tablespoon olive oil
- 1 cup water

1. Place potatoes, chicken, onions, and garlic into the inner pot of the Instant Pot, then sprinkle with seasonings. Top with oil and water. 2. Secure the lid and make sure vent is set to sealing. Cook on Manual mode for 20 minutes. 3. When cook time is over, let the pressure release naturally for 5 minutes, then release the rest manually.

Pulled Chicken

Prep time: 5 minutes | Cook time: 14 minutes | Serves 4

- ½ teaspoon salt
- ½ teaspoon pepper
- ½ teaspoon dried oregano
- ½ teaspoon dried basil
- ½ teaspoon garlic powder
- 2 (6-ounce / 170-g) boneless, skinless chicken breasts
- 1 tablespoon coconut oil
- 1 cup water

1. In a small bowl, combine the salt, pepper, oregano, basil, and garlic powder. Rub this mix over both sides of the chicken. 2. Set your Instant Pot to Sauté and heat the coconut oil until sizzling. 3. Add the chicken and sear for 3 to 4 minutes until golden on both sides. 4. Remove the chicken and set aside. 5. Pour the water into the Instant Pot and use a wooden spoon or rubber spatula to make sure no seasoning is stuck to bottom of pot. 6. Add the trivet to the Instant Pot and place the chicken on top. 7. Secure the lid. Select the Manual mode and set the cooking time for 10 minutes at High Pressure. 8. Once cooking is complete, do a natural pressure release for 5 minutes, then release any remaining pressure. Carefully open the lid. 9. Remove the chicken and shred, then serve.

Mushroom and Tomato Braised Chicken

Prep time: 20 minutes | Cook time: 25 minutes | Serves 4

- 1 tablespoon extra-virgin olive oil
- 1 pound (454 g) portobello mushroom caps, gills removed, caps halved and sliced ½ inch thick
- 1 onion, chopped fine
- ¾ teaspoon salt, divided
- 4 garlic cloves, minced
- 1 tablespoon tomato paste
- 1 tablespoon all-purpose flour
- 2 teaspoons minced fresh sage
- ½ cup dry red wine
- 1 (14½ ounces / 411 g) can diced tomatoes, drained
- 4 (5 to 7 ounces / 142 to 198 g) bone-in chicken thighs, skin removed, trimmed
- ¼ teaspoon pepper
- 2 tablespoons chopped fresh parsley
- Shaved Parmesan cheese

1. Using highest sauté function, heat oil in Instant Pot until shimmering. Add mushrooms, onion, and ¼ teaspoon salt. Partially cover and cook until mushrooms are softened and have released their liquid, about 5 minutes. Stir in garlic, tomato paste, flour, and sage and cook until fragrant, about 1 minute. Stir in wine, scraping up any browned bits, then stir in tomatoes. 2. Sprinkle chicken with remaining ½ teaspoon salt and pepper. Nestle chicken skinned side up into pot and spoon some of sauce on top. Lock lid in place and close pressure release valve. Select high pressure cook function and cook for 15 minutes. 3. Turn off Instant Pot and quick-release pressure. Carefully remove lid, allowing steam to escape away from you. Transfer chicken to serving dish, tent with aluminum foil, and let rest while finishing sauce. 4. Using highest sauté function, bring sauce to simmer and cook until thickened slightly, about 5 minutes. Season sauce with salt and pepper to taste. Spoon sauce over chicken and sprinkle with parsley and Parmesan. Serve.

Dijon-Glazed Turkey

Prep time: 15 minutes | Cook time: 14 minutes | Serves 4

- 14 ounces (397 g) ground turkey
- 1 tablespoon Dijon mustard
- ½ cup coconut flour
- 1 teaspoon onion powder
- 1 teaspoon salt
- ½ cup chicken broth
- 1 tablespoon avocado oil

1. In the mixing bowl, mix up ground turkey, Dijon mustard, coconut flour, onion powder, and salt. 2. Make the meatballs with the help of the fingertips. 3. Then pour avocado oil in the instant pot and heat it up for 1 minute. 4. Add the meatballs and cook them for 2 minutes from each side. 5. Then add chicken broth. Close and seal the lid. 6. Cook the meatballs for 10 minutes. Make a quick pressure release.

Divan-Style Broccoli Chicken

Prep time: 15 minutes | Cook time: 10 minutes | Serves 4

- 1 cup chopped broccoli
- 2 tablespoons cream cheese
- ½ cup heavy cream
- 1 tablespoon curry powder
- ¼ cup chicken broth
- ½ cup grated Cheddar cheese
- 6 ounces (170 g) chicken fillet, cooked and chopped

1. Mix up broccoli and curry powder and put the mixture in the instant pot. 2. Add heavy cream and cream cheese. 3. Then add chicken and mix up the ingredients. 4. Then add chicken broth and heavy cream. 5. Top the mixture with Cheddar cheese. Close and seal the lid. 6. Cook the meal on Manual mode (High Pressure) for 10 minutes. Allow the natural pressure release for 5 minutes, open the lid and cool the meal for 10 minutes.

Spicy Crack Chicken Breasts

Prep time: 5 minutes | Cook time: 15 minutes | Serves 2

- ½ pound (227 g) boneless, skinless chicken breasts
- 2 ounces (57 g) cream cheese, softened
- ½ cup grass-fed bone broth
- ¼ cup tablespoons keto-friendly ranch dressing
- ½ cup shredded full-fat Cheddar cheese
- 3 slices bacon, cooked and chopped into small pieces

1. Combine all the ingredients except the Cheddar cheese and bacon in the Instant Pot. 2. Secure the lid. Select the Manual mode and set the cooking time for 15 minutes at High Pressure. 3. Once cooking is complete, do a quick pressure release. Carefully open the lid. 4. Add the Cheddar cheese and bacon and stir well, then serve.

Turkey Tetrazzini

Prep time: 5 minutes | Cook time: 20 minutes | Serves 6

- 1 tablespoon extra-virgin olive oil
- 2 garlic cloves, minced
- 1 yellow onion, diced
- 8 ounces cremini or button mushrooms, sliced
- ½ teaspoon fine sea salt
- ¼ teaspoon freshly ground black pepper
- 1 pound 93 percent lean ground turkey
- 1 teaspoon poultry seasoning
- 6 ounces whole-grain extra-broad egg-white pasta (such as No Yolks brand) or whole-wheat elbow pasta
- 2 cups low-sodium chicken broth
- 1½ cups frozen green peas, thawed
- 3 cups baby spinach
- Three ¾-ounce wedges Laughing Cow creamy light Swiss cheese, or 2 tablespoons Neufchâtel cheese, at room temperature
- ⅓ cup grated Parmesan cheese
- 1 tablespoon chopped fresh flat-leaf parsley

1. Select the Sauté setting on the Instant Pot and heat the oil and garlic for 2 minutes, until the garlic is bubbling but not browned. Add the onion, mushrooms, salt, and pepper and sauté for about 5 minutes, until the mushrooms have wilted and begun to give up their liquid. Add the turkey and poultry seasoning and sauté, using a wooden spoon or spatula to break up the meat as it cooks, for about 4 minutes more, until cooked through and no streaks of pink remain. 2. Stir in the pasta. Pour in the broth and use the spoon or spatula to nudge the pasta into the liquid as much as possible. It's fine if some pieces are not completely submerged. 3. Secure the lid and set the Pressure Release to Sealing. Press the Cancel button to reset the cooking program, then select the Pressure Cook or Manual setting and set the cooking time for 5 minutes at high pressure. (The pot will take about 5 minutes to come up to pressure before the cooking program begins.) 4. When the cooking program ends, let the pressure release naturally for 5 minutes, then move the Pressure Release to Venting to release any remaining steam. Open the pot and stir in the peas, spinach, Laughing Cow cheese, and Parmesan. Let stand for 2 minutes, then stir the mixture once more. 5. Ladle into bowls or onto plates and sprinkle with the parsley. Serve right away.

Feta-Topped Chicken Thighs

Prep time: 7 minutes | Cook time: 15 minutes | Serves 2

- 4 lemon slices
- 2 chicken thighs
- 1 tablespoon Greek seasoning
- 4 ounces (113 g) feta, crumbled
- 1 teaspoon butter
- ½ cup water

1. Rub the chicken thighs with Greek seasoning. 2. Then spread the chicken with butter. 3. Pour water in the instant pot and place the trivet. 4. Place the chicken on the foil and top with the lemon slices. Top it with feta. 5. Wrap the chicken in the foil and transfer on the trivet. 6. Cook on the Sauté mode for 10 minutes. Then make a quick pressure release for 5 minutes. 7. Discard the foil from the chicken thighs and serve!

Crispy Parmesan Chicken

Prep time: 15 minutes | Cook time: 13 minutes | Serves 2

- 1 tomato, sliced
- 8 ounces (227 g) chicken fillets
- 2 ounces (57 g) Parmesan, sliced
- 1 teaspoon butter
- 4 tablespoons water, for sprinkling
- 1 cup water, for cooking

1. Pour water and insert the steamer rack in the instant pot. 2. Then grease the baking mold with butter. 3. Slice the chicken fillets into halves and put them in the mold. 4. Sprinkle the chicken with water and top with tomato and Parmesan. 5. Cover the baking mold with foil and place it on the rack. 6. Close and seal the lid. 7. Cook the meal in Manual mode for 13 minutes. Then allow the natural pressure release for 10 minutes.

Chicken and Green Cabbage Meatballs

Prep time: 15 minutes | Cook time: 4 minutes | Serves 4

- 1 pound (454 g) ground chicken
- ¼ cup heavy (whipping) cream
- 2 teaspoons salt, divided
- ½ teaspoon ground caraway seeds
- 1½ teaspoons freshly ground black pepper, divided
- ¼ teaspoon ground allspice
- 4 to 6 cups thickly chopped green cabbage
- ½ cup coconut milk
- 2 tablespoons unsalted butter

1. To make the meatballs, put the chicken in a bowl. Add the cream, 1 teaspoon of salt, the caraway, ½ teaspoon of pepper, and the allspice. Mix thoroughly. Refrigerate the mixture for 30 minutes. Once the mixture has cooled, it is easier to form the meatballs. 2. Using a small scoop, form the chicken mixture into small-to medium-size meatballs. Place half the meatballs in the inner cooking pot of your Instant Pot and cover them with half the cabbage. Place the remaining meatballs on top of the cabbage, then cover them with the rest of the cabbage. 3. Pour in the milk, place pats of the butter here and there, and sprinkle with the remaining 1 teaspoon of salt and 1 teaspoon of pepper. 4. Lock the lid into place. Select Manual and adjust the pressure to High. Cook for 4 minutes. When the cooking is complete, quick-release the pressure. Unlock the lid. Serve the meatballs on top of the cabbage.

Tomato-Braised Chicken Legs

Prep time: 10 minutes | Cook time: 35 minutes | Serves 2

- 2 chicken legs
- 2 tomatoes, chopped
- 1 cup chicken stock
- 1 teaspoon peppercorns

1. Put all ingredients in the instant pot. 2. Close and seal the lid. Set Manual mode (High Pressure). 3. Cook the chicken legs for 35 minutes. 4. Make a quick pressure release. 5. Transfer the cooked chicken legs in the serving bowls and add 1 ladle of the chicken stock.

Easy Chicken Masala

Prep time: 10 minutes | Cook time: 17 minutes | Serves 3

- 12 ounces (340 g) chicken fillet
- 1 tablespoon masala spices
- 1 tablespoon avocado oil
- 3 tablespoons organic almond milk

1. Heat up avocado oil in the instant pot on Sauté mode for 2 minutes. 2. Meanwhile, chop the chicken fillet roughly and mix it up with masala spices. 3. Add almond milk and transfer the chicken in the instant pot. 4. Cook the chicken bites on Sauté mode for 15 minutes. Stir the meal occasionally.

Apple Cider Pecan Chicken

Prep time: 10 minutes | Cook time: 15 minutes | Serves 2

- 6 ounces (170 g) chicken fillet, cubed
- 2 pecans, chopped
- 1 teaspoon coconut aminos
- ½ bell pepper, chopped
- 1 tablespoon coconut oil
- ¼ cup apple cider vinegar
- ¼ cup chicken broth

1. Melt coconut oil on Sauté mode and add chicken cubes. 2. Add bell pepper, and pecans. 3. Sauté the ingredients for 10 minutes and add apple cider vinegar, chicken broth, and coconut aminos. 4. Sauté the chicken for 5 minutes more.

Chicken Stuffed with Bruschetta and Cheese

Prep time: 10 minutes | Cook time: 10 minutes | Serves 4

- 6 ounces (170 g) diced Roma tomatoes
- 2 tablespoons avocado oil
- 1 tablespoon thinly sliced fresh basil, plus more for garnish
- 1½ teaspoons balsamic vinegar
- Pinch of salt
- Pinch of black pepper
- 4 boneless, skinless chicken breasts (about 2 pounds / 907 g)
- 12 ounces (340 g) goat cheese, divided
- 2 teaspoons Italian seasoning, divided
- 1 cup water

1. Prepare the bruschetta by mixing the tomatoes, avocado oil, basil, vinegar, salt, and pepper in a small bowl. Let it marinate until the chicken is done. 2. Pat the chicken dry with a paper towel. Butterfly the breast open but do not cut all the way through. Stuff each breast with 3 ounces (85 g) of the goat cheese. Use toothpicks to close the edges. 3. Sprinkle ½ teaspoon of the Italian seasoning on top of each breast. 4. Pour the water into the pot. Place the trivet inside. Lay a piece of aluminum foil on top of the trivet and place the chicken breasts on top. It is okay if they overlap. 5. Close the lid and seal the vent. Cook on High Pressure for 10 minutes. Quick release the steam. 6. Remove the toothpicks and top each breast with one-fourth of the bruschetta.

Garlic-Infused Rotisserie Chicken

Prep time: 5 minutes | Cook time: 3 minutes | Serves 4

- 3 pounds whole chicken
- 2 tablespoons olive oil, divided
- Salt to taste
- Pepper to taste
- 20 to 30 cloves fresh garlic, peeled and left whole
- 1 cup low-sodium chicken stock, broth, or water
- 2 tablespoons garlic powder
- 2 teaspoons onion powder
- ½ teaspoon basil
- ½ teaspoon cumin
- ½ teaspoon chili powder

1. Rub chicken with one tablespoon of the olive oil and sprinkle with salt and pepper. 2. Place the garlic cloves inside the chicken. Use butcher's twine to secure the legs. 3. Press the Sauté button on the Instant Pot, then add the rest of the olive oil to the inner pot. 4. When the pot is hot, place the chicken inside. You are just trying to sear it, so leave it for about 4 minutes on each side. 5. Remove the chicken and set aside. Place the trivet at the bottom of the inner pot and pour in the chicken stock. 6. Mix together the remaining seasonings and rub them all over the entire chicken. 7. Place the chicken back inside the inner pot, breast-side up, on top of the trivet and secure the lid to the sealing position. 8. Press the Manual button and use the +/- to set it for 25 minutes. 9. When the timer beeps, allow the pressure to release naturally for 15 minutes. If the lid will not open at this point, quick release the remaining pressure and remove the chicken. 10. Let the chicken rest for 5–10 minutes before serving.

Poblano-Spiced Chicken

Prep time: 10 minutes | Cook time: 29 minutes | Serves 4

- 2 Poblano peppers, sliced
- 16 ounces (454 g) chicken fillet
- ½ teaspoon salt
- ½ cup coconut cream
- 1 tablespoon butter
- ½ teaspoon chili powder

1. Heat up the butter on Sauté mode for 3 minutes. 2. Add Poblano and cook them for 3 minutes. 3. Meanwhile, cut the chicken fillet into the strips and sprinkle with salt and chili powder. 4. Add the chicken strips to the instant pot. 5. Then add coconut cream and close the lid. Cook the meal on Sauté mode for 20 minutes.

Chicken Meatball Thai Yellow Curry

Prep time: 5 minutes | Cook time: 30 minutes | Serves 4

- 1 pound 95 percent lean ground chicken
- ⅓ cup gluten-free panko (Japanese bread crumbs)
- 1 egg white
- 1 tablespoon coconut oil
- 1 yellow onion, cut into 1-inch pieces
- One 14-ounce can light coconut milk
- 3 tablespoons yellow curry paste
- ¾ cup water
- 8 ounces carrots, halved lengthwise, then cut crosswise into 1-inch lengths (or quartered if very large)
- 8 ounces zucchini, quartered lengthwise, then cut crosswise into 1-inch lengths (or cut into halves, then thirds if large)
- 8 ounces cremini mushrooms, quartered
- Fresh Thai basil leaves for serving (optional)
- Fresno or jalapeño chile, thinly sliced, for serving (optional)
- 1 lime, cut into wedges
- Cooked cauliflower "rice" for serving

1. In a medium bowl, combine the chicken, panko, and egg white and mix until evenly combined. Set aside. 2. Select the Sauté setting on the Instant Pot and heat the oil for 2 minutes. Add the onion and sauté for 5 minutes, until it begins to soften and brown. Add ½ cup of the coconut milk and the curry paste and sauté for 1 minute more, until bubbling and fragrant. Press the Cancel button to turn off the pot, then stir in the water. 3. Using a 1½-tablespoon cookie scoop, shape and drop meatballs into the pot in a single layer. 4. Secure the lid and set the Pressure Release to Sealing. Select the Pressure Cook or Manual setting and set the cooking time for 5 minutes at high pressure. (The pot will take about 5 minutes to come up to pressure before the cooking program begins.) 5. When the cooking program ends, perform a quick pressure release by moving the Pressure Release to Venting, or let the pressure release naturally. Open the pot and stir in the carrots, zucchini, mushrooms, and remaining 1¼ cups coconut milk. 6. Press the Cancel button to reset the cooking program, then select the Sauté setting. Bring the curry to a simmer (this will take about 2 minutes), then let cook, uncovered, for about 8 minutes, until the carrots are fork-tender. Press the Cancel button to turn off the pot. 7. Ladle the curry into bowls. Serve piping hot, topped with basil leaves and chile slices, if desired, and the lime wedges and cauliflower "rice" on the side.

Wine-Braised Chicken

Prep time: 10 minutes | Cook time: 12 minutes | Serves 6

- 2 pounds chicken breasts, trimmed of skin and fat
- 10¾-ounce can 98% fat-free, reduced-sodium cream of mushroom soup
- 10¾-ounce can French onion soup
- 1 cup dry white wine or chicken broth

1. Place the chicken into the Instant Pot. 2. Combine soups and wine. Pour over chicken. 3. Secure the lid and make sure vent is set to sealing. Cook on Manual mode for 12 minutes. 4. When cook time is up, let the pressure release naturally for 5 minutes and then release the rest manually.

Chapter 4
Fish and Seafood

Chili and Turmeric Haddock

Prep time: 10 minutes | Cook time: 5 minutes | Serves 4

- 1 chili pepper, minced
- 1 pound (454 g) haddock, chopped
- ½ teaspoon ground turmeric
- ½ cup fish stock
- 1 cup water

1. Combine chili pepper, ground turmeric, and fish stock in a mixing bowl. 2. Add chopped haddock to the mixture and transfer it to a baking mold. 3. Pour water into the Instant Pot and insert a trivet. 4. Place the baking mold with the fish on the trivet and close the lid. 5. Cook the meal on Manual (High Pressure) for 5 minutes, then perform a quick pressure release.

Fish Tagine

Prep time: 25 minutes | Cook time: 12 minutes | Serves 4

- 2 tablespoons extra-virgin olive oil, plus extra for drizzling
- 1 large onion, halved and sliced ¼ inch thick
- 1 pound (454 g) carrots, peeled, halved lengthwise, and sliced ¼ inch thick
- 2 (2-inch) strips orange zest, plus 1 teaspoon grated zest
- ¾ teaspoon table salt, divided
- 2 tablespoons tomato paste
- 4 garlic cloves, minced, divided
- 1¼ teaspoons paprika
- 1 teaspoon ground cumin
- ¼ teaspoon red pepper flakes
- ¼ teaspoon saffron threads, crumbled
- 1 (8-ounce / 227-g) bottle clam juice
- 1½ pounds (680 g) skinless halibut fillets, 1½ inches thick, cut into 2-inch pieces
- ¼ cup pitted oil-cured black olives, quartered
- 2 tablespoons chopped fresh parsley
- 1 teaspoon sherry vinegar

1. Using the highest sauté setting to heat oil in the Instant Pot until it shimmers. Incorporate onion, carrots, orange zest strips, and ¼ teaspoon of salt, cooking until the vegetables are tender and slightly browned, approximately 10 to 12 minutes. Blend in tomato paste, three-quarters of the garlic, paprika, cumin, pepper flakes, and saffron, and cook until aromatic, around 30 seconds. Stir in clam juice, ensuring to scrape up any browned residues. 2. Season the halibut with the remaining ½ teaspoon of salt. Place the halibut within the onion mixture and ladle some of the cooking liquid over the pieces. Secure the lid and close the pressure release valve. Choose the high-pressure cook function and set the cooking time to 0 minutes. As soon as the Instant Pot reaches the desired pressure, immediately switch it off and perform a quick pressure release. 3. Discard the orange zest. Gently mix in olive s, parsley, vinegar, grated orange zest, and the remaining garlic. Taste and adjust seasoning with salt and pepper as needed. Before serving, drizzle a bit of extra oil over each portion.

Rosemary Baked Haddock

Prep time: 7 minutes | Cook time: 10 minutes | Serves 2

- 2 eggs, beaten
- 12 ounces (340 g) haddock fillet, chopped
- 1 tablespoon cream cheese
- ¾ teaspoon dried rosemary
- 2 ounces (57 g) Parmesan, grated
- 1 teaspoon butter

1. Stir the beaten eggs until they are a uniform mixture. Incorporate the cream cheese, dried rosemary, and dill into the eggs. 2. Apply butter to the inside of the springform pan and put the haddock in it. 3. Pour the egg mixture over the haddock and top with a sprinkle of Parmesan cheese. 4. Select Manual mode with high pressure and cook for 5 minutes. After that, allow the pressure to release naturally for 5 minutes.

Haddock and Veggie Foil Packets

Prep time: 5 minutes | Cook time: 10 minutes | Serves 4

- 1½ cups water
- 1 lemon, sliced
- 2 bell peppers, sliced
- 1 brown onion, sliced into rings
- 4 sprigs parsley
- 2 sprigs thyme
- 2 sprigs rosemary
- 4 haddock fillets
- Sea salt, to taste
- ⅓ teaspoon ground black pepper, or more to taste
- 2 tablespoons extra-virgin olive oil

1. Pour water and lemon into your Instant Pot, then insert a steamer basket. 2. Assemble packets using large sheets of heavy-duty foil. 3. Put peppers, onion rings, parsley, thyme, and rosemary in the center of each foil sheet. Place fish fillets on top of the vegetables. 4. Season with salt and black pepper, and drizzle olive oil over the fillets. Place the packets in the steamer basket. 5. Lock the lid. Choose Manual mode and set cooking time for 10 minutes at Low Pressure. 6. When the timer sounds, do a quick pressure release. Carefully remove the lid. 7. Serve warm.

Fish Bake with Veggies

Prep time: 10 minutes | Cook time: 5 minutes | Serves 4

- 1½ cups water
- Cooking spray
- 2 ripe tomatoes, sliced
- 2 cloves garlic, minced
- 1 teaspoon dried oregano
- 1 teaspoon dried basil
- ½ teaspoon dried rosemary
- 1 red onion, sliced
- 1 head cauliflower, cut into florets
- 1 pound (454 g) tilapia fillets, sliced
- Sea salt, to taste
- 1 tablespoon olive oil
- 1 cup crumbled feta cheese
- ⅓ cup Kalamata olives, pitted and halved

1. 1. Pour water into the Instant Pot and insert a trivet. 2. Spray a casserole dish with cooking spray, add tomato slices, and top with garlic, oregano, basil, and rosemary. 3. Mix in onions and cauliflower, arrange fish fillets on top, sprinkle with salt, and drizzle with olive oil. 4. Add feta cheese and Kalamata olives on top, then lower the dish onto the trivet. 5. Lock the lid, select Manual mode, and set cooking time for 5 minutes at High Pressure. 6. When the timer beeps, perform a quick pressure release and carefully remove the lid. 7. Let it cool for 5 minutes before serving.

Garam Masala Fish

Prep time: 10 minutes | Cook time: 10 minutes | Serves 4

- 2 tablespoons sesame oil
- ½ teaspoon cumin seeds
- ½ cup chopped leeks
- 1 teaspoon ginger-garlic paste
- 1 pound (454 g) cod fillets, boneless and sliced
- 2 ripe tomatoes, chopped
- 1½ tablespoons fresh lemon juice
- ½ teaspoon garam masala
- ½ teaspoon turmeric powder
- 1 tablespoon chopped fresh dill leaves
- 1 tablespoon chopped fresh curry leaves
- 1 tablespoon chopped fresh parsley leaves
- Coarse sea salt, to taste
- ½ teaspoon smoked cayenne pepper
- ¼ teaspoon ground black pepper, or more to taste

1. Set the Instant Pot on to the Sauté setting. Pour in the sesame oil and heat it until it's piping hot. Add the cumin seeds and sauté them for half a minute. 2. Throw in the leeks and let them cook for another couple of minutes until they become translucent. Add the ginger-garlic paste and give it another 40 seconds on the stove. 3. Mix in all the remaining ingredients. 4. Seal the lid tightly. Choose the Manual mode and set the cooking time to 6 minutes at low pressure. 5. As soon as the timer goes off, do a quick pressure release. Be careful when lifting the lid. 6. Serve the dish while it's still hot.

Aromatic Monkfish Stew

Prep time: 5 minutes | Cook time: 6 minutes | Serves 6

- Juice of 1 lemon
- 1 tablespoon fresh basil
- 1 tablespoon fresh parsley
- 1 tablespoon olive oil
- 1 teaspoon garlic, minced
- 1½ pounds (680 g) monkfish
- 1 tablespoon butter
- 1 bell pepper, chopped
- 1 onion, sliced
- ½ teaspoon cayenne pepper
- ½ teaspoon mixed peppercorns
- ¼ teaspoon turmeric powder
- ¼ teaspoon ground cumin
- Sea salt and ground black pepper, to taste
- 2 cups fish stock
- ½ cup water
- ¼ cup dry white wine
- 2 bay leaves
- 1 ripe tomato, crushed

1. In a ceramic dish, whisk together the lemon juice, basil, parsley, olive oil, and garlic. Add the monkfish and let it marinate for 30 minutes. 2. Turn on your Instant Pot's Sauté function. Add and melt the butter. Once it's hot, cook the bell pepper and onion until they become fragrant. 3. Stir in the remaining ingredients. 4. Lock the lid in place. Choose the Manual mode and set the cooking time to 6 minutes at High Pressure. 5. When the timer sounds, execute a quick pressure release. Carefully take off the lid. 6. Throw away the bay leaves and portion your stew into serving bowls. Serve while it's still hot.

Lemon Shrimp Skewers

Prep time: 10 minutes | Cook time: 2 minutes | Serves 4

- 1 tablespoon lemon juice
- 1 teaspoon coconut aminos
- 12 ounces (340 g) shrimp, peeled
- 1 teaspoon olive oil
- 1 cup water

1. Place the shrimp in a mixing bowl. 2. Add lemon juice, coconut aminos, and olive oil to the bowl. 3. Thread the shrimp onto skewers. 4. Pour water into the Instant Pot. 5. Insert a trivet into the pot. 6. Place the shrimp skewers on top of the trivet. 7. Close the lid and cook the seafood on Manual mode (High Pressure) for 2 minutes. 8. Once the cooking time is complete, perform a quick pressure release.

Coconut Milk-Braised Squid

Prep time: 10 minutes | Cook time: 20 minutes | Serves 3

- 1 pound (454 g) squid, sliced
- 1 teaspoon sugar-free tomato paste
- 1 cup coconut milk
- 1 teaspoon cayenne pepper
- ½ teaspoon salt

1. Add all the listed ingredients to the Instant Pot. 2. Close and seal the lid, then cook the squid on Manual (High Pressure) for 20 minutes. 3. Once the cooking time is complete, perform a quick pressure release. 4. Serve the squid accompanied by coconut milk gravy.

Braised Striped Bass with Zucchini and Tomatoes

Prep time: 20 minutes | Cook time: 16 minutes | Serves 4

- 2 tablespoons extra-virgin olive oil, divided, plus extra for drizzling
- 3 zucchini (8 ounces / 227 g each), halved lengthwise and sliced ¼ inch thick
- 1 onion, chopped
- ¾ teaspoon table salt, divided
- 3 garlic cloves, minced
- 1 teaspoon minced fresh oregano or ¼ teaspoon dried
- ¼ teaspoon red pepper flakes
- 1 (28-ounce / 794-g) can whole peeled tomatoes, drained with juice reserved, halved
- 1½ pounds (680 g) skinless striped bass, 1½ inches thick, cut into 2-inch pieces
- ¼ teaspoon pepper
- 2 tablespoons chopped pitted kalamata olives
- 2 tablespoons shredded fresh mint

1. Utilize the highest sauté setting to heat 1 tablespoon of oil in the Instant Pot for 5 minutes (or until it starts to smoke). Add the zucchini and cook until it becomes tender, approximately 5 minutes; then transfer it to a bowl and set it aside. 2. Add the remaining 1 tablespoon of oil, onion, and ¼ teaspoon of salt to the now-empty pot, and cook using the highest sauté function until the onion is softened, about 5 minutes. Stir in garlic, oregano, and pepper flakes, and cook until fragrant, around 30 seconds. Mix in the tomatoes and reserved juice. 3. Season the bass with the remaining ½ teaspoon of salt and pepper. Place the bass into the tomato mixture and spoon some of the cooking liquid over the pieces. Secure the lid and close the pressure release valve. Choose the high-pressure cook function and set the cooking time to 0 minutes. As soon as the Instant Pot reaches pressure, immediately turn it off and perform a quick pressure release. Carefully remove the lid, making sure the steam escapes away from you. 4. Transfer the bass to a plate, cover it with aluminum foil, and let it rest while finishing the vegetables. Stir the zucchini back into the pot and allow it to heat through for about 5 minutes. Mix in the olives and season with salt and pepper to taste. Serve the bass with the vegetables, sprinkling individual portions with mint and drizzling with extra oil.

Cayenne Cod

Prep time: 10 minutes | Cook time: 10 minutes | Serves 2

- 2 cod fillets
- ¼ teaspoon chili powder
- ½ teaspoon cayenne pepper
- ½ teaspoon dried oregano
- 1 tablespoon lime juice
- 2 tablespoons avocado oil

1. Season the cod fillets with chili powder, cayenne pepper, dried oregano, and a sprinkle of lime juice. 2. Pour avocado oil into the Instant Pot and heat it on Sauté mode for 2 minutes. 3. Add the cod fillets to the hot oil and cook for 5 minutes. 4. Flip the fish over to the other side and cook for an additional 5 minutes.

Mahi-Mahi Fillets with Peppers

Prep time: 10 minutes | Cook time: 3 minutes | Serves 3

- 2 sprigs fresh rosemary
- 2 sprigs dill, tarragon
- 1 sprig fresh thyme
- 1 cup water
- 1 lemon, sliced
- 3 mahi-mahi fillets
- 2 tablespoons coconut oil, melted
- Sea salt and ground black pepper, to taste
- 1 serrano pepper, seeded and sliced
- 1 green bell pepper, sliced
- 1 red bell pepper, sliced

1. Start by adding the herbs, water, and lemon slices to the Instant Pot and inserting a steamer basket, then place the mahi-mahi fillets inside the basket. 2. Drizzle the melted coconut oil over them, followed by seasoning with salt and black pepper. 3. Lock the lid, choose the Manual mode, and set the cooking time to 3 minutes at Low Pressure. 4. After the timer sounds, do a natural pressure release for 10 minutes and release any extra pressure before carefully taking off the lid. 5. Put the peppers on top, select the Sauté mode, and let it simmer for another minute before serving right away.

Foil-Packet Salmon

Prep time: 2 minutes | Cook time: 7 minutes | Serves 2

- 2 (3-ounce / 85-g) salmon fillets
- ¼ teaspoon garlic powder
- 1 teaspoon salt
- ¼ teaspoon pepper
- ¼ teaspoon dried dill
- ½ lemon
- 1 cup water

1. Position every piece of salmon filet on a square of foil with the skin facing downward. 2. Season using garlic powder, salt, and pepper, then pour lemon juice over the fish. 3. Slice the lemon into four parts and put two slices on each filet. Fold over the edges to seal the foil packages. 4. Pour water into the Instant Pot and insert a trivet. Put the foil packages on top of the trivet. 5. Fasten the lid. Choose the Steam mode and set the cooking duration to 7 minutes at Low Pressure. 6. After cooking finishes, carry out a quick pressure release. Open the lid cautiously. 7. Use a meat thermometer to examine the internal temperature to confirm the thickest section of the filets has attained at least 145°F (63°C). Fully cooked salmon should flake readily. Serve without delay.

Lemon Salmon with Tomatoes

Prep time: 7 minutes | Cook time: 21 minutes | Serves 4

- 1 tablespoon unsalted butter
- 3 cloves garlic, minced
- ¼ cup lemon juice
- 1¼ cups fresh or canned diced tomatoes
- 1 tablespoon chopped fresh flat-leaf parsley, plus more for garnish
- ¼ teaspoon ground black pepper
- 4 (6-ounce / 170-g) skinless salmon fillets
- 1 teaspoon fine sea salt
- Lemon wedges, for garnish

1. Place the butter in your Instant Pot and choose the Sauté mode. After it melts, add the garlic (if using) and cook for 1 minute. 2. Stir in the roasted garlic, lemon juice, tomatoes, parsley, and pepper. Allow it to simmer for about 5 minutes, or until the liquid has slightly reduced. 3. In the meantime, rinse the salmon and gently pat it dry with a paper towel. Season all sides with salt. 4. Use a spatula to push the reduced sauce to one side of the pot, then place the salmon on the opposite side. Spoon some of the sauce over the salmon. 5. Continue cooking uncovered for an additional 15 minutes, or until the salmon flakes easily when tested with a fork. The cooking time may vary depending on the thickness of the fillets. 6. Finally, transfer the salmon to a serving plate, serve with the sauce, and garnish with parsley and lemon wedges.

Mascarpone Tilapia with Nutmeg

Prep time: 10 minutes | Cook time: 20 minutes | Serves 2

- 10 ounces (283 g) tilapia
- ½ cup mascarpone
- 1 garlic clove, diced
- 1 teaspoon ground nutmeg
- 1 tablespoon olive oil
- ½ teaspoon salt

1. Pour olive oil into the Instant Pot. 2. Add diced garlic and sauté for 4 minutes. 3. Add tilapia and sprinkle with ground nutmeg. Sauté the fish for 3 minutes on each side. 4. Add mascarpone and close the lid. 5. Cook the tilapia on Sauté mode for an additional 10 minutes.

Shrimp Louie Salad with Thousand Island Dressing

Prep time: 5 minutes | Cook time: 20 minutes | Serves 4

- 2 cups water
- 1½ teaspoons fine sea salt
- 1 pound medium shrimp, peeled and deveined
- 4 large eggs
- Thousand island Dressing
- ¼ cup no-sugar-added ketchup
- ¼ cup mayonnaise
- 1 tablespoon fresh lemon juice
- 1 teaspoon Worcestershire sauce
- ⅛ teaspoon cayenne pepper
- Freshly ground black pepper
- 2 green onions, white and green parts, sliced thinly
- 2 hearts romaine lettuce or 1 head iceberg lettuce, shredded
- 1 English cucumber, sliced
- 8 radishes, sliced
- 1 cup cherry tomatoes, sliced
- 1 large avocado, pitted, peeled, and sliced

1. Mix water and salt in the Instant Pot, stirring until the salt dissolves. 2. Lock the lid and set the Pressure Release to Sealing. Choose the Steam setting and set the cooking time to 0 minutes at low pressure. (The pot will take roughly 10 minutes to reach pressure before cooking begins.) 3. Prepare an ice bath while waiting. 4. After the cooking program finishes, quickly release pressure by moving the Pressure Release to Venting. Open the pot, stir in the shrimp with a wooden spoon, cover, and let them cook on Keep Warm for 2 minutes. The shrimp will gently poach. Remove the inner pot with heat-resistant mitts, drain the shrimp in a colander, cool

them in an ice bath for 5 minutes, then drain and refrigerate. 5. Clean the inner pot, add 1 cup of water, and place a wire metal steam rack inside. Put the eggs on the rack. 6. Lock the lid and set the Pressure Release to Sealing. Reset the cooking program with the Cancel button, then select Egg, Pressure Cook, or Manual mode and cook for 5 minutes at high pressure. (The pot will take about 5 minutes to reach pressure.) 7. Prepare another ice bath during cooking. 8. When done, let the pressure release naturally for 5 minutes, then vent any remaining steam. Use tongs to move the eggs to the ice bath to cool for 5 minutes. 9. Make the dressing by mixing ketchup, mayonnaise, lemon juice, Worcestershire sauce, cayenne, ¼ teaspoon black pepper, and green onions in a small bowl. 10. Arrange lettuce, cucumber, radishes, tomatoes, and avocado on plates or bowls. Place cooked shrimp in the center and surround with quartered, peeled eggs. 11. Spoon dressing over salads and add more black pepper if desired. Serve immediately.

Rosemary Catfish

Prep time: 10 minutes | Cook time: 20 minutes | Serves 4

- 16 ounces (454 g) catfish fillet
- 1 tablespoon dried rosemary
- 1 teaspoon garlic powder
- 1 tablespoon avocado oil
- 1 teaspoon salt
- 1 cup water, for cooking

1. Cut the catfish fillet into 4 steaks. 2. Then sprinkle them with dried rosemary, garlic powder, avocado oil, and salt. 3. Place the fish steak in the baking mold in one layer. 4. After this, pour water and insert the steamer rack in the instant pot. 5. Put the baking mold with fish on the rack. Close and seal the lid. 6. Cook the meal on Manual (High Pressure) for 20 minutes. Make a quick pressure release.

Mediterranean Salmon with Whole-Wheat Couscous

Prep time: 5 minutes | Cook time: 30 minutes | Serves 4

- Couscous
- 1 cup whole-wheat couscous
- 1 cup water
- 1 tablespoon extra-virgin olive oil
- 1 teaspoon dried basil
- ¼ teaspoon fine sea salt
- 1 pint cherry or grape tomatoes, halved
- 8 ounces zucchini, halved lengthwise, then sliced crosswise ¼ inch thick
- Salmon
- 1 pound skinless salmon fillet
- 2 teaspoons extra-virgin olive oil
- 1 tablespoon fresh lemon juice
- 1 garlic clove, minced
- ¼ teaspoon dried oregano
- ¼ teaspoon fine sea salt
- ¼ teaspoon freshly ground black pepper
- 1 tablespoon capers, drained
- Lemon wedges for serving

1. Pour 1 cup of water into the Instant Pot and have two-tier stackable stainless-steel containers ready. 2. To make the couscous: In one container, combine the couscous, water, oil, basil, and salt. Top with tomatoes and zucchini. 3. To make the salmon: Place the salmon fillet in the second container. In a small bowl, whisk together the oil, lemon juice, garlic, oregano, salt, pepper, and capers. Spread the mixture over the salmon. 4. Position the couscous and vegetables container at the bottom and the salmon container on top. Cover the top container with its lid and secure the containers together. Holding the handle, lower them into the Instant Pot. 5. Lock the lid and set the Pressure Release to Sealing. Choose Pressure Cook or Manual mode and set the cooking time to 20 minutes at high pressure. (The pot will take approximately 10 minutes to reach pressure before cooking begins.) 6. When the cooking program finishes, allow the pressure to release naturally for 5 minutes, then switch the Pressure Release to Venting to release any remaining steam. Open the pot and, wearing heat-resistant mitts, lift out the stacked containers. Unlock, unstack, and open the containers, being cautious of the steam. 7. Fluff the couscous with a fork and mix in the vegetables. Serve the couscous on plates, topped with a piece of salmon cut into four pieces. Garnish with lemon wedges on the side and serve immediately.

Turmeric Salmon

Prep time: 10 minutes | Cook time: 4 minutes | Serves 3

- 1 pound (454 g) salmon fillet
- 1 teaspoon ground black pepper
- ½ teaspoon salt
- 1 teaspoon ground turmeric
- 1 teaspoon lemon juice
- 1 cup water

1. In a shallow bowl, combine salt, ground black pepper, and ground turmeric. 2. Sprinkle lemon juice over the salmon fillet and rub it with the spice mixture. 3. Pour water into the Instant Pot and insert the steamer rack. 4. Wrap the salmon fillet in foil and place it on the rack. 5. Close and seal the lid. 6. Cook the fish on Manual mode (High Pressure) for 4 minutes. 7. Perform a quick pressure release and cut the fish into servings.

Dill Salmon Cakes

Prep time: 15 minutes | Cook time: 10 minutes | Serves 4

- 1 pound (454 g) salmon fillet, chopped
- 1 tablespoon chopped dill
- 2 eggs, beaten
- ½ cup almond flour
- 1 tablespoon coconut oil

1. Add the chopped salmon, dill, eggs, and almond flour to the food processor. 2. Blend the mixture until smooth. 3. Form small balls (cakes) from the salmon mixture. 4. Heat coconut oil on Sauté mode for 3 minutes. 5. Place the salmon cakes in the Instant Pot in a single layer and cook on Sauté mode for 2 minutes on each side or until they turn light brown.

Salmon with Dill Butter

Prep time: 7 minutes | Cook time: 8 minutes | Serves 2

- 1 teaspoon salt
- 2 tablespoons chopped fresh dill
- 10 ounces (283 g) salmon fillet
- ¼ cup butter
- ½ cup water

1. Place a generous amount of butter and a pinch of salt in the baking dish. 2. Carefully lay the salmon fillet on top and sprinkle with fresh dill. Cover the dish securely with aluminum foil. 3. Fill the Instant Pot with water and gently lower the baking dish containing the fish into it. 4. Activate the Steam function and let the salmon cook for exactly 8 minutes. 5. Once cooked, remove the foil from the salmon and serve it hot!

Halibut Stew with Bacon and Cheese

Prep time: 10 minutes | Cook time: 10 minutes | Serves 4

- 1½ cups water
- Cooking spray
- 4 slices bacon, chopped
- 1 celery, chopped
- ½ cup chopped shallots
- 1 teaspoon garlic, smashed
- 1 pound (454 g) halibut
- 2 cups fish stock
- 1 tablespoon coconut oil, softened
- ¼ teaspoon ground allspice
- Sea salt and crushed black peppercorns, to taste
- 1 cup Cottage cheese, at room temperature
- 1 cup heavy cream

1. Turn on the Instant Pot's Sauté function and cook the bacon until it's nice and crispy. 2. Add the celery, shallots, and garlic to the pot and sauté for an additional 2 minutes, or until the veggies are just tender. 3. Stir in the halibut, stock, coconut oil, allspice, salt, and black peppercorns until well combined. 4. Lock the lid in place, select Manual mode, and set the cooking time to 7 minutes at Low Pressure. 5. When the timer goes off, let the pressure release naturally for 10 minutes before releasing any remaining pressure. Carefully remove the lid. 6. Mix in the cheese and heavy cream, then switch back to Sauté mode and let it simmer for a few minutes until heated through. Serve immediately.

Louisiana Shrimp Gumbo

Prep time: 10 minutes | Cook time: 4 minutes | Serves 6

- 1 pound (454 g) shrimp
- ¼ cup chopped celery stalk
- 1 chili pepper, chopped
- ¼ cup chopped okra
- 1 tablespoon coconut oil
- 2 cups chicken broth
- 1 teaspoon sugar-free tomato paste

1. Add all the ingredients to the Instant Pot and stir until the mixture turns light red. 2. Close and seal the lid. 3. Cook the meal on Manual mode (High Pressure) for 4 minutes. 4. Once the cooking time is complete, let the natural pressure release for 10 minutes.

Trout Casserole

Prep time: 5 minutes | Cook time: 10 minutes | Serves 3

- 1½ cups water
- 1½ tablespoons olive oil
- 3 plum tomatoes, sliced
- ½ teaspoon dried oregano
- 1 teaspoon dried basil
- 3 trout fillets
- ½ teaspoon cayenne pepper, or more to taste
- ⅓ teaspoon black pepper
- Salt, to taste
- 1 bay leaf
- 1 cup shredded Pepper Jack cheese

1. Pour water into the Instant Pot and insert a trivet. 2. Grease a baking dish with olive oil, add tomato slices, and sprinkle with oregano and basil. 3. Place fish fillets in the dish, season with cayenne pepper, black pepper, and salt, and add a bay leaf. Lower the dish onto the trivet. 4. Lock the lid, select Manual mode, and set cooking time for 10 minutes at High Pressure. 5. When the timer beeps, perform a quick pressure release and carefully remove the lid. 6. Scatter Pepper Jack cheese on top, lock the lid, and let the cheese melt. 7. Serve warm.

Shrimp and Asparagus Risotto

Prep time: 15 minutes | Cook time: 20 minutes | Serves 4

- ¼ cup extra-virgin olive oil, divided
- 8 ounces (227 g) asparagus, trimmed and cut on bias into 1-inch lengths
- ½ onion, chopped fine
- ¼ teaspoon table salt
- 1½ cups Arborio rice
- 3 garlic cloves, minced
- ½ cup dry white wine
- 3 cups chicken or vegetable broth, plus extra as needed
- 1 pound (454 g) large shrimp (26 to 30 per pound), peeled and deveined
- 2 ounces (57 g) Parmesan cheese, grated (1 cup)
- 1 tablespoon lemon juice
- 1 tablespoon minced fresh chives

1. Using the highest sauté setting to heat 1 tablespoon of oil in the Instant Pot until it shimmers. Add asparagus, partially cover, and cook until just crisp-tender, approximately 4 minutes. Use a slotted spoon to transfer the asparagus to a bowl and set it aside. 2. Add onion, 2 tablespoons of oil, and salt to the now-empty pot and cook using the highest sauté function until the onion is softened, about 5 minutes. Stir in rice and garlic and cook until the grains are translucent around the edges, about 3 minutes. Stir in wine and cook until nearly evaporated, about 1 minute. 3. Stir in broth, scraping up any rice that sticks to the bottom of the pot. Lock the lid in place and close the pressure release valve. Select the high-pressure cook function and cook for 7 minutes. 4. Turn off the Instant Pot and perform a quick pressure release. Carefully remove the lid, allowing steam to escape away from you. Stir shrimp and asparagus into the risotto, cover, and let sit until the shrimp are opaque throughout, 5 to 7 minutes. Add Parmesan and the remaining 1 tablespoon of oil, and stir vigorously until the risotto becomes creamy. Adjust consistency with extra hot broth as needed. Stir in lemon juice and season with salt and pepper to taste. Sprinkle individual portions with chives before serving.

Tuna Stuffed Poblano Peppers

Prep time: 15 minutes | Cook time: 12 minutes | Serves 4

- 7 ounces (198 g) canned tuna, shredded
- 1 teaspoon cream cheese
- ¼ teaspoon minced garlic
- 2 ounces (57 g) Provolone cheese, grated
- 4 poblano pepper
- 1 cup water, for cooking

1. Extract the seeds from the poblano peppers, 2. then blend shredded tuna, cream cheese, minced garlic, and grated cheese in a mixing bowl, 3. subsequently fill the peppers with this tuna mixture and arrange them in a baking pan, 4. after that pour water into the instant pot and insert the baking pan into it, 5. finally cook the meal on Manual mode (High Pressure) for 12 minutes and carry out a quick pressure release.

Cajun Cod Fillet

Prep time: 10 minutes | Cook time: 4 minutes | Serves 2

- 10 ounces (283 g) cod fillet
- 1 tablespoon olive oil
- 1 teaspoon Cajun seasoning
- 2 tablespoons coconut aminos

1. Lightly season the cod fillet with coconut aminos and Cajun seasoning. 2. Next, heat olive oil in the Instant Pot on Sauté mode until shimmering. 3. Carefully add the spiced cod fillet to the pot and cook for 4 minutes on each side, ensuring even cooking. 4. Once cooked, gently cut the cod fillet into halves and drizzle with the flavorful oily liquid from the Instant Pot for added taste.

Fish Packets with Pesto and Cheese

Prep time: 8 minutes | Cook time: 6 minutes | Serves 4

- 1½ cups cold water.
- 4 (4-ounce / 113-g) white fish fillets, such as cod or haddock
- 1 teaspoon fine sea salt
- ½ teaspoon ground black pepper
- 1 (4-ounce / 113-g) jar pesto
- ½ cup shredded Parmesan cheese (about 2 ounces / 57 g)
- Halved cherry tomatoes, for garnish

1. Pour water into the Instant Pot and insert a steamer basket. 2. Season the fish fillets with salt and pepper on all sides. Take four sheets of parchment paper and place a fillet in the center of each. 3. Add 2 tablespoons of pesto on top of each fillet and sprinkle with 2 tablespoons of Parmesan cheese. 4. Wrap the fish in the parchment by folding in the edges and folding down the top like an envelope to seal tightly. 5. Stack the packets in the steamer basket, seam-side down. 6. Lock the lid and select Manual mode, setting the cooking time for 6 minutes at Low Pressure. 7. After cooking, perform a natural pressure release for 10 minutes, then release any remaining pressure. Carefully open the lid. 8. Remove the fish packets from the pot and transfer them to a serving plate. Garnish with cherry tomatoes. 9. Serve immediately.

Perch Fillets with Red Curry

Prep time: 5 minutes | Cook time: 6 minutes | Serves 4

- 1 cup water
- 2 sprigs rosemary
- 1 large-sized lemon, sliced
- 1 pound (454 g) perch fillets
- 1 teaspoon cayenne pepper
- Sea salt and ground black pepper, to taste
- 1 tablespoon red curry paste
- 1 tablespoons butter

1. Pour water into the Instant Pot, add rosemary and lemon slices, then insert a trivet. 2. Season the perch fillets with cayenne pepper, salt, and black pepper. Spread red curry paste and butter evenly over the fillets. 3. Place the fish fillets on the trivet. 4. Lock the lid in place. Choose Manual mode and set the cooking time to 6 minutes at Low Pressure. 5. When the timer sounds, do a quick pressure release. Carefully lift off the lid. Serve with your favorite keto sides.

Salade Niçoise with Oil-Packed Tuna

Prep time: 5 minutes | Cook time: 20 minutes | Serves 4

- 8 ounces small red potatoes, quartered
- 8 ounces green beans, trimmed
- 4 large eggs
- french vinaigrette
- 2 tablespoons extra-virgin olive oil
- 2 tablespoons cold-pressed avocado oil
- 2 tablespoons white wine vinegar
- 1 tablespoon water
- 1 teaspoon Dijon mustard
- ½ teaspoon dried oregano
- ¼ teaspoon fine sea salt
- 1 tablespoon minced shallot
- 2 hearts romaine lettuce, leaves separated and torn into bite-size pieces
- ½ cup grape tomatoes, halved
- ¼ cup pitted Niçoise or Greek olives
- One 7 ounces can oil-packed tuna, drained and flaked
- Freshly ground black pepper
- 1 tablespoon chopped fresh flat-leaf parsley

1. Pour 1 cup of water into the Instant Pot and insert a steamer basket. Add potatoes, green beans, and eggs to the basket. 2. Lock the lid and set the Pressure Release to Sealing. Choose the Steam setting and set the cooking time to 3 minutes at high pressure. (Note: The pot will take approximately 15 minutes to reach pressure before the cooking cycle begins.) 3. Prepare the vinaigrette: While the vegetables and eggs steam, combine olive oil, avocado oil, vinegar, water, mustard, oregano, salt, and shallot in a small jar with a tight lid. Shake vigorously to emulsify and set aside. 4. Prepare an ice bath. 5. Upon completion of the cooking cycle, quickly release pressure by switching the Pressure Release to Venting. Open the pot and, wearing heat-resistant mitts, remove the steamer basket. Use tongs to transfer eggs and green beans to the ice bath, leaving potatoes in the basket. 6. As the eggs and green beans cool, divide lettuce, tomatoes, olives, and tuna among four shallow bowls. Drain the eggs and green beans, peel and halve the eggs lengthwise, and arrange them on the salads with the green beans and potatoes. 7. Drizzle the vinaigrette over the salads and sprinkle with pepper and parsley. Serve immediately.

Mackerel and Broccoli Casserole

Prep time: 15 minutes | Cook time: 15 minutes | Serves 5

- 1 cup shredded broccoli
- 10 ounces (283 g) mackerel, chopped
- ½ cup shredded Cheddar cheese
- 1 cup coconut milk
- 1 teaspoon ground cumin
- 1 teaspoon salt

1. Season the chopped mackerel with ground cumin and salt, then place it in the Instant Pot. 2. Cover the fish with shredded broccoli and Cheddar cheese. 3. Pour in the coconut milk and ensure the lid is closed and sealed properly. 4. Cook the casserole on Manual mode (High Pressure) for 15 minutes. 5. Let the natural pressure release for 10 minutes before opening the lid.

Herb-Crusted Cod Steaks

Prep time: 5 minutes | Cook time: 4 minutes | Serves 4

- 1½ cups water
- 2 tablespoons garlic-infused oil
- 4 cod steaks, 1½-inch thick
- Sea salt, to taste
- ½ teaspoon mixed peppercorns, crushed
- 2 sprigs thyme
- 1 sprig rosemary
- 1 yellow onion, sliced

1. Pour water into the Instant Pot and insert a trivet. 2. Rub the garlic-infused oil into the cod steaks and season with salt and crushed peppercorns. 3. Place the cod steaks on the trivet, skin-side down, and top with thyme, rosemary, and onion. 4. Lock the lid and select Manual mode, setting the cooking time to 4 minutes at High Pressure. 5. When the timer beeps, perform a quick pressure release and carefully remove the lid. 6. Serve immediately.

Garlic Tuna Casserole

Prep time: 7 minutes | Cook time: 9 minutes | Serves 4

- 1 cup grated Parmesan or shredded Cheddar cheese, plus more for topping
- 1 (8-ounce / 227-g) package cream cheese (1 cup), softened
- ½ cup chicken broth
- 1 tablespoon unsalted butter
- ½ small head cauliflower, cut into 1-inch pieces
- 1 cup diced onions
- 2 cloves garlic, minced, or more to taste
- 2 (4-ounce / 113-g) cans chunk tuna packed in water, drained
- 1½ cups cold water
- For Garnish:
- Chopped fresh flat-leaf parsley
- Sliced green onions
- Cherry tomatoes, halved
- Ground black pepper

1. In a blender, add the Parmesan cheese, cream cheese, and broth and blitz until smooth. Set aside. 2. Set your Instant Pot to Sauté. Add and melt the butter. Add the cauliflower and onions and sauté for 4 minutes, or until the onions are softened. Fold in the garlic and sauté for an additional 1 minute. 3. Place the cheese sauce and tuna in a large bowl. Mix in the veggies and stir well. Transfer the mixture to a casserole dish. 4. Place a trivet in the bottom of your Instant Pot and add the cold water. Use a foil sling, lower the casserole dish onto the trivet. Tuck in the sides of the sling. 5. Lock the lid. Select the Manual mode and set the cooking time for 5 minutes for al dente cauliflower or 8 minutes for softer cauliflower at High Pressure. 6. Once cooking is complete, do a quick pressure release. Carefully open the lid. 7. Serve topped with the cheese and garnished with the parsley, green onions, cherry tomatoes, and freshly ground pepper.

Shrimp Zoodle Alfredo

Prep time: 10 minutes | Cook time: 10 minutes | Serves 4

- 10 ounces (283 g) salmon fillet (2 fillets)
- 4 ounces (113 g) Mozzarella, sliced
- 4 cherry tomatoes, sliced
- 1 teaspoon erythritol
- 1 teaspoon dried basil
- ½ teaspoon ground black pepper
- 1 tablespoon apple cider vinegar
- 1 tablespoon butter
- 1 cup water, for cooking

1. Melt the butter on Sauté mode and add shrimp. 2. Sprinkle them with seafood seasoning and sauté them for 2 minutes. 3. After this, use the spiralizer to create zucchini noodles and add them to the shrimp. 4. Add coconut cream, close the lid, and cook the meal on Sauté mode for 8 minutes.

Ahi Tuna and Cherry Tomato Salad

Prep time: 5 minutes | Cook time: 4 minutes | Serves 4

- 1 cup water
- 2 sprigs thyme
- 2 sprigs rosemary
- 2 sprigs parsley
- 1 lemon, sliced
- 1 pound (454 g) ahi tuna
- ⅓ teaspoon ground black pepper
- 1 head lettuce
- 1 cup cherry tomatoes, halved
- 1 red bell pepper, julienned
- 2 tablespoons extra-virgin olive oil
- 1 teaspoon Dijon mustard
- Sea salt, to taste

1. Pour water into the Instant Pot, then add thyme, rosemary, parsley, and lemon slices, and insert a trivet. 2. Place the fish on the trivet and season with ground black pepper. 3. Lock the lid, select Manual mode, and set the cooking time for 4 minutes at High Pressure. 4. When the timer beeps, perform a quick pressure release and carefully remove the lid. 5. In a salad bowl, combine the remaining ingredients and toss well. Add the flaked tuna and toss again. 6. Serve chilled.

Chunky Fish Soup with Tomatoes

Prep time: 10 minutes | Cook time: 8 minutes | Serves 4

- 2 teaspoons olive oil
- 1 yellow onion, chopped
- 1 bell pepper, sliced
- 1 celery, diced
- 2 garlic cloves, minced
- 3 cups fish stock
- 2 ripe tomatoes, crushed
- ¾ pound (340 g) haddock fillets
- 1 cup shrimp
- 1 tablespoon sweet Hungarian paprika
- 1 teaspoon hot Hungarian paprika
- ½ teaspoon caraway seeds

1. Switch the Instant Pot to the Sauté function and add the oil, heating it until it reaches the desired temperature. Once hot, incorporate the onions and sauté them until they become tender and aromatic. 2. Add the pepper, celery, and garlic to the pan and continue the sautéing process until these ingredients are also soft. 3. Gradually stir in the remaining components of the recipe. 4. Secure the lid in place, select the Manual mode, and adjust the cooking time to 5 minutes at High Pressure. 5. Upon the timer sounding, execute a quick pressure release and carefully lift the lid. 6. Portion the contents into serving bowls and serve while still hot.

Foil-Pack Haddock with Spinach

Prep time: 15 minutes | Cook time: 15 minutes | Serves 4

- 12 ounces (340 g) haddock fillet
- 1 cup spinach
- 1 tablespoon avocado oil
- 1 teaspoon minced garlic
- ½ teaspoon ground coriander
- 1 cup water, for cooking

1. Blend the spinach until smooth and mix it with avocado oil, ground coriander, and minced garlic. 2. Cut the haddock into 4 fillets and place them on foil. 3. Top the fish fillets with the spinach mixture and place them on a rack. 4. Pour water into the Instant Pot and insert the rack. 5. Close and seal the lid, then cook the haddock on Manual (High Pressure) for 15 minutes. 6. Perform a quick pressure release.

Cod with Warm Tabbouleh Salad

Prep time: 10 minutes | Cook time: 6 minutes | Serves 4

- 1 cup medium-grind bulgur, rinsed
- 1 teaspoon table salt, divided
- 1 lemon, sliced ¼ inch thick, plus 2 tablespoons juice
- 4 (6-ounce / 170-g) skinless cod fillets, 1½ inches thick
- 3 tablespoons extra-virgin olive oil, divided, plus extra for drizzling
- ¼ teaspoon pepper
- 1 small shallot, minced
- 10 ounces (283 g) cherry tomatoes, halved
- 1 cup chopped fresh parsley
- ½ cup chopped fresh mint

1. Place the trivet that comes with the Instant Pot at the bottom of the insert and add ½ cup of water. Fold a sheet of aluminum foil into a 16 by 6-inch sling, then position a 1½-quart round soufflé dish in the center of the sling. Mix 1 cup of water, bulgur, and ½ teaspoon of salt in the dish. Utilizing the sling, lower the soufflé dish into the pot and onto the trivet, letting the narrow edges of the sling rest along the sides of the insert. 2. Lock the lid in place and close the pressure release valve. Choose the high-pressure cook function and cook for 3 minutes. Switch off the Instant Pot and perform a quick pressure release. Carefully remove the lid, making sure the steam escapes away from you. Using the sling, transfer the soufflé dish to a wire rack; let it cool. Remove the trivet; do not discard the sling or the water in the pot. 3. Arrange lemon slices widthwise in two rows across the center of the sling. Brush the cod with 1 tablespoon of oil and season with the remaining ½ teaspoon of salt and pepper. Place the cod, skin side down, in an even layer on top of the lemon slices. Using the sling, lower the cod into the Instant Pot; allow the narrow edges of the sling to rest along the sides of the insert. Lock the lid in place and close the pressure release valve. Select the high-pressure cook function and cook for 3 minutes. 4. In the meantime, whisk together the remaining 2 tablespoons of oil, lemon juice, and shallot in a large bowl. Add the bulgur, tomatoes, parsley, and mint, and gently toss to combine. Season with salt and pepper to taste. 5. Turn off the Instant Pot and quick-release pressure. Carefully remove the lid, ensuring the steam escapes away from you. Using the sling, transfer the cod to a large plate. Gently lift and tilt the fillets with a spatula to remove the lemon slices. Serve the cod with the salad, drizzling individual portions with extra oil.

Tilapia Fillets with Arugula

Prep time: 5 minutes | Cook time: 4 minutes | Serves 4

- 1 lemon, juiced
- 1 cup water
- 1 pound (454 g) tilapia fillets
- ½ teaspoon cayenne pepper, or more to taste
- 2 teaspoons butter, melted
- Sea salt and ground black pepper, to taste
- ½ teaspoon dried basil
- 2 cups arugula

1. Add the fresh lemon juice and water to your Instant Pot, then insert a steamer basket into the pot. 2. Use a brush to apply melted butter evenly over the fish fillets. 3. Season the fillets with cayenne pepper, salt, and black pepper. Put the tilapia fillets into the steamer basket and sprinkle dried basil on top of them. 4. Lock the lid of the Instant Pot. Choose the Manual mode and set the cooking time to 4 minutes at Low Pressure. 5. When the timer sounds, carry out a quick pressure release. After that, carefully take off the lid. 6. Finally, serve the fish with fresh arugula.

Lemon Butter Mahi Mahi

Prep time: 10 minutes | Cook time: 9 minutes | Serves 4

- 1 pound (454 g) mahi-mahi fillet
- 1 teaspoon grated lemon zest
- 1 tablespoon lemon juice
- 1 tablespoon butter, softened
- ½ teaspoon salt
- 1 cup water, for cooking

1. Divide the fish into four portions and season with lemon zest, lemon juice, salt, and a light coating of softened butter. 2. Arrange the fish slices in a single layer within a baking pan. 3. Fill the Instant Pot with water and insert a steamer rack. 4. Place the baking pan containing the fish on top of the steamer rack. Securely close and seal the lid of the Instant Pot. 5. Cook the Mahi Mahi using the Manual mode at High Pressure for 9 minutes, followed by a quick pressure release.

Chapter 5
Snacks and Appetizers

Fast Spring Kale Appetizer

Prep time: 5 minutes | Cook time: 2 minutes | Serves 6

- 3 teaspoons butter
- 1 cup chopped spring onions
- 1 pound (454 g) kale, torn into pieces
- 1 cup water
- ½ teaspoon cayenne pepper
- Himalayan salt and ground black pepper, to taste
- ½ cup shredded Colby cheese, for serving

1. Begin by switching your Instant Pot to the Sauté function and allow the butter to melt completely. 2. Incorporate the spring onions into the pot and cook for approximately 60 seconds, or until they appear soft and translucent. 3. Pour in all the remaining ingredients, excluding the cheese, into the Instant Pot and stir thoroughly to combine. 4. Secure the lid in place, choose the Manual setting, and adjust the cooking time to 1 minute under High Pressure. 5. Upon the timer's signal, execute a rapid pressure release, then cautiously lift off the lid. 6. Finally, spoon the kale mixture into a serving bowl and garnish generously with cheese before serving.

Layered Seven Dip

Prep time: 10 minutes | Cook time: 35 minutes | Serves 6

- Cashew Sour Cream
- 1 cup raw whole cashews, soaked in water to cover for 1 to 2 hours and then drained
- ½ cup avocado oil
- ½ cup water
- ¼ cup fresh lemon juice
- 2 tablespoons nutritional yeast
- 1 teaspoon fine sea salt
- Beans
- ½ cup dried black beans
- 2 cups water
- ½ teaspoon fine sea salt
- ½ teaspoon chili powder
- ¼ teaspoon garlic powder
- ½ cup grape or cherry tomatoes, halved
- 1 avocado, diced
- ¼ cup chopped yellow onion
- 1 jalapeño chile, sliced
- 2 tablespoons chopped cilantro
- 6 ounces baked corn tortilla chips
- 1 English cucumber, sliced
- 2 carrots, sliced
- 6 celery stalks, cut into sticks

1. To make the cashew sour cream: In a blender, combine the cashews, oil, water, lemon juice, nutritional yeast, and salt. Blend on high speed, stopping to scrape down the sides of the container as needed, for about 2 minutes, until very smooth. (The sour cream can be made in advance and stored in an airtight container in the refrigerator for up to 5 days.) 2. To make the beans: Pour 1 cup water into the Instant Pot. In a 1½-quart stainless-steel bowl, combine the beans, the 2 cups water, and salt and stir to dissolve the salt. Place the bowl on a long-handled silicone steam rack, then, holding the handles of the steam rack, lower it into the Instant Pot. (If you don't have the long-handled rack, use the wire metal steam rack and a homemade sling) 3. Secure the lid and set the Pressure Release to Sealing. Select the Bean/Chili, Pressure Cook, or Manual setting and set the cooking time for 25 minutes at high pressure. (The pot will take about 10 minutes to come up to pressure before the cooking program begins.) 4. When the cooking program ends, let the pressure release naturally for at least 20 minutes, then move the Pressure Release to Venting to release any remaining steam. 5. Place a colander over a bowl. Open the pot and, wearing heat-resistant mitts, lift out the inner pot and drain the beans in the colander. Transfer the liquid captured in the bowl to a measuring cup, and pour the beans into the bowl. Add ¼ cup of the cooking liquid to the beans and, using a potato masher or fork, mash the beans to your desired consistency, adding more cooking liquid as needed. Stir in the chili powder and garlic powder. 6. Using a rubber spatula, spread the black beans in an even layer in a clear-glass serving dish. Spread the cashew sour cream in an even layer on top of the beans. Add layers of the tomatoes, avocado, onion, jalapeño, and cilantro. (At this point, you can cover and refrigerate the assembled dip for up to 1 day.) Serve accompanied with the tortilla chips, cucumber, carrots, and celery on the side.

Parmesan Chicken Balls with Chives

Prep time: 10 minutes | Cook time: 15 minutes | Serves 4

- 1 teaspoon coconut oil, softened
- 1 cup ground chicken
- ¼ cup chicken broth
- 1 tablespoon chopped chives
- 1 teaspoon cayenne pepper
- 3 ounces (85 g) Parmesan cheese, grated

1. Activate the Sauté mode on your Instant Pot and melt the coconut oil. 2. Pour in all the ingredients except for the cheese into the Instant Pot, ensuring they are well mixed by stirring. 3. Place the lid securely on the pot, select Manual mode, and program it to cook for 15 minutes at High Pressure. 4. After the cooking cycle finishes, perform a swift pressure release before carefully removing the lid. 5. Incorporate the grated cheese into the mixture and stir until evenly distributed. Shape the cooked chicken mixture into balls, let them cool for a duration of 10 minutes, and then they are ready to be served.

Cheese Stuffed Bell Peppers

Prep time: 10 minutes | Cook time: 5 minutes | Serves 5

- 1 cup water
- 10 baby bell peppers, seeded and sliced lengthwise
- 4 ounces (113 g) Monterey Jack cheese, shredded
- 4 ounces (113 g) cream cheese
- 2 tablespoons chopped scallions
- 1 tablespoon olive oil
- 1 teaspoon minced garlic
- ½ teaspoon cayenne pepper
- ¼ teaspoon ground black pepper, or more to taste

1. Fill the Instant Pot with water and insert a steamer basket. 2. In a separate mixing bowl, combine all the ingredients except the bell peppers, stirring until well mixed. Evenly fill the peppers with this mixture and then place them in the steamer basket. 3. Secure the lid, select Manual mode, and set the cooking time to 5 minutes at High Pressure. 4. Upon the timer's alarm, execute a quick pressure release and then carefully lift the lid. 5. Allow the peppers to cool for about 5 minutes before serving.

Ground Turkey Lettuce Cups

Prep time: 5 minutes | Cook time: 30 minutes | Serves 8

- 3 tablespoons water
- 2 tablespoons soy sauce, tamari, or coconut aminos
- 3 tablespoons fresh lime juice
- 2 teaspoons Sriracha, plus more for serving
- 2 tablespoons cold-pressed avocado oil
- 2 teaspoons toasted sesame oil
- 4 garlic cloves, minced
- 1-inch piece fresh ginger, peeled and minced
- 2 carrots, diced
- 2 celery stalks, diced
- 1 yellow onion, diced
- 2 pounds 93 percent lean ground turkey
- ½ teaspoon fine sea salt
- Two 8-ounce cans sliced water chestnuts, drained and chopped
- 1 tablespoon cornstarch
- 2 hearts romaine lettuce or 2 heads butter lettuce, leaves separated
- ½ cup roasted cashews (whole or halves and pieces), chopped
- 1 cup loosely packed fresh cilantro leaves

1. In a small bowl, whisk together the water, soy sauce, 2 tablespoons of lime juice, and Sriracha until well blended. Set this sauce aside for later use. 2. Turn on the Instant Pot's Sauté mode and heat the avocado oil, sesame oil, garlic, and ginger for approximately 2 minutes, or until the garlic is bubbling but not yet browned. Next, add the carrots, celery, and onion, and continue sautéing for about 3 minutes, or until the onion starts to become translucent and soft. 3. Add the ground turkey and a pinch of salt to the pot, breaking up the meat with a wooden spoon or spatula as it cooks, for around 5 minutes, or until the turkey is fully cooked and free of any pink color. Then, incorporate the water chestnuts and the reserved soy sauce mixture, stirring quickly to combine all ingredients before too much steam escapes. 4. Secure the lid on the pot and ensure the Pressure Release is set to Sealing. Press the Cancel button to reset the cooking cycle, then choose either the Pressure Cook or Manual setting and set the cooking time to 5 minutes at high pressure. Note that the pot will take roughly 10 minutes to reach the desired pressure before the cooking cycle begins. 5. Once the cooking cycle is complete, either perform a quick pressure release by switching the Pressure Release to Venting or opt for a natural pressure release. Afterward, carefully open the pot. 6. In another small bowl, mix together the remaining 1 tablespoon of lime juice and cornstarch until smooth, then add this mixture to the pot and stir well to combine. Press the Cancel button to reset the cooking cycle again, then select the Sauté mode. Allow the mixture to come to a boil and thicken, stirring frequently, for about 2 minutes, before pressing the Cancel button to turn off the pot. 7. Finally, spoon the turkey mixture onto lettuce leaves and garnish with crushed cashews and chopped cilantro. Serve immediately, with extra Sriracha provided at the table for those who wish to add more heat to their dish.

Jalapeño Poppers with Bacon

Prep time: 10 minutes | Cook time: 3 minutes | Serves 4

- 6 jalapeños
- 4 ounces (113 g) cream cheese
- ¼ cup shredded sharp Cheddar cheese
- 1 cup water
- ¼ cup cooked crumbled bacon

1. Make a lengthwise incision in the jalapeños and carefully remove the seeds and membrane, setting them aside for later use. 2. In a small mixing bowl, combine cream cheese and Cheddar cheese until smooth. Use a spoon to fill the hollowed-out jalapeños with this cheese mixture. 3. Pour a sufficient amount of water into the Instant Pot and insert a steamer basket at the bottom. 4. Arrange the stuffed jalapeños on the steamer rack within the pot. Close the lid securely. 5. Select the Manual mode on the Instant Pot and set the cooking time to 3 minutes. 6. When the timer sounds, perform a quick pressure release to safely open the pot. 7. Serve the jalapeños topped with crumbled bacon for an added burst of flavor.

Chinese Spare Ribs

Prep time: 3 minutes | Cook time: 24 minutes | Serves 6

- 1½ pounds (680 g) spare ribs
- Salt and ground black pepper, to taste
- 2 tablespoons sesame oil
- ½ cup chopped green onions
- ½ cup chicken stock
- 2 tomatoes, crushed
- 2 tablespoons sherry
- 1 tablespoon coconut aminos
- 1 teaspoon ginger-garlic paste
- ½ teaspoon crushed red pepper flakes
- ½ teaspoon dried parsley
- 2 tablespoons sesame seeds, for serving

1. Season the spare ribs generously with salt and black pepper according to your preference. 2. Switch the Instant Pot to the Sauté function and warm the sesame oil. 3. Place the seasoned ribs in the pot and sear on each side for roughly three minutes, or until they achieve a nice golden crust. 4. Incorporate the rest of the ingredients, excluding the sesame seeds, into the Instant Pot and stir thoroughly to ensure they are well mixed. 5. Lock the lid into place, choose the Meat/Stew setting, and set the cooking time to 18 minutes at High Pressure. 6. Once the cooking cycle concludes, let the pot undergo a natural pressure release for ten minutes, followed by a quick release of any residual pressure before carefully opening the lid. 7. Finally, dish out the ribs and sprinkle sesame seeds on top before serving.

Blackberry Baked Brie

Prep time: 5 minutes | Cook time: 15 minutes | Serves 5

- 8-ounce round Brie
- 1 cup water
- ¼ cup sugar-free blackberry preserves
- 2 teaspoons chopped fresh mint

1. Use a knife to carve a grid pattern into the top surface of the Brie cheese. 2. Position the Brie in a 7-inch round baking dish and cover it tightly with aluminum foil. 3. Place a trivet inside the Instant Pot's inner pot and pour water into the bottom. 4. Create a sling using foil, positioning it on top of the trivet, and then place the baking dish on the sling. 5. Lock the Instant Pot's lid in place and switch the vent to the sealed position. 6. Select the Manual setting and program the Instant Pot for 15 minutes of cooking at high pressure. 7. Upon completion of the cooking cycle, turn off the Instant Pot and perform a quick pressure release. 8. Once the pressure indicator has dropped, remove the lid and carefully take out the baking dish. 9. Peel off the top layer of the Brie cheese, spread preserves over the exposed cheese, and finish with a sprinkle of fresh mint.

Buffalo Chicken Meatballs

Prep time: 5 minutes | Cook time: 10 minutes | Serves 4

- 1 pound (454 g) ground chicken
- ½ cup almond flour
- 2 tablespoons cream cheese
- 1 packet dry ranch dressing mix
- ½ teaspoon salt
- ¼ teaspoon pepper
- ¼ teaspoon garlic powder
- 1 cup water
- 2 tablespoons butter, melted
- ⅓ cup hot sauce
- ¼ cup crumbled feta cheese
- ¼ cup sliced green onion

1. In a large mixing bowl, combine ground chicken, almond flour, cream cheese, ranch dressing, salt, pepper, and garlic powder until the ingredients are well integrated. 2. Roll the mixture into sixteen evenly sized meatballs. 3. Arrange the meatballs on a steam rack and pour one cup of water into the Instant Pot. Close the lid securely. Select the Meat/Stew mode and set the cooking time to 10 minutes. 4. While the meatballs are cooking, mix butter and hot sauce in a separate bowl. 5. When the Instant Pot's timer sounds, carefully remove the meatballs using tongs or a slotted spoon and transfer them to a clean, large bowl. 6. Toss the meatballs in the hot sauce mixture to coat them evenly. 7. Garnish with crumbled feta cheese and chopped green onions before serving.

Cauliflower Fritters with Cheese

Prep time: 10 minutes | Cook time: 8 minutes | Serves 4

- 1 cup cauliflower, boiled
- 2 eggs, beaten
- 2 tablespoons almond flour
- 2 ounces (57 g) Cheddar cheese, shredded
- ½ teaspoon garlic powder
- 1 tablespoon avocado oil

1. Within a medium-sized bowl, crush the cauliflower finely. Incorporate the beaten eggs, flour, cheese, and garlic powder into the cauliflower, stirring vigorously until all components are uniformly blended. Proceed to form the mixture into fritters. 2. Turn on the Instant Pot's Sauté feature and warm up the avocado oil. 3. Carefully place the fritters into the heated oil, cooking each side for approximately three minutes or until they achieve a golden-brown hue. 4. Once prepared, serve the fritters while they are still hot.

Crispy Brussels Sprouts with Bacon

Prep time: 5 minutes | Cook time: 10 minutes | Serves 4

- ½ pound (227 g) bacon
- 1 pound (454 g) Brussels sprouts
- 4 tablespoons butter
- 1 teaspoon salt
- ½ teaspoon pepper
- ½ cup water

1. Initiate the Sauté function on the Instant Pot and reduce the heat to the lowest setting by pressing the Adjust button. Add bacon strips into the pot and cook for a duration of 3 to 5 minutes, or until the fat starts to liquefy. Discontinue the cooking process by pressing the Cancel button. 2. Reactivate the Sauté mode with the heat set at normal level and continue to cook the bacon until it achieves a crispy texture. During this phase, thoroughly wash the Brussels sprouts and discard any damaged outer leaves. Cut them into halves or quarters for even cooking. 3. Once the bacon is perfectly cooked, remove it from the pot and keep it aside. Add the prepared Brussels sprouts to the hot bacon fat, followed by the addition of butter. Season with salt and pepper, and continue to sauté for approximately 8 to 10 minutes, or until the Brussels sprouts are caramelized and crispy. If necessary, add small amounts of water to the pot occasionally to prevent sticking and to facilitate the deglazing process. Serve the dish while it is still warm for optimal flavor and texture.

Mushrooms Filled with Cheese

Prep time: 15 minutes | Cook time: 8 minutes | Serves 4

- 1 cup cremini mushroom caps
- 1 tablespoon chopped scallions
- 1 tablespoon chopped chives
- 1 teaspoon cream cheese
- 1 teaspoon sour cream
- 1 ounce (28 g) Monterey Jack cheese, shredded
- 1 teaspoon butter, softened
- ½ teaspoon smoked paprika
- 1 cup water, for cooking

1. Trim the mushroom caps if needed and wash them well. 2. After this, in the mixing bowl, mix up scallions, chives, cream cheese, sour cream, butter, and smoked paprika. 3. Then fill the mushroom caps with the cream cheese mixture and top with shredded Monterey Jack cheese. 4. Pour water and insert the trivet in the instant pot. 5. Arrange the stuffed mushrooms caps on the trivet and close the lid. 6. Cook the meal on Manual (High Pressure) for 8 minutes. 7. Then make a quick pressure release.

Boiled Peanuts

Prep time: 5 minutes | Cook time: 1 hour 20 minutes | Makes 8 cups

- 1 pound raw jumbo peanuts in the shell
- 3 tablespoons fine sea salt

1. Remove the inner pot from the Instant Pot and add the peanuts to it. Cover the peanuts with water and use your hands to agitate them, loosening any dirt. Drain the peanuts in a colander, rinse out the pot, and return the peanuts to it. Return the inner pot to the Instant Pot housing. 2. Add the salt and 9 cups water to the pot and stir to dissolve the salt. Select a salad plate just small enough to fit inside the pot and set it on top of the peanuts to weight them down, submerging them all in the water. 3. Secure the lid and set the Pressure Release to Sealing. Select the Steam setting and set the cooking time for 1 hour at low pressure. (The pot will take about 20 minutes to come up to pressure before the cooking program begins.) 4. When the cooking program ends, let the pressure release naturally (this will take about 1 hour). Open the pot and, wearing heat-resistant mitts, remove the inner pot from the housing. Let the peanuts cool to room temperature in the brine (this will take about 1½ hours). 5. Serve at room temperature or chilled. Transfer the peanuts with their brine to an airtight container and refrigerate for up to 1 week.

Sweet Candied Pecans

Prep time: 5 minutes | Cook time: 20 minutes | Serves 10

- 4 cups raw pecans
- 1½ teaspoons liquid stevia
- ½ cup plus 1 tablespoon water, divided
- 1 teaspoon vanilla extract
- 1 teaspoon cinnamon
- ¼ teaspoon nutmeg
- ⅛ teaspoon ground ginger
- ⅛ teaspoon sea salt

1. Place the raw pecans, liquid stevia, 1 tablespoon water, vanilla, cinnamon, nutmeg, ground ginger, and sea salt into the inner pot of the Instant Pot. 2. Press the Sauté button on the Instant Pot and sauté the pecans and other ingredients until the pecans are soft. 3. Pour in the ½ cup water and secure the lid to the locked position. Set the vent to sealing. 4. Press Manual and set the Instant Pot for 15 minutes. 5. Preheat the oven to 350°F. 6. When cooking time is up, turn off the Instant Pot, then do a quick release. 7. Spread the pecans onto a greased, lined baking sheet. 8. Bake the pecans for 5 minutes or less in the oven, checking on them frequently so they do not burn.

Coconut Cajun Shrimp

Prep time: 10 minutes | Cook time: 6 minutes | Serves 2

- 4 Royal tiger shrimps
- 3 tablespoons coconut shred
- 2 eggs, beaten
- ½ teaspoon Cajun seasoning
- 1 teaspoon olive oil

1. Begin by heating olive oil in the Instant Pot using the Sauté setting. 2. In the meantime, blend Cajun seasoning with coconut flakes to create a coating mixture. 3. Coat the shrimp in beaten eggs and then cover them with the coconut and seasoning mixture. 4. Subsequently, add the shrimp to the hot olive oil and continue cooking on Sauté mode, turning them over halfway through to ensure even cooking for a total of approximately six minutes (three minutes per side).

Creamy Onion and Spinach

Prep time: 3 minutes | Cook time: 5 minutes | Serves 6

- 4 tablespoons butter
- ¼ cup diced onion
- 8 ounces (227 g) cream cheese
- 1 (12 ounces / 340 g) bag frozen spinach
- ½ cup chicken broth
- 1 cup shredded whole-milk Mozzarella cheese

1. Press the Sauté button and add butter. Once butter is melted, add onion to Instant Pot and sauté for 2 minutes or until onion begins to turn translucent. 2. Break cream cheese into pieces and add to Instant Pot. Press the Cancel button. Add frozen spinach and broth. Click lid closed. Press the Manual button and adjust time for 5 minutes. When timer beeps, quick-release the pressure and stir in shredded Mozzarella. If mixture is too watery, press the Sauté button and reduce for additional 5 minutes, stirring constantly.

Colby Pepper Cheese Dip

Prep time: 5 minutes | Cook time: 5 minutes | Serves 8

- 1 tablespoon butter
- 2 red bell peppers, sliced
- 2 cups shredded Colby cheese
- 1 cup cream cheese, room temperature
- 1 cup chicken broth
- 2 garlic cloves, minced
- 1 teaspoon red Aleppo pepper flakes
- 1 teaspoon sumac
- Salt and ground black pepper, to taste

1. Set your Instant Pot to Sauté and melt the butter. 2. Add the bell peppers and sauté for about 2 minutes until just tender. 3. Add the remaining ingredients to the Instant Pot and gently stir to incorporate. 4. Lock the lid. Select the Manual mode and set the cooking time for 3 minutes at High Pressure. 5. When the timer beeps, perform a quick pressure release. Carefully remove the lid. 6. Allow to cool for 5 minutes and serve warm.

Jalapeño Cream Chicken Dip

Prep time: 5 minutes | Cook time: 12 minutes | Serves 10

- 1 pound boneless chicken breast
- 8 ounces low-fat cream cheese
- 3 jalapeños, seeded and sliced
- ½ cup water
- 8 ounces reduced-fat shredded cheddar cheese
- ¾ cup low-fat sour cream

1. Place the chicken, cream cheese, jalapeños, and water in the inner pot of the Instant Pot. 2. Secure the lid so it's locked and turn the vent to sealing. 3. Press Manual and set the Instant Pot for 12 minutes on high pressure. 4. When cooking time is up, turn off Instant Pot, do a quick release of the remaining pressure, then remove lid. 5. Shred the chicken between 2 forks, either in the pot or on a cutting board, then place back in the inner pot. 6. Stir in the shredded cheese and sour cream.

Hearty Porcupine Meatballs

Prep time: 20 minutes | Cook time: 15 minutes | Serves 8

- 1 pound ground sirloin or turkey
- ½ cup raw brown rice, parboiled
- 1 egg
- ¼ cup finely minced onion
- 1 or 2 cloves garlic, minced
- ¼ teaspoon dried basil and/or oregano, optional
- 10¾-ounce can reduced-fat condensed tomato soup
- ½ soup can of water

1. Mix all ingredients, except tomato soup and water, in a bowl to combine well. 2. Form into balls about 1½-inch in diameter. 3. Mix tomato soup and water in the inner pot of the Instant Pot, then add the meatballs. 4. Secure the lid and make sure the vent is turned to sealing. 5. Press the Meat button and set for 15 minutes on high pressure. 6. Allow the pressure to release naturally after cook time is up.

Cheesy Cauliflower Bites

Prep time: 5 minutes | Cook time: 21 minutes | Serves 8

- 1 cup water
- 1 head cauliflower, broken into florets
- 1 cup shredded Asiago cheese
- ½ cup grated Parmesan cheese
- 2 eggs, beaten
- 2 tablespoons butter
- 2 tablespoons minced fresh chives
- 1 garlic clove, minced
- ½ teaspoon cayenne pepper
- Coarse sea salt and white pepper, to taste

1. Pour the water into the Instant Pot and insert a steamer basket. Place the cauliflower in the basket. 2. Lock the lid. Select the Manual mode and set the cooking time for 3 minutes at High Pressure. 3. When the timer beeps, perform a quick pressure release. Carefully remove the lid. 4. Transfer the cauliflower to a food processor, along with the remaining ingredients. Pulse until everything is well combined. 5. Form the mixture into bite-sized balls and place them on a baking sheet. 6. Bake in the preheated oven at 400ºF (205ºC) for 18 minutes until golden brown. Flip the balls halfway through the cooking time. Cool for 5 minutes before serving.

Shrimp and Bok Choy Salad Boats

Prep time: 8 minutes | Cook time: 2 minutes | Serves 8

- 26 shrimp, cleaned and deveined
- 2 tablespoons fresh lemon juice
- 1 cup water
- Sea salt and ground black pepper, to taste
- 4 ounces (113 g) feta cheese, crumbled
- 2 tomatoes, diced
- ⅓ cup olives, pitted and sliced
- 4 tablespoons olive oil
- 2 tablespoons apple cider vinegar
- 8 Bok choy leaves
- 2 tablespoons fresh basil leaves, snipped
- 2 tablespoons chopped fresh mint leaves

1. Toss the shrimp and lemon juice in the Instant Pot until well coated. Pour in the water. 2. Lock the lid. Select the Manual mode and set the cooking time for 2 minutes at Low Pressure. 3. When the timer beeps, perform a quick pressure release. Carefully remove the lid. 4. Season the shrimp with salt and pepper to taste, then let them cool completely. 5. Toss the shrimp with the feta cheese, tomatoes, olives, olive oil, and vinegar until well incorporated. 6. Divide the salad evenly onto each Bok choy leaf and place them on a serving plate. Scatter the basil and mint leaves on top and serve immediately.

Lemon-Flavored Artichokes

Prep time: 5 minutes | Cook time: 5 to 15 minutes | Serves 4

- 4 artichokes
- 1 cup water
- 2 tablespoons lemon juice
- 1 teaspoon salt

1. Wash and trim artichokes by cutting off the stems flush with the bottoms of the artichokes and by cutting ¾–1 inch off the tops. Stand upright in the bottom of the inner pot of the Instant Pot. 2. Pour water, lemon juice, and salt over artichokes. 3. Secure the lid and make sure the vent is set to sealing. On Manual, set the Instant Pot for 15 minutes for large artichokes, 10 minutes for medium artichokes, or 5 minutes for small artichokes. 4. When cook time is up, perform a quick release by releasing the pressure manually.

Garlic Herb Butter

Prep time: 10 minutes | Cook time: 8 minutes | Serves 4

- ⅓ cup butter
- 1 teaspoon dried parsley
- 1 tablespoon dried dill
- ½ teaspoon minced garlic
- ¼ teaspoon dried thyme

1. Begin by preheating the Instant Pot on the Sauté setting. 2. Once heated, introduce butter into the pot and allow it to melt completely. 3. Incorporate dried parsley, dill, minced garlic, and thyme into the pot, ensuring that the butter mixture is thoroughly stirred to combine all the ingredients. 4. After the mixture has reached a uniform consistency, pour it into a butter mold. 5. Place the mold in the refrigerator and let it chill until the butter has solidified.

Creamy Spinach Dish

Prep time: 5 minutes | Cook time: 4 minutes | Serves 4

- 2 cups chopped spinach
- 2 ounces (57 g) Monterey Jack cheese, shredded
- 1 cup almond milk
- 1 tablespoon butter
- 1 teaspoon minced garlic
- ½ teaspoon salt

1. Combine all the ingredients in the Instant Pot. 2. Secure the lid. Select the Manual mode and set the cooking time for 4 minutes at High Pressure. 3. Once cooking is complete, do a quick pressure release. Carefully open the lid. 4. Give the mixture a good stir and serve warm.

Cheese Zucchini Tots

Prep time: 15 minutes | Cook time: 10 minutes | Serves 6

- 4 ounces (113 g) Parmesan, grated
- 4 ounces (113 g) Cheddar cheese, grated
- 1 zucchini, grated
- 1 egg, beaten
- 1 teaspoon dried oregano
- 1 tablespoon coconut oil

1. In the mixing bowl, mix up Parmesan, Cheddar cheese, zucchini, egg, and dried oregano. 2. Make the small tots with the help of the fingertips. 3. Then melt the coconut oil in the instant pot on Sauté mode. 4. Put the prepared zucchini tots in the hot coconut oil and cook them for 3 minutes from each side or until they are light brown. Cool the zucchini tots for 5 minutes.

Savory Italian Tomatillos

Prep time: 10 minutes | Cook time: 10 minutes | Serves 4

- 1 tablespoon Italian seasoning
- 4 tomatillos, sliced
- 4 teaspoons olive oil
- 4 tablespoons water

1. Sprinkle the tomatillos with Italian seasoning. 2. Then pour the olive oil in the instant pot and heat it up on Sauté mode for 1 minute. 3. Put the tomatillos in the instant pot in one layer and cook them for 2 minutes from each side. 4. Then add water and close the lid. 5. Sauté the vegetables for 3 minutes more.

Herb-Infused Shrimp

Prep time: 5 minutes | Cook time: 5 minutes | Serves 4

- 2 tablespoons olive oil
- ¾ pound (340 g) shrimp, peeled and deveined
- 1 teaspoon paprika
- 1 teaspoon garlic powder
- 1 teaspoon onion powder
- 1 teaspoon dried parsley flakes
- ½ teaspoon dried oregano
- ½ teaspoon dried thyme
- ½ teaspoon dried basil
- ½ teaspoon dried rosemary
- ¼ teaspoon red pepper flakes
- Coarse sea salt and ground black pepper, to taste
- 1 cup chicken broth

1. Set your Instant Pot to Sauté and heat the olive oil. 2. Add the shrimp and sauté for 2 to 3 minutes. 3. Add the remaining ingredients to the Instant Pot and stir to combine. 4. Secure the lid. Select the Manual mode and set the cooking time for 2 minutes at Low Pressure. 5. When the timer beeps, perform a quick pressure release. Carefully remove the lid. 6. Transfer the shrimp to a plate and serve.

Broccoli in Garlic-Herb & Cheese Sauce

Prep time: 5 minutes | Cook time: 3 minutes | Serves 4

- ½ cup water
- 1 pound (454 g) broccoli (frozen or fresh)
- ½ cup heavy cream
- 1 tablespoon butter
- ½ cup shredded Cheddar cheese
- 3 tablespoons garlic and herb cheese spread
- Pinch of salt
- Pinch of black pepper

1. Add the water to the pot and place the trivet inside. 2. Put the steamer basket on top of the trivet. Place the broccoli in the basket. 3. Close the lid and seal the vent. Cook on Low Pressure for 1 minute. Quick release the steam. Press Cancel. 4. Carefully remove the steamer basket from the pot and drain the water. If you steamed a full bunch of broccoli, pull the florets off the stem. (Chop the stem into bite-size pieces, it's surprisingly creamy.) 5. Turn the pot to Sauté mode. Add the cream and butter. Stir continuously while the butter melts and the cream warms up. 6. When the cream begins to bubble on the edges, add the Cheddar cheese, cheese spread, salt, and pepper. Whisk continuously until the cheeses are melted and a sauce consistency is reached, 1 to 2 minutes. 7. Top one-fourth of the broccoli with 2 tablespoons cheese sauce.

Savory Garlic Meatballs

Prep time: 20 minutes | Cook time: 15 minutes | Serves 6

- 7 ounces (198 g) ground beef
- 7 ounces (198 g) ground pork
- 1 teaspoon minced garlic
- 3 tablespoons water
- 1 teaspoon chili flakes
- 1 teaspoon dried parsley
- 1 tablespoon coconut oil
- ¼ cup beef broth

1. In the mixing bowl, mix up ground beef, ground pork, minced garlic, water, chili flakes, and dried parsley. 2. Make the medium size meatballs from the mixture. 3. After this, heat up coconut oil in the instant pot on Sauté mode. 4. Put the meatballs in the hot coconut oil in one layer and cook them for 2 minutes from each side. 5. Then add beef broth and close the lid. 6. Cook the meatballs for 10 minutes on Manual mode (High Pressure). 7. Then make a quick pressure release and transfer the meatballs on the plate.

Delicious Roasted Garlic Bulbs

Prep time: 2 minutes | Cook time: 25 minutes | Serves 4

- 4 bulbs garlic
- 1 tablespoon avocado oil
- 1 teaspoon salt
- Pinch of black pepper
- 1 cup water

1. Slice the pointy tops off the bulbs of garlic to expose the cloves. 2. Drizzle the avocado oil on top of the garlic and sprinkle with the salt and pepper. 3. Place the bulbs in the steamer basket, cut-side up. Alternatively, you may place them on a piece of aluminum foil with the sides pulled up and resting on top of the trivet. Place the steamer basket in the pot. 4. Close the lid and seal the vent. Cook on High Pressure for 25 minutes. Quick release the steam. 5. Let the garlic cool completely before removing the bulbs from the pot. 6. Hold the stem end (bottom) of the bulb and squeeze out all the garlic. Mash the cloves with a fork to make a paste.

Herb-Infused Sausage Balls

Prep time: 10 minutes | Cook time: 16 minutes | Serves 10

- 15 ounces (425 g) ground pork sausage
- 1 teaspoon dried oregano
- 4 ounces (113 g) Mozzarella, shredded
- 1 cup coconut flour
- 1 garlic clove, grated
- 1 teaspoon coconut oil, melted

1. In the bowl mix up ground pork sausages, dried oregano, shredded Mozzarella, coconut flour, and garlic clove. 2. When the mixture is homogenous, make the balls. 3. After this, pour coconut oil in the instant pot. 4. Arrange the balls in the instant pot and cook them on Sauté mode for 8 minutes from each side.

Fiery Baked Feta Foil Packets

Prep time: 10 minutes | Cook time: 6 minutes | Serves 6

- 12 ounces (340 g) feta cheese
- ½ tomato, sliced
- 1 ounce (28 g) bell pepper, sliced
- 1 teaspoon ground paprika
- 1 tablespoon olive oil
- 1 cup water, for cooking

1. Sprinkle the cheese with olive oil and ground paprika and place it on the foil. 2. Then top feta cheese with sliced tomato and bell pepper. Wrap it in the foil well. 3. After this, pour water and insert the steamer rack in the instant pot. 4. Put the wrapped cheese on the rack. Close and seal the lid. 5. Cook the cheese on Manual mode (High Pressure) for 6 minutes. Then make a quick pressure release. 6. Discard the foil and transfer the cheese on the serving plates.

Cheesy Pancetta & Pizza Dip

Prep time: 10 minutes | Cook time: 4 minutes | Serves 10

- 10 ounces (283 g) Pepper Jack cheese
- 10 ounces (283 g) cream cheese
- 10 ounces (283 g) pancetta, chopped
- 1 pound (454 g) tomatoes, puréed
- 1 cup green olives, pitted and halved
- 1 teaspoon dried oregano
- ½ teaspoon garlic powder
- 1 cup chicken broth
- 4 ounces (113 g) Mozzarella cheese, thinly sliced

1. Mix together the Pepper Jack cheese, cream cheese, pancetta, tomatoes, olives, oregano, and garlic powder in the Instant Pot. Pour in the chicken broth. 2. Lock the lid. Select the Manual mode and set the cooking time for 4 minutes at High Pressure. 3. When the timer beeps, perform a quick pressure release. Carefully remove the lid. 4. Scatter the Mozzarella cheese on top. Cover and allow to sit in the residual heat. Serve warm.

Tuna-Stuffed Deviled Eggs

Prep time: 10 minutes | Cook time: 8 minutes | Serves 3

- 1 cup water
- 6 eggs
- 1 (5 ounces / 142 g) can tuna, drained
- 4 tablespoons mayonnaise
- 1 teaspoon lemon juice
- 1 celery stalk, diced finely
- ¼ teaspoon Dijon mustard
- ¼ teaspoon chopped fresh dill
- ¼ teaspoon salt
- ⅛ teaspoon garlic powder

1. Add water to Instant Pot. Place steam rack or steamer basket inside pot. Carefully put eggs into steamer basket. Click lid closed. Press the Manual button and adjust time for 8 minutes. 2. Add remaining ingredients to medium bowl and mix. 3. When timer beeps, quick-release the steam and remove eggs. Place in bowl of cool water for 10 minutes, then remove shells. 4. Cut eggs in half and remove hard-boiled yolks, setting whites aside. Place yolks in food processor and pulse until smooth, or mash with fork. Add yolks to bowl with tuna and mayo, mixing until smooth. 5. Spoon mixture into egg-white halves. Serve chilled.

Crispy Parmesan Zucchini Fries

Prep time: 15 minutes | Cook time: 5 minutes | Serves 4

- 1 zucchini
- 1 ounce (28 g) Parmesan, grated
- 1 tablespoon almond flour
- ½ teaspoon Italian seasoning
- 1 tablespoon coconut oil

1. Trim the zucchini and cut it into the French fries. 2. Then sprinkle them with grated Parmesan, almond flour, and Italian seasoning. 3. Put coconut oil in the instant pot and melt it on Sauté mode. 4. Put the zucchini in the hot oil in one layer and cook for 2 minutes from each side or until they are golden brown. 5. Dry the zucchini fries with paper towels.

Chicken Celery Salad with Mayo

Prep time: 15 minutes | Cook time: 15 minutes | Serves 4

- 14 ounces (397 g) chicken breast, skinless, boneless
- 1 cup water
- 4 celery stalks
- 1 teaspoon salt
- ½ teaspoon onion powder
- 1 teaspoon mayonnaise

1. Combine all the ingredients except the mayo in the Instant Pot. 2. Secure the lid. Select the Manual mode and set the cooking time for 15 minutes at High Pressure. 3. Once cooking is complete, do a natural pressure release for 6 minutes, then release any remaining pressure. Carefully open the lid. 4. Remove the chicken and shred with two forks, then return to the Instant Pot. 5. Add the mayo and stir well. Serve immediately.

Cheesy Broccoli Dip

Prep time: 5 minutes | Cook time: 10 minutes | Serves 6

- 4 tablespoons butter
- ½ medium onion, diced
- 1½ cups chopped broccoli
- 8 ounces (227 g) cream cheese
- ½ cup mayonnaise
- ½ cup chicken broth
- 1 cup shredded Cheddar cheese

1. Press the Sauté button and then press the Adjust button to set heat to Less. Add butter to Instant Pot. Add onion and sauté until softened, about 5 minutes. Press the Cancel button. 2. Add broccoli, cream cheese, mayo, and broth to pot. Press the Manual button and adjust time for 4 minutes. 3. When timer beeps, quick-release the pressure and stir in Cheddar. Serve warm.

Quick Popcorn

Prep time: 1 minutes | Cook time: 5 minutes | Serves 5

- 2 tablespoons coconut oil
- ½ cup popcorn kernels
- ¼ cup margarine spread, melted, optional
- Sea salt to taste

1. Set the Instant Pot to Sauté. 2. Melt the coconut oil in the inner pot, then add the popcorn kernels and stir. 3. Press Adjust to bring the temperature up to high. 4. When the corn starts popping, secure the lid on the Instant Pot. 5. When you no longer hear popping, turn off the Instant Pot, remove the lid, and pour the popcorn into a bowl. 6. Top with the optional melted margarine and season the popcorn with sea salt to your liking.

Broccoli and Cabbage Slaw

Prep time: 5 minutes | Cook time: 10 minutes | Serves 6

- 2 cups broccoli slaw
- ½ head cabbage, thinly sliced
- ¼ cup chopped kale
- 4 tablespoons butter
- 1 teaspoon salt
- ¼ teaspoon pepper

1. Press the Sauté button and add all ingredients to Instant Pot. Stir-fry for 7 to 10 minutes until cabbage softens. Serve warm.

Chicken Cabbage Salad

Prep time: 15 minutes | Cook time: 10 minutes | Serves 4

- 12 ounces (340 g) chicken fillet, chopped
- 1 teaspoon Cajun seasoning
- 1 tablespoon coconut oil
- 1 cup chopped Chinese cabbage
- 1 tablespoon avocado oil
- 1 teaspoon sesame seeds

1. Sprinkle the chopped chicken with the Cajun seasoning. 2. Set your Instant Pot to Sauté and heat the coconut oil. Add the chicken and cook for 10 minutes, stirring occasionally. 3. When the chicken is cooked, transfer to a salad bowl. Add the cabbage, avocado oil, and sesame seeds and gently toss to combine. Serve immediately.

Chapter 6
Stews and Soups

Chicken Zucchini Soup

Prep time: 8 minutes | Cook time: 14 minutes | Serves 6

- ¼ cup coconut oil or unsalted butter
- 1 cup chopped celery
- ¼ cup chopped onions
- 2 cloves garlic, minced
- 1 pound (454 g) boneless, skinless chicken breasts, cut into 1-inch cubes
- 6 cups chicken broth
- 1 tablespoon dried parsley
- 1 teaspoon fine sea salt
- ½ teaspoon dried marjoram
- ½ teaspoon ground black pepper
- 1 bay leaf
- 2 cups zucchini noodles

1. Put the coconut oil into the Instant Pot and select the Sauté function. After the oil has melted, add the celery, onions, and garlic, cooking while stirring occasionally for 4 minutes or until the onions become soft. Then press Cancel to halt the Sauté process. 2. Add the cubed chicken, broth, parsley, salt, marjoram, pepper, and bay leaf. Seal the lid properly, choose the Manual mode, and set a timer for 10 minutes. When the cooking is done, allow the pressure to release naturally. 3. Take off the lid and stir thoroughly. Put the noodles into bowls, using ⅓ cup for each bowl. Pour the soup over the noodles and serve right away; if it is left for too long, the noodles will become overly soft.

Chicken Noodle Soup

Prep time: 15 minutes | Cook time: 20 minutes | Serves 12

- 2 tablespoons avocado oil
- 1 medium onion, chopped
- 3 celery stalks, chopped
- 1 teaspoon kosher salt
- ¼ teaspoon freshly ground black pepper
- 2 teaspoons minced garlic
- 5 large carrots, peeled and cut into ¼-inch-thick rounds
- 3 pounds bone-in chicken breasts (about 3)
- 4 cups Chicken Bone Broth or low-sodium store-bought chicken broth
- 4 cups water
- 2 tablespoons soy sauce
- 6 ounces whole grain wide egg noodles

1. Switch the electric pressure cooker to the Sauté mode. Once the pot reaches the desired temperature, pour in the avocado oil. 2. Add the onion, celery, salt, and pepper to the pot, and sauté for 3 to 5 minutes, or until the vegetables start to become tender. 3. Incorporate the garlic and carrots into the pot, stirring well to ensure that all ingredients are evenly mixed. Press the Cancel button to stop the cooking process at this stage. 4. Place the chicken breasts into the pot, meat-side down. Pour in the broth, water, and soy sauce. Close and lock the lid of the pressure cooker, ensuring that the valve is set to sealing. 5. Cook the chicken at high pressure for 20 minutes to ensure thorough cooking. 6. After the cooking cycle is complete, press the Cancel button and perform a quick release of the pressure. Unlock and remove the lid carefully. 7. Use tongs to transfer the chicken breasts to a cutting board. Switch the pot back to Sauté/More mode and bring the liquid to a boil. 8. Add the noodles to the boiling liquid and cook for 4 to 5 minutes, or until they reach an al dente texture. 9. While the noodles are cooking, shred the chicken breasts using two forks. Return the shredded chicken to the pot and reserve the bones for making additional bone broth later. 10. Taste the soup and season with more pepper if desired. Serve hot, enjoying your homemade chicken noodle soup.

Creamy Chicken Wild Rice Soup

Prep time: 15 minutes | Cook time: 15 minutes | Serves 5

- 2 tablespoons margarine
- ½ cup yellow onion, diced
- ¾ cup carrots, diced
- ¾ cup sliced mushrooms (about 3–4 mushrooms)
- ½ pound chicken breast, diced into 1-inch cubes
- 6.2-ounce box Uncle Ben's Long Grain &
- Wild Rice Fast Cook
- 2 14-ounce cans low-sodium chicken broth
- 1 cup skim milk
- 1 cup evaporated skim milk
- 2 ounces fat-free cream cheese
- 2 tablespoons cornstarch

1. Activate the Sauté feature and include the margarine, onion, carrots, and mushrooms in the inner pot. Sauté for approximately 5 minutes, or until the onions become translucent and tender. 2. Add the cubed chicken along with the seasoning packet from the Uncle Ben's box, stirring to integrate well. 3. Incorporate the rice and chicken broth into the pot. Switch to Manual mode, set to high pressure, then lock the lid and confirm the vent is set to sealing. Establish a cooking time of 5 minutes. 4. Once the cooking period concludes, let it remain on Keep Warm for an additional 5 minutes before executing a quick pressure release. 5. Remove the lid and revert the setting back to Sauté. 6. Add the skim milk, evaporated milk, and cream cheese, stirring until fully melted. 7. In a separate small bowl, mix cornstarch with a small quantity of water to ensure it dissolves properly, then incorporate it into the soup to achieve the desired thickness.

Buffalo Chicken Soup

Prep time: 7 minutes | Cook time: 10 minutes | Serves 2

- 1 ounce (28 g) celery stalk, chopped
- 4 tablespoons coconut milk
- ¾ teaspoon salt
- ¼ teaspoon white pepper
- 1 cup water
- 2 ounces (57 g) Mozzarella, shredded
- 6 ounces (170 g) cooked chicken, shredded
- 2 tablespoons keto-friendly Buffalo sauce

1. Add the chopped celery stalk, coconut milk, salt, white pepper, water, and Mozzarella into the Instant Pot, stirring thoroughly to ensure all ingredients are well incorporated. 2. Activate the Manual mode on the Instant Pot and program it to cook for 7 minutes at High Pressure. 3. Upon hearing the timer beep, perform a quick pressure release to safely open the lid. 4. Pour the soup into bowls, mix in the chicken and Buffalo sauce until well blended, and serve the warm and savory soup.

Provençal Chicken Soup

Prep time: 20 minutes | Cook time: 30 minutes | Serves 6 to 8

- 1 tablespoon extra-virgin olive oil
- 2 fennel bulbs, 2 tablespoons fronds minced, stalks discarded, bulbs halved, cored, and cut into ½-inch pieces
- 1 onion, chopped
- 1¾ teaspoons table salt
- 2 tablespoons tomato paste
- 4 garlic cloves, minced
- 1 tablespoon minced fresh thyme or 1 teaspoon dried
- 2 anchovy fillets, minced
- 7 cups water, divided
- 1 (14½-ounce / 411-g) can diced tomatoes, drained
- 2 carrots, peeled, halved lengthwise, and sliced ½ inch thick
- 2 (12-ounce / 340-g) bone-in split chicken breasts, trimmed
- 4 (5- to 7-ounce / 142- to 198-g) bone-in chicken thighs, trimmed
- ½ cup pitted brine-cured green olives, chopped
- 1 teaspoon grated orange zest

1. Utilize the highest Sauté setting on the Instant Pot to heat oil until it glistens. Add fennel pieces, onion, and salt, cooking until the vegetables are tender, approximately 5 minutes. Incorporate tomato paste, garlic, thyme, and anchovies, stirring until the aroma is noticeable, about 30 seconds. Pour in 5 cups of water, scraping the bottom to loosen any browned bits, then add tomatoes and carrots. Carefully place chicken breasts and thighs into the pot. 2. Lock the lid securely and ensure the pressure release valve is closed. Choose the high-pressure cook function and set the cooking time to 20 minutes. Afterward, turn off the Instant Pot and perform a quick-release of the pressure. Open the lid carefully, ensuring that steam escapes away from you. 3. Move the chicken to a cutting board, allowing it to cool slightly before shredding it into bite-sized pieces with two forks; discard the skin and bones. 4. Use a wide, shallow spoon to remove excess fat from the surface of the soup. Stir in the shredded chicken along with any collected juices, olives, and the remaining 2 cups of water. Allow the soup to sit until heated through, about 3 minutes. Incorporate fennel fronds and orange zest, and season with salt and pepper according to taste. Serve hot.

Spicy Sausage and Chicken Stew

Prep time: 10 minutes | Cook time: 25 minutes | Serves 10

- 1 tablespoon coconut oil
- 2 pounds (907 g) bulk Italian sausage
- 2 boneless, skinless chicken thighs, cut into ½-inch pieces
- ½ cup chopped onions
- 1 (28 ounces / 794 g) can whole peeled tomatoes, drained
- 1 cup sugar-free tomato sauce
- 1 (4½ ounces / 128 g) can green chilies
- 3 tablespoons minced garlic
- 2 tablespoons smoked paprika
- 1 tablespoon ground cumin
- 1 tablespoon dried oregano leaves
- 2 teaspoons fine sea salt
- 1 teaspoon cayenne pepper
- 1 cup chicken broth
- 1 ounce (28 g) unsweetened baking chocolate, chopped
- ¼ cup lime juice
- Chopped fresh cilantro leaves, for garnish
- Red pepper flakes, for garnish

1. Pour the coconut oil into the Instant Pot and select the Sauté function; once it melts, add the sausage, chicken, and onions, stirring occasionally until the sausage is partially cooked and the onions are tender, approximately 5 minutes. 2. Meanwhile, combine tomatoes, tomato sauce, and chilies in a food processor and process until smooth. 3. Next, incorporate garlic, paprika, cumin, oregano, salt, and cayenne pepper into the Instant Pot, stirring well, then add the tomato purée, broth, and chocolate, ensuring thorough mixing before pressing Cancel to halt the Sauté mode. 4. Seal the lid, choose Manual mode, set a timer for 20 minutes, and after completion, allow the pressure to release naturally. 5. Just prior to serving, stir in the lime juice, ladle the stew into bowls, and garnish with cilantro and red pepper flakes.

Unstuffed Cabbage Soup

Prep time: 15 minutes | Cook time: 20 minutes | Serves 5

- 2 tablespoons coconut oil
- 1 pound ground sirloin or turkey
- 1 medium onion, diced
- 2 cloves garlic, minced
- 1 small head cabbage, chopped, cored, cut into roughly 2-inch pieces.
- 6-ounce can low-sodium tomato paste
- 32-ounce can low-sodium diced tomatoes, with liquid
- 2 cups low-sodium beef broth
- 1½ cups water
- ¾ cup brown rice
- 1–2 teaspoons salt
- ½ teaspoon black pepper
- 1 teaspoon oregano
- 1 teaspoon parsley

1. Utilize the Sauté function in the Instant Pot's inner pot to melt the coconut oil. Add the ground meat and stir frequently until it loses its color, approximately 2 minutes. 2. Incorporate the onion and garlic, continuing to sauté for an additional 2 minutes while stirring regularly. 3. Add the chopped cabbage to the pot. 4. Layer on top of the cabbage the tomato paste, tomatoes with their liquid, beef broth, water, rice, and desired spices. 5. Secure the lid and adjust the vent to the sealing position. Choose the Manual setting and set the cooking time to 20 minutes. 6. Once the cooking time has elapsed, allow the pressure to release naturally for 10 minutes before performing a quick release.

Instantly Good Beef Stew

Prep time: 20 minutes | Cook time: 35 minutes | Serves 6

- 3 tablespoons olive oil, divided
- 2 pounds stewing beef, cubed
- 2 cloves garlic, minced
- 1 large onion, chopped
- 3 ribs celery, sliced
- 3 large potatoes, cubed
- 2–3 carrots, sliced
- 8 ounces no-salt-added tomato sauce
- 10 ounces low-sodium beef broth
- 2 teaspoons Worcestershire sauce
- ¼ teaspoon pepper
- 1 bay leaf

1. Set the Instant Pot to the Sauté mode and add 1 tablespoon of oil. Add ⅓ of the beef cubes and cook until they are browned and seared on all sides. Repeat this process two more times with the remaining oil and beef cubes. Set the beef aside. 2. Add the garlic, onion, and celery to the pot and sauté for a few minutes. Press Cancel to stop the cooking process. 3. Return the beef to the pot along with all the remaining ingredients. 4. Secure the lid and ensure the vent is set to sealing. Select Manual mode and set the cooking time for 35 minutes. 5. When the cooking time is up, let the pressure release naturally for 15 minutes, then manually release any remaining pressure. 6. Remove the lid, discard the bay leaf, and serve the dish.

Spiced Chicken Soup with Squash and Chickpeas

Prep time: 15 minutes | Cook time: 30 minutes | Serves 6 to 8

- 2 tablespoons extra-virgin olive oil
- 1 onion, chopped
- 1¾ teaspoons table salt
- 2 tablespoons tomato paste
- 4 garlic cloves, minced
- 1 tablespoon ground coriander
- 1½ teaspoons ground cumin
- 1 teaspoon ground cardamom
- ½ teaspoon ground allspice
- ¼ teaspoon cayenne pepper
- 7 cups water, divided
- 2 (12 ounces / 340 g) bone-in split chicken breasts, trimmed
- 4 (5 to 7 ounces / 142 to 198 g) bone-in chicken thighs, trimmed
- 1½ pounds (680 g) butternut squash, peeled, seeded, and cut into 1½-inch pieces (4 cups)
- 1 (15 ounces / 425 g) can chickpeas, rinsed
- ½ cup chopped fresh cilantro

1. Utilize the highest Sauté setting on the Instant Pot to heat oil until it glistens. Add onions and salt, cooking until the onions are tender, approximately 5 minutes. Incorporate tomato paste, garlic, coriander, cumin, cardamom, allspice, and cayenne, stirring until the mixture is fragrant, about 30 seconds. Pour in 5 cups of water, scraping the bottom to loosen any browned bits. Carefully place chicken breasts and thighs into the pot, then surround them with evenly arranged squash pieces. 2. Lock the lid securely and ensure the pressure release valve is closed. Choose the high-pressure cook function and set the cooking time to 20 minutes. Afterward, turn off the Instant Pot and perform a quick-release of the pressure. Open the lid carefully, ensuring that steam escapes away from you. 3. Transfer the chicken to a cutting board, allowing it to cool slightly before shredding it into bite-sized pieces with two forks; discard the skin and bones. 4. Use a wide, shallow spoon to remove excess fat from the surface of the soup, then break the squash into bite-size pieces. Stir in the shredded chicken along with any collected juices, chickpeas, and the remaining 2 cups of water. Allow the soup to sit until heated through, about 3 minutes. Incorporate chopped cilantro and season with salt and pepper according to taste. Serve hot.

Swiss Chard and Chicken Soup

Prep time: 10 minutes | Cook time: 5 minutes | Serves 4

- 1 onion, chopped
- 6 garlic cloves, peeled
- 1 (2-inch) piece fresh ginger, chopped
- 1 (10-ounce / 283-g) can tomatoes with chiles
- 1½ cups full-fat coconut milk, divided
- 1 tablespoon powdered chicken broth base
- 1 pound (454 g) boneless chicken thighs, cut into large bite-size pieces
- 1½ cups chopped celery
- 2 cups chopped Swiss chard
- 1 teaspoon ground turmeric

1. Place the onion, garlic, ginger, tomatoes, ½ cup of coconut milk, and chicken broth base into a blender jar. Process the ingredients until they form a smooth sauce. 2. Transfer the puréed mixture into the inner cooking pot of the Instant Pot, followed by adding the chicken, celery, and chard. 3. Secure the lid and select Manual mode, setting the pressure to High. Cook for 5 minutes, then allow the pressure to release naturally for 10 minutes after cooking is complete, followed by a quick-release of any residual pressure. 4. Unlock the lid and stir in the remaining 1 cup of coconut milk and turmeric. Heat through and serve.

Buttercup Squash Soup

Prep time: 15 minutes | Cook time: 10 minutes | Serves 6

- 2 tablespoons extra-virgin olive oil
- 1 medium onion, chopped
- 4 to 5 cups Vegetable Broth or Chicken Bone Broth
- 1½ pounds buttercup squash, peeled, seeded, and cut into 1-inch chunks
- ½ teaspoon kosher salt
- ¼ teaspoon ground white pepper
- Whole nutmeg, for grating

1. Switch the electric pressure cooker to the Sauté mode. Once the pot reaches the desired temperature, pour in the olive oil. 2. Incorporate the onion and sauté for a duration of 3 to 5 minutes, or until it starts to become tender. Press Cancel to stop the cooking process. 3. Add the broth, squash, salt, and pepper to the pot, stirring well to combine. Adjust the broth quantity based on your preferred soup consistency: 4 cups for a thicker soup or 5 cups for a thinner, more drinkable option. 4. Close and lock the pressure cooker's lid securely. Ensure the valve is set to the sealing position. 5. Cook the mixture under high pressure for 10 minutes. 6. Upon completion of the cooking cycle, press Cancel and wait for the pressure to release naturally. 7. After the pin drops, unlock and remove the lid carefully. 8. Utilize an immersion blender to purée the soup directly in the pot. If an immersion blender is unavailable, transfer the soup to a blender or food processor for puréeing, adhering to the manufacturer's guidelines for blending hot foods. 9. Finally, pour the puréed soup into serving bowls and garnish with freshly grated nutmeg on top.

Chicken and Kale Soup

Prep time: 5 minutes | Cook time: 5 minutes | Serves 4

- 2 cups chopped cooked chicken breast
- 12 ounces (340 g) frozen kale
- 1 onion, chopped
- 2 cups water
- 1 tablespoon powdered chicken broth base
- ½ teaspoon ground cinnamon
- Pinch ground cloves
- 2 teaspoons minced garlic
- 1 teaspoon freshly ground black pepper
- 1 teaspoon salt
- 2 cups full-fat coconut milk

1. Add the chicken, kale, onion, water, chicken broth base, cinnamon, cloves, garlic, pepper, and salt to the inner cooking pot of the Instant Pot. 2. Secure the lid in position. Choose Manual mode and set the pressure to High. Cook for a duration of 5 minutes. Upon completion of cooking, allow the pressure to release naturally for 10 minutes, followed by a quick-release of any remaining pressure. Unlock the lid. 3. Incorporate the coconut milk into the pot. Taste the dish and adjust any seasonings as necessary prior to serving.

Beef and Eggplant Tagine

Prep time: 15 minutes | Cook time: 25 minutes | Serves 6

- 1 pound (454 g) beef fillet, chopped
- 1 eggplant, chopped
- 6 ounces (170 g) scallions, chopped
- 4 cups beef broth
- 1 teaspoon ground allspices
- 1 teaspoon erythritol
- 1 teaspoon coconut oil

1. Add all the ingredients to the Instant Pot and stir thoroughly to ensure they are well combined. 2. Close the lid securely. Choose Manual mode and set the cooking time to 25 minutes at High Pressure. 3. When the timer sounds, allow the pressure to release naturally for 15 minutes before quickly releasing any remaining pressure. Open the lid once it is safe to do so. 4. Serve the dish while it is still warm for the best flavor experience.

Butternut Squash Soup

Prep time: 30 minutes | Cook time: 15 minutes | Serves 4

- 2 tablespoons margarine
- 1 large onion, chopped
- 2 cloves garlic, minced
- 1 teaspoon thyme
- ½ teaspoon sage
- Salt and pepper to taste
- 2 large butternut squash, peeled, seeded, and cubed (about 4 pounds)
- 4 cups low-sodium chicken stock

1. In the inner pot of the Instant Pot, melt the margarine by selecting the Sauté function. 2. Add the onion and garlic, cooking until they become soft, which should take about 3 to 5 minutes. 3. Incorporate the thyme and sage, and continue cooking for another minute. Season the mixture with salt and pepper. 4. Stir in the butternut squash and then add the chicken stock. 5. Secure the lid and ensure the vent is set to sealing. Choose the Manual setting and cook the squash and seasonings for 10 minutes at high pressure. 6. When the cooking time is up, perform a quick release of the pressure. 7. Puree the soup in a food processor or use an immersion blender directly in the inner pot. If the soup is too thick, add more stock as needed. Adjust the seasoning with salt and pepper to taste.

Spanish-Style Turkey Meatball Soup

Prep time: 10 minutes | Cook time: 15 minutes | Serves 6 to 8

- 1 slice hearty white sandwich bread, torn into quarters
- ¼ cup whole milk
- 1 ounce (28 g) Manchego cheese, grated (½ cup), plus extra for serving
- 5 tablespoons minced fresh parsley, divided
- ½ teaspoon table salt
- 1 pound (454 g) ground turkey
- 1 tablespoon extra-virgin olive oil
- 1 onion, chopped
- 1 red bell pepper, stemmed, seeded, and cut into ¾-inch pieces
- 4 garlic cloves, minced
- 2 teaspoons smoked paprika
- ½ cup dry white wine
- 8 cups chicken broth
- 8 ounces (227 g) kale, stemmed and chopped

1. With a fork, mash the bread and milk together in a large bowl to form a paste. Stir in the Manchego cheese, 3 tablespoons of parsley, and salt until well mixed. Add the turkey and knead the mixture with your hands until thoroughly combined. Pinch off and roll the mixture into 2-teaspoon-size balls, arranging them on a large plate (you should end up with approximately 35 meatballs); set them aside. 2. Using the highest sauté setting, heat the oil in the Instant Pot until it shimmers. Add the onion and bell pepper, cooking until they are softened and lightly browned, about 5 to 7 minutes. Stir in the garlic and paprika and cook until fragrant, approximately 30 seconds. Stir in the wine, scraping up any browned bits, and cook until it is almost completely evaporated, around 5 minutes. Stir in the broth and kale, then gently submerge the meatballs. 3. Lock the lid into place and close the pressure release valve. Select the high-pressure cook function and cook for 3 minutes. Turn off the Instant Pot and perform a quick-release of the pressure. Carefully remove the lid, making sure the steam escapes away from you. 4. Stir in the remaining 2 tablespoons of parsley and season with salt and pepper to taste. Serve the dish, passing extra Manchego cheese separately for guests to add as desired.

Bacon, Leek, and Cauliflower Soup

Prep time: 15 minutes | Cook time: 15 minutes | Serves 6

- 6 slices bacon
- 1 leek, remove the dark green end and roots, sliced in half lengthwise, rinsed, cut into ½-inch-thick slices crosswise
- ½ medium yellow onion, sliced
- 4 cloves garlic, minced
- 3 cups chicken broth
- 1 large head cauliflower, roughly chopped into florets
- 1 cup water
- 1 teaspoon kosher salt
- 1 teaspoon ground black pepper
- ⅔ cup shredded sharp Cheddar cheese, divided
- ½ cup heavy whipping cream

1. Turn on the Instant Pot's Sauté mode. Once it's heated up, put the bacon on the bottom of the pot and cook for about 5 minutes or until it becomes crispy. 2. Move the bacon slices onto a plate. Let them sit until they are cool enough to touch, then crumble them with forks. 3. Add the leek and onion to the pot where the bacon fat is left. Sauté for around 5 minutes or until they give off a fragrant aroma and the onion starts to caramelize. Then add the garlic and sauté for another 30 seconds or until it smells fragrant. 4. Mix in the chicken broth, cauliflower florets, water, salt, pepper, and three - quarters of the crumbled bacon. 5. Fasten the lid. Push the Manual button and set the cooking time to 3 minutes at High Pressure. 6. When the timer goes off, do a quick pressure release. Open the lid. 7. Stir in ½ cup of the Cheddar cheese and the cream. Use an immersion blender to blend the soup until it's smooth. 8. Serve the soup by ladling it into bowls and sprinkle with the remaining Cheddar cheese and crumbled bacon. Serve right away.

Blue Cheese Mushroom Soup

Prep time: 15 minutes | Cook time: 20 minutes | Serves 4

- 2 cups chopped white mushrooms
- 3 tablespoons cream cheese
- 4 ounces (113 g) scallions, diced
- 4 cups chicken broth
- 1 teaspoon olive oil
- ½ teaspoon ground cumin
- 1 teaspoon salt
- 2 ounces (57 g) blue cheese, crumbled

1. Mix the mushrooms, cream cheese, scallions, chicken broth, olive oil, and ground cumin together in the Instant Pot. 2. Lock the lid in place. Choose Manual mode and set the cooking time to 20 minutes at High Pressure. 3. After the timer sounds, perform a quick pressure release and then open the lid. 4. Season with salt and use an immersion blender to blend the soup until smooth. 5. Serve the soup warm by ladling it into bowls and garnishing each serving with crumbled blue cheese on top.

Bacon Broccoli Soup

Prep time: 12 minutes | Cook time: 12 minutes | Serves 6

- 2 large heads broccoli
- 2 strips bacon, chopped
- 2 tablespoons unsalted butter
- ¼ cup diced onions
- Cloves squeezed from 1 head roasted garlic, or 2 cloves garlic, minced
- 3 cups chicken broth or beef broth
- 6 ounces (170 g) extra-sharp Cheddar cheese, shredded (about 1½ cups)
- 2 ounces (57 g) cream cheese, softened
- ½ teaspoon fine sea salt
- ¼ teaspoon ground black pepper
- Pinch of ground nutmeg

1. First, detach the broccoli florets from the stems, preserving as much of the stem as possible for other uses. Set the florets aside for a different recipe. Trim the bottom of each stem to create a flat surface. Utilize a spiral slicer to transform the stems into "noodles." 2. Begin by placing bacon in the Instant Pot and selecting the Sauté function. Cook, stirring occasionally, for approximately 4 minutes or until the bacon is crispy. Remove the bacon using a slotted spoon and place it on a plate lined with paper towels to drain, ensuring the fat remains in the pot. 3. Add butter and onions to the Instant Pot and cook for about 4 minutes, or until the onions are tender. Incorporate garlic (and additional minute of sautéing if using raw garlic). Next, add broth, Cheddar cheese, cream cheese, salt, pepper, and nutmeg. Sauté until all cheeses have melted, which should take around 3 minutes. Press Cancel to halt the Sauté process. 4. Employ a stick blender to blend the soup until smooth. Alternatively, pour the soup into a conventional blender or food processor for blending, then return it to the Instant Pot. If using a standard blender, consider blending in batches to avoid overfilling, which can prevent proper puréeing. 5. Incorporate broccoli noodles into the puréed soup within the Instant Pot. Seal the lid, select Manual mode, and set a timer for 1 minute. After completion, allow the pressure to release naturally. 6. Finally, remove the lid and stir thoroughly. Serve the soup by ladling it into bowls and garnish each serving with a sprinkle of bacon.

Broccoli and Red Feta Soup

Prep time: 10 minutes | Cook time: 25 minutes | Serves 4

- 1 cup broccoli, chopped
- ½ cup coconut cream
- 1 teaspoon unsweetened tomato purée
- 4 cups beef broth
- 1 teaspoon chili flakes
- 6 ounces (170 g) feta, crumbled

1. Add broccoli, coconut cream, tomato purée, and beef broth to the Instant Pot. Season with chili flakes and stir until well combined. 2. Seal the lid and choose Manual mode. Set the cooking time to 8 minutes on High Pressure. 3. When the timer sounds, perform a quick pressure release and open the lid. 4. Incorporate the feta cheese and stir the soup on Sauté mode for 5 minutes or until the cheese has melted. 5. Serve the soup immediately.

Kale Curry Soup

Prep time: 10 minutes | Cook time: 15 minutes | Serves 3

- 2 cups kale
- 1 teaspoon almond butter
- 1 tablespoon fresh cilantro
- ½ cup ground chicken
- 1 teaspoon curry paste
- ½ cup heavy cream
- 1 cup chicken stock
- ½ teaspoon salt

1. Insert the kale into the Instant Pot. 2. Toss in the almond butter, cilantro, and minced chicken. Sauté this amalgamation for approximately five minutes. 3. In the interim, blend the curry paste with the heavy cream in the Instant Pot till it acquires a creamy texture. 4. Pour in the chicken stock and add salt, then shut the lid. 5. Pick the Manual mode and establish a cooking duration of ten minutes under High Pressure. 6. Upon the timer's beep, execute a swift pressure release. Subsequently, unlatch the lid. 7. Present while still warm.

Chicken Poblano Pepper Soup

Prep time: 10 minutes | Cook time: 20 minutes | Serves 8

- 1 cup diced onion
- 3 poblano peppers, chopped
- 5 garlic cloves
- 2 cups diced cauliflower
- 1½ pounds (680 g) chicken breast, cut into large chunks
- ¼ cup chopped fresh cilantro
- 1 teaspoon ground coriander
- 1 teaspoon ground cumin
- 1 to 2 teaspoons salt
- 2 cups water
- 2 ounces (57 g) cream cheese, cut into small chunks
- 1 cup sour cream

1. Add the onion, poblanos, garlic, cauliflower, chicken, cilantro, coriander, cumin, salt, and water to the inner cooking pot of the Instant Pot. 2. Lock the lid into position. Select Manual mode and set the pressure to High. Cook for 15 minutes. After the cooking is done, allow the pressure to release naturally for 10 minutes, then perform a quick release for any remaining pressure. Unlock the lid. 3. Use tongs to remove the chicken and place it in a bowl. 4. Tilt the pot and use an immersion blender to roughly puree the vegetable mixture, leaving it slightly chunky. 5. Switch the Instant Pot to Sauté mode and increase the heat to high. Once the broth is hot and bubbling, add the cream cheese and stir until it melts. If necessary, use a whisk to blend in the cream cheese. 6. Shred the chicken and stir it back into the pot. Heat through and serve, topped with sour cream for an enjoyable meal.

Easy Southern Brunswick Stew

Prep time: 20 minutes | Cook time: 8 minutes | Serves 12

- 2 pounds pork butt, visible fat removed
- 17-ounce can white corn
- 1¼ cups ketchup
- 2 cups diced, cooked potatoes
- 10-ounce package frozen peas
- 2 10¾-ounce cans reduced-sodium tomato soup
- Hot sauce to taste, optional

1. Position the pork inside the Instant Pot and ensure the lid is properly secured. 2. Activate the Slow Cook function and set the temperature to low, allowing it to cook for a period of 6–8 hours. 3. Upon completion of the cooking time, carefully remove the pork from the bone, shred it, and discard any visible fat. 4. Mix all the shredded meat with the remaining ingredients (excluding the hot sauce) inside the Instant Pot's inner pot. 5. Lock the lid back into place and continue cooking in Slow Cook mode on low for an additional 30 minutes. Afterward, hot sauce can be added according to your preference.

Chicken Vegetable Soup

Prep time: 12 to 25 minutes | Cook time: 4 minutes | Serves 6

- 1 to 2 raw chicken breasts, cubed
- ½ medium onion, chopped
- 4 cloves garlic, minced
- ½ sweet potato, small cubes
- 1 large carrot, peeled and cubed
- 4 stalks celery, chopped, leaves included
- ½ cup frozen corn
- ¼ cup frozen peas
- ¼ cup frozen lima beans
- 1 cup frozen green beans (bite-sized)
- ¼ to ½ cup chopped savoy cabbage
- 14½ ounces can low-sodium petite diced tomatoes
- 3 cups low-sodium chicken bone broth
- ½ teaspoon black pepper
- 1 teaspoon garlic powder
- ¼ cup chopped fresh parsley
- ¼ to ½ teaspoon red pepper flakes

1. Add all of the ingredients, following the order listed, into the inner pot of the Instant Pot. 2. Lock the lid securely in place, set the vent to sealing, press Manual, and cook at high pressure for 4 minutes. 3. Manually release the pressure immediately after the cooking time is finished.

Broccoli Cheddar Soup

Prep time: 5 minutes | Cook time: 10 minutes | Serves 4

- 2 tablespoons butter
- ⅛ cup onion, diced
- ½ teaspoon garlic powder
- ½ teaspoon salt
- ¼ teaspoon pepper
- 2 cups chicken broth
- 1 cup chopped broccoli
- 1 tablespoon cream cheese, softened
- ¼ cup heavy cream
- 1 cup shredded Cheddar cheese

1. Press the Sauté button on the Instant Pot and add butter. Then add onion and sauté until it becomes translucent. Press the Cancel button. Subsequently, add garlic powder, salt, pepper, broth, and broccoli to the pot. 2. Close the lid by clicking it. Press the Soup button and set the cooking time for 5 minutes. When the timer beeps, stir in heavy cream, cream cheese, and Cheddar.

Cabbage and Pork Soup

Prep time: 10 minutes | Cook time: 12 minutes | Serves 3

- 1 teaspoon butter
- ½ cup shredded white cabbage
- ½ teaspoon ground coriander
- ½ teaspoon salt
- ½ teaspoon chili flakes
- 2 cups chicken broth
- ½ cup ground pork

1. On the Instant Pot, select Sauté mode and melt the butter. 2. Add the cabbage to the pot and season with ground coriander, salt, and chili flakes. 3. Gently mix in the chicken broth and ground pork. 4. Close the lid securely and choose Manual mode. Set the cooking time to 12 minutes at High Pressure. 5. When the timer sounds, perform a quick pressure release. Open the lid carefully. 6. Ladle out the soup and serve it warm.

Beef Meatball Minestrone

Prep time: 5 minutes | Cook time: 35 minutes | Serves 6

- 1 pound (454 g) ground beef
- 1 large egg
- 1½ tablespoons golden flaxseed meal
- ⅓ cup shredded Mozzarella cheese
- ¼ cup unsweetened tomato purée
- 1½ tablespoons Italian seasoning, divided
- 1½ teaspoons garlic powder, divided
- 1½ teaspoons sea salt, divided
- 1 tablespoon olive oil
- 2 garlic cloves, minced
- ½ medium yellow onion, minced
- ¼ cup pancetta, diced
- 1 cup sliced yellow squash
- 1 cup sliced zucchini
- ½ cup sliced turnips
- 4 cups beef broth
- 14 ounces (397 g) can diced tomatoes
- ½ teaspoon ground black pepper
- 3 tablespoons shredded Parmesan cheese

1. Heat the oven to 400°F (205°C). Line a large baking sheet with foil. 2. In a large bowl, mix ground beef, egg, flaxseed meal, Mozzarella, unsweetened tomato purée, ½ tablespoon Italian seasoning, ½ teaspoon garlic powder, and ½ teaspoon sea salt until combined. 3. Shape 1 heaping tablespoon of the mixture into a meatball. Repeat with the rest and place on the baking sheet. 4. Bake the meatballs for 15 minutes. Remove and let cool. 5. Turn on the Instant Pot's Sauté mode. Add olive oil, garlic, onion, and pancetta. Cook for 2 minutes or until garlic is fragrant and onions soften. 6. Add yellow squash, zucchini, and turnips. Sauté for 3 more minutes. 7. Pour in beef broth, diced tomatoes, black pepper, and the remaining seasonings. Stir and add meatballs. 8. Lock the lid. Choose Manual mode and cook for 15 minutes at High Pressure. 9. Let the pressure release naturally for 10 minutes, then quick-release any remaining pressure. 10. Open the lid and stir the soup gently. Serve in bowls topped with Parmesan. Enjoy hot.

Chicken Brunswick Stew

Prep time: 0 minutes | Cook time: 30 minutes | Serves 6

- 2 tablespoons extra-virgin olive oil
- 2 garlic cloves, chopped
- 1 large yellow onion, diced
- 2 pounds boneless, skinless chicken (breasts, tenders, or thighs), cut into bite-size pieces
- 1 teaspoon dried thyme
- 1 teaspoon smoked paprika
- 1 teaspoon fine sea salt
- ½ teaspoon freshly ground black pepper
- 1 cup low-sodium chicken broth
- 1 tablespoon hot sauce (such as Tabasco or Crystal)
- 1 tablespoon raw apple cider vinegar
- 1½ cups frozen corn
- 1½ cups frozen baby lima beans
- One 14½ ounces can fire-roasted diced tomatoes and their liquid
- 2 tablespoons tomato paste
- Cornbread, for serving

1. Choose the Sauté option on the Instant Pot. Heat the oil and garlic for 2 minutes, till the garlic gets bubbly but not brown. Add the onion and sauté for 3 minutes, until it starts to get soft. Put in the chicken and sauté for another 3 minutes, until it's mostly opaque (it doesn't need to be fully cooked at this point). Add thyme, paprika, salt, and pepper and sauté for an additional 1 minute. 2. Stir in the broth, hot sauce, vinegar, corn, and lima beans. Add the diced tomatoes and their liquid in an even layer, and place the tomato paste on top without stirring them in. 3. Fasten the lid and set the Pressure Release to Sealing. Push the Cancel button to reset the cooking program, then pick the Pressure Cook or Manual setting and set the cooking time to 5 minutes at high pressure. (Note that the pot will take around 15 minutes to reach the required pressure before the cooking program starts.) 4. When the cooking program is done, let the pressure release naturally for at least 10 minutes. Then move the Pressure Release to Venting to let out any remaining steam. Open the pot and stir the stew to combine all the ingredients. 5. Serve the stew hot by ladling it into bowls, accompanied by cornbread on the side.

Hot and Sour Soup

Prep time: 0 minutes | Cook time: 30 minutes | Serves 6

- 4 cups boiling water
- 1 ounce dried shiitake mushrooms
- 2 tablespoons cold-pressed avocado oil
- 3 garlic cloves, chopped
- 4 ounces cremini or button mushrooms, sliced
- 1 pound boneless pork loin, sirloin, or tip, thinly sliced against the grain into ¼-inch-thick, ½-inch-wide, 2-inch-long strips
- 1 teaspoon ground ginger
- ½ teaspoon ground white pepper
- 2 cups low-sodium chicken broth or vegetable broth
- One 8-ounce can sliced bamboo shoots, drained and rinsed
- 2 tablespoons low-sodium soy sauce
- 1 tablespoon chile garlic sauce
- 1 teaspoon toasted sesame oil
- 2 teaspoons Lakanto Monkfruit Sweetener Classic
- 2 large eggs
- ¼ cup rice vinegar
- 2 tablespoons cornstarch
- 4 green onions, white and green parts, thinly sliced
- ¼ cup chopped fresh cilantro

1. In a large liquid measuring cup or heatproof bowl, pour boiling water over shiitake mushrooms. Cover and let soak for 30 minutes. Drain the mushrooms, reserving the soaking liquid. Remove and discard stems, then thinly slice mushroom caps. 2. Select Sauté setting on Instant Pot. Heat avocado oil and garlic for 2 minutes, until garlic is bubbling but not browned. Add cremini and shiitake mushrooms and sauté for 3 minutes, until mushrooms begin to wilt. Add pork, ginger, and white pepper and sauté for about 5 minutes, until pork is opaque and cooked through. 3. Pour mushroom soaking liquid into pot, being careful to leave any sediment behind. Use wooden spoon to nudge any browned bits from bottom of pot. Stir in broth, bamboo shoots, soy sauce, chile garlic sauce, sesame oil, and sweetener. 4. Secure lid and set Pressure Release to Sealing. Press Cancel button to reset cooking program, then select Pressure Cook or Manual setting and set cooking time for 5 minutes at high pressure. (Pot will take about 10 minutes to reach pressure before cooking begins.) 5. While soup is cooking, beat eggs in a small bowl until no yolk streaks remain. 6. When cooking program ends, let pressure release naturally for at least 15 minutes, then move Pressure Release to Venting to release any remaining steam. 7. In a small bowl, stir together vinegar and cornstarch until cornstarch dissolves. Open pot and stir vinegar mixture into soup. Press Cancel button to reset cooking program, then select Sauté setting. Bring soup to simmer and cook, stirring occasionally, for about 3 minutes, until slightly thickened. While stirring constantly, pour in beaten eggs in a thin stream. Press Cancel button to turn off pot, then stir in green onions and cilantro. 8. Ladle soup into bowls and serve hot.

Hearty Hamburger and Lentil Stew

Prep time: 0 minutes | Cook time: 55 minutes | Serves 8

- 2 tablespoons cold-pressed avocado oil
- 2 garlic cloves, chopped
- 1 large yellow onion, diced
- 2 carrots, diced
- 2 celery stalks, diced
- 2 pounds 95 percent lean ground beef
- ½ cup small green lentils
- 2 cups low-sodium roasted beef bone broth or vegetable broth
- 1 tablespoon Italian seasoning
- 1 tablespoon paprika
- 1½ teaspoons fine sea salt
- 1 extra-large russet potato, diced
- 1 cup frozen green peas
- 1 cup frozen corn
- One 14½-ounce can no-salt petite diced tomatoes and their liquid
- ¼ cup tomato paste

1. Choose the Sauté option on the Instant Pot. Heat the oil and garlic for a duration of 3 minutes, or until the garlic begins to bubble but remains unburnt. Next, incorporate the onion, carrots, and celery into the pot and continue to sauté for an additional 5 minutes, or until the onion starts to show signs of softening. Then, add the beef to the mixture and sauté, utilizing a wooden spoon or spatula to break up the meat as it cooks, for approximately 6 minutes, or until the beef is fully cooked through and free of any pink streaks. 2. Stir in the lentils, broth, Italian seasoning, paprika, and salt until well combined. Add the potato, peas, corn, and tomatoes, along with their accompanying liquid, in layers on top of the lentils and beef. Finally, place a dollop of tomato paste on the very top. Be careful not to stir in the vegetables and tomato paste at this stage. 3. Ensure that the lid is securely fastened and set the Pressure Release to Sealing. Press the Cancel button to reset the cooking program, then select either the Pressure Cook or Manual setting and set the cooking time for 20 minutes at high pressure. Note that the pot will require approximately 20 minutes to reach the desired pressure level before the cooking program commences. 4. Once the cooking program has concluded, allow the pressure to release naturally for a minimum of 15 minutes. Subsequently, move the Pressure Release to Venting to release any remaining steam. Open the pot carefully and stir the stew thoroughly to ensure that all ingredients are evenly mixed. 5. Finally, ladle the stew into individual bowls and serve while still hot for the best flavor experience.

Curried Chicken Soup

Prep time: 10 minutes | Cook time: 10 minutes | Serves 6

- 1 pound (454 g) boneless, skinless chicken thighs
- 1½ cups unsweetened coconut milk
- ½ onion, finely diced
- 3 or 4 garlic cloves, crushed
- 1 (2-inch) piece ginger, finely chopped
- 1 cup sliced mushrooms, such as cremini and shiitake
- 4 ounces (113 g) baby spinach
- 1 teaspoon salt
- ½ teaspoon ground turmeric
- ½ teaspoon cayenne
- 1 teaspoon garam masala
- ¼ cup chopped fresh cilantro

1. Add chicken, coconut milk, onion, garlic, ginger, mushrooms, spinach, salt, turmeric, cayenne, garam masala, and cilantro to the inner pot of the Instant Pot. 2. Lock the lid and choose Manual mode with high pressure. Cook for ten minutes, then allow the pressure to release naturally before unlocking the lid. 3. Use tongs to remove the chicken to a bowl. Shred it and stir back into the soup. 4. Enjoy your meal!

Chicken and Asparagus Soup

Prep time: 7 minutes | Cook time: 11 minutes | Serves 8

- 1 tablespoon unsalted butter (or coconut oil for dairy-free)
- ¼ cup finely chopped onions
- 2 cloves garlic, minced
- 1 (14-ounce / 397-g) can full-fat coconut milk
- 1 (14-ounce / 397-g) can sugar-free tomato sauce
- 1 cup chicken broth
- 1 tablespoon red curry paste
- 1 teaspoon fine sea salt
- ½ teaspoon ground black pepper
- 2 pounds (907 g) boneless, skinless chicken breasts, cut into ½-inch chunks
- 2 cups asparagus, trimmed and cut into 2-inch pieces
- Fresh cilantro leaves, for garnish
- Lime wedges, for garnish

1. Put the butter into the Instant Pot and select Sauté. When it has melted, add onions and garlic and cook for 4 minutes or until the onions are tender. Then press Cancel to end the Sautéing. 2. Pour in the coconut milk, tomato sauce, broth, curry paste, salt, and pepper, and whisk until well mixed. Stir in the chicken and asparagus. 3. Close the lid, choose Manual mode, and set a 7 - minute timer. After it finishes, turn the valve to vent for a rapid pressure release. 4. Take off the lid and stir thoroughly. Taste and modify the seasoning if necessary. Serve the soup in bowls, garnished with cilantro, and pair it with lime wedges or a squeeze of lime juice.

French Market Soup

Prep time: 20 minutes | Cook time: 1 hour | Serves 8

- 2 cups mixed dry beans, washed with stones removed
- 7 cups water
- 1 ham hock, all visible fat removed
- 1 teaspoon salt
- ¼ teaspoon pepper
- 16-ounce can low-sodium tomatoes
- 1 large onion, chopped
- 1 garlic clove, minced
- 1 chile, chopped, or 1 teaspoon chili powder
- ¼ cup lemon juice

1. Mix all the ingredients together in the inner pot of the Instant Pot. 2. Tighten the lid and ensure that the vent is set to the sealing position. Select the Manual mode on the Instant Pot and set the cooking time to 60 minutes. 3. Once the cooking time has elapsed, allow the pressure to release naturally. When the Instant Pot indicates it is safe to do so, unlock the lid. Remove any bones and pieces that are hard or fatty from the pot. Use your hands or a utensil to pull the meat away from the bone and chop it into small pieces. Place the ham back into the Instant Pot.

Cabbage Roll Soup

Prep time: 10 minutes | Cook time: 8 minutes | Serves 4

- ½ pound (227 g) 84% lean ground pork
- ½ pound (227 g) 85% lean ground beef
- ½ medium onion, diced
- ½ medium head cabbage, thinly sliced
- 2 tablespoons sugar-free tomato paste
- ½ cup diced tomatoes
- 2 cups chicken broth
- 1 teaspoon salt
- ½ teaspoon thyme
- ½ teaspoon garlic powder
- ¼ teaspoon pepper

1. First, press the Sauté button on the Instant Pot and add beef and pork to it. Cook the meat until it is fully browned, with no pink color remaining. Then add onions and keep cooking until they become fragrant and soft. After that, press the Cancel button. 2. Add the remaining ingredients to the Instant Pot. Press the Manual button and set the cooking time to 8 minutes. 3. When the timer beeps, let the pressure release naturally for 15 minutes and then perform a quick release of the remaining pressure. Serve the dish warm.

Green Chile Corn Chowder

Prep time: 20 minutes | Cook time: 7 to 8 hours | Serves 8

- 16-ounce can cream-style corn
- 3 potatoes, peeled and diced
- 2 tablespoons chopped fresh chives
- 4-ounce can diced green chilies, drained
- 2-ounce jar chopped pimentos, drained
- ½ cup chopped cooked ham
- 2 10½-ounce cans 100% fat-free lower-sodium chicken broth
- Pepper to taste
- Tabasco sauce to taste
- 1 cup fat-free milk

1. Mix all the ingredients, excluding milk, in the inner pot of the Instant Pot. 2. Fasten the lid and utilize the Slow Cook function on a low setting for 7–8 hours, or until the potatoes become soft. 3. Once the cooking time elapses, take off the lid and stir in the milk. Cover again and allow it to simmer for an additional 20 minutes.

Sicilian Fish Stew

Prep time: 10 minutes | Cook time: 10 minutes | Serves 4 to 6

- 2 tablespoons extra-virgin olive oil
- 2 onions, chopped fine
- 1 teaspoon table salt
- ½ teaspoon pepper
- 1 teaspoon minced fresh thyme or ¼ teaspoon dried
- Pinch red pepper flakes
- 4 garlic cloves, minced, divided
- 1 (28-ounce / 794-g) can whole peeled tomatoes, drained with juice reserved, chopped coarse
- 1 (8-ounce / 227-g) bottle clam juice
- ¼ cup dry white wine
- ¼ cup golden raisins
- 2 tablespoons capers, rinsed
- 1½ pounds (680 g) skinless swordfish steak, 1 to 1½ inches thick, cut into 1-inch pieces
- ¼ cup pine nuts, toasted
- ¼ cup minced fresh mint
- 1 teaspoon grated orange zest

1. Utilize the highest sauté function of the Instant Pot to heat oil until it shimmers. Add onions, salt, and pepper, and cook until the onions are softened, approximately 5 minutes. Stir in thyme, pepper flakes, and three - quarters of the garlic, and cook until fragrant, about 30 seconds. Stir in tomatoes and their reserved juice, clam juice, wine, raisins, and capers. Place swordfish into the pot and spoon some of the cooking liquid over it. 2. Lock the lid into position and close the pressure release valve. Select the high - pressure cook function and cook for 1 minute. Turn off the Instant Pot and perform a quick - release of the pressure. Carefully remove the lid, making sure that the steam escapes away from you. 3. Combine pine nuts, mint, orange zest, and the remaining garlic in a bowl. Season the stew with salt and pepper according to taste. Sprinkle each individual portion with the pine nut mixture prior to serving.

Garlicky Chicken Soup

Prep time: 5 minutes | Cook time: 20 minutes | Serves 6

- 10 roasted garlic cloves
- ½ medium onion, diced
- 4 tablespoons butter
- 4 cups chicken broth
- ½ teaspoon salt
- ¼ teaspoon pepper
- 1 teaspoon thyme
- 1 pound (454 g) boneless, skinless chicken thighs, cubed
- ½ cup heavy cream
- 2 ounces (57 g) cream cheese

1. In a small bowl, mash the roasted garlic into a paste. Press the Sauté button and add garlic, onion, and butter to the Instant Pot. Sauté for 2 to 3 minutes until the onion begins to soften. Press the Cancel button. 2. Add chicken broth, salt, pepper, thyme, and chicken to the Instant Pot. Click the lid closed. Press the Manual button and adjust the time for 20 minutes. 3. When the timer beeps, quick - release the pressure. Stir in heavy cream and cream cheese until smooth. Serve warm.

Bacon Curry Soup

Prep time: 10 minutes | Cook time: 20 minutes | Serves 4

- 3 ounces (85 g) bacon, chopped
- 1 tablespoon chopped scallions
- 1 teaspoon curry powder
- 1 cup coconut milk
- 3 cups beef broth
- 1 cup Cheddar cheese, shredded

1. Turn on the Instant Pot's Sauté mode and let it heat up for 3 minutes. Add the bacon and cook for 5 minutes, flipping it constantly to ensure even cooking. 2. Add the scallions and curry powder to the pot and sauté for an additional 5 minutes, allowing the flavors to meld together. 3. Pour in the coconut milk and beef broth, followed by the Cheddar cheese. Stir everything together until well combined. 4. Switch to Manual mode on the Instant Pot and set the cooking time to 10 minutes at high pressure. 5. Once the timer goes off, perform a quick pressure release to safely open the lid. 6. Use an immersion blender to blend the soup until it reaches a smooth consistency. Serve the soup warm and enjoy!

Avocado and Serrano Chile Soup

Prep time: 10 minutes | Cook time: 7 minutes | Serves 4

- 2 avocados
- 1 small fresh tomatillo, quartered
- 2 cups chicken broth
- 2 tablespoons avocado oil
- 1 tablespoon butter
- 2 tablespoons finely minced onion
- 1 clove garlic, minced
- ½ Serrano chile, deseeded and ribs removed, minced, plus thin slices for garnish
- ¼ teaspoon sea salt
- Pinch of ground white pepper
- ½ cup full-fat coconut milk
- Fresh cilantro sprigs, for garnish

1. Use a spoon to scoop the flesh of the avocado into a food processor. Add the tomatillo and chicken broth to the food processor as well, and then purée the mixture until it is smooth. Set this puréed mixture aside. 2. Turn the Instant Pot on to the Sauté mode. Add the avocado oil and butter to the pot. Wait until the butter has completely melted, then add the onion and garlic to the pot. Sauté them for about 1 minute, or until they become softened. After that, add the Serrano chile and continue to sauté for another minute. 3. Pour the previously puréed avocado mixture into the Instant Pot. Add salt and pepper to taste, and then stir all the ingredients together until they are well combined. 4. Close and secure the lid of the Instant Pot properly. Press the Manual button on the control panel, and set the cooking time to 5 minutes at High Pressure. 5. When the timer sounds, perform a quick pressure release. After the pressure has been released, open the lid of the Instant Pot. Then, stir in the coconut milk until it is fully incorporated into the soup. 6. Serve the soup while it is still hot. Garnish each serving with thin slices of Serrano chile and a sprig of cilantro.

Creamy Sweet Potato Soup

Prep time: 15 minutes | Cook time: 10 minutes | Serves 6

- 2 tablespoons avocado oil
- 1 small onion, chopped
- 2 celery stalks, chopped
- 2 teaspoons minced garlic
- 1 teaspoon kosher salt
- ½ teaspoon freshly ground black pepper
- 1 teaspoon ground turmeric
- ½ teaspoon ground cinnamon
- 2 pounds sweet potatoes, peeled and cut into 1-inch cubes
- 3 cups Vegetable Broth or Chicken Bone Broth
- Plain Greek yogurt, to garnish (optional)
- Chopped fresh parsley, to garnish (optional)
- Pumpkin seeds (pepitas), to garnish (optional)

1. Turn on the electric pressure cooker and select the Sauté setting. Once the pot is heated up, pour in the avocado oil. 2. Add the onion and celery to the pot and sauté for 3 to 5 minutes, or until they start to become tender. 3. Stir in the garlic, salt, pepper, turmeric, and cinnamon. Then, press Cancel to stop the sautéing process. 4. Add the sweet potatoes and broth to the pot and stir well to combine. 5. Close and lock the lid of the pressure cooker, ensuring that the valve is set to sealing. 6. Cook the soup on high pressure for 10 minutes. 7. When the cooking time is up, press Cancel and let the pressure release naturally. 8. Once the pin drops, unlock and remove the lid. 9. Use an immersion blender to purée the soup directly in the pot. If you don't have an immersion blender, transfer the soup to a blender or food processor and purée according to the manufacturer's instructions for blending hot foods. 10. Serve the soup by spooning it into bowls and topping it with Greek yogurt, parsley, and/or pumpkin seeds (if using).

Beef and Mushroom Stew

Prep time: 15 minutes | Cook time: 30 minutes | Serves 4

- 2 tablespoons coconut oil
- 1 pound (454 g) cubed chuck roast
- 1 cup sliced button mushrooms
- ½ medium onion, chopped
- 2 cups beef broth
- ½ cup chopped celery
- 1 tablespoon sugar-free tomato paste
- 1 teaspoon thyme
- 2 garlic cloves, minced
- ½ teaspoon xanthan gum

1. Press the Sauté button on the Instant Pot and add coconut oil. Place cubes of chuck roast into the pot and brown them until they are golden in color. If there are too many pieces and the pan is overcrowded, they may not brown properly, so work in batches if needed. Once browning is complete, set the roast aside. 2. Add mushrooms and onions to the pot. Sauté them until the mushrooms start to brown and the onions become translucent. Then press the Cancel button to stop the Sauté cycle. 3. Pour broth into the Instant Pot. If there are any bits stuck to the bottom of the pot, use a wooden spoon to scrape them off. Add celery, tomato paste, thyme, and garlic to the pot. Close the lid by clicking it into place. Press the Manual button and set the cooking time for 35 minutes. When the timer beeps, allow the pressure to release naturally. 4. When the pressure valve drops, indicating that the pressure has been released, stir in xanthan gum. Allow the soup to thicken for a moment. Serve the soup warm.

Nancy's Vegetable Beef Soup

Prep time: 25 minutes | Cook time: 8 hours | Serves 8

- 2 pounds roast, cubed, or 2 pounds stewing meat
- 15 ounces can corn
- 15 ounces can green beans
- 1 pound bag frozen peas
- 40 ounces can no-added-salt stewed tomatoes
- 5 teaspoons salt-free beef bouillon powder
- Tabasco, to taste
- ½ teaspoons salt

1. Mix all the ingredients together in the Instant Pot. Do not drain the vegetables. 2. Add water to the inner pot, making sure not to exceed the fill line. 3. Secure the lid (or use the glass lid if preferred) and set the Instant Pot to Slow Cook mode on Low for 8 hours, or until the meat is tender and the vegetables are soft.

Venison and Tomato Stew

Prep time: 12 minutes | Cook time: 42 minutes | Serves 8

- 1 tablespoon unsalted butter
- 1 cup diced onions
- 2 cups button mushrooms, sliced in half
- 2 large stalks celery, cut into ¼-inch pieces
- Cloves squeezed from 2 heads roasted garlic or 4 cloves garlic, minced
- 2 pounds (907 g) boneless venison or beef roast, cut into 4 large pieces
- 5 cups beef broth
- 1 (14½-ounce / 411-g) can diced tomatoes
- 1 teaspoon fine sea salt
- 1 teaspoon ground black pepper
- ½ teaspoon dried rosemary, or 1 teaspoon fresh rosemary, finely chopped
- ½ teaspoon dried thyme leaves, or 1 teaspoon fresh thyme leaves, finely chopped
- ½ head cauliflower, cut into large florets
- Fresh thyme leaves, for garnish

1. Put the butter into the Instant Pot and select Sauté. After it melts, add the onions and cook for 4 minutes or until they are soft. 2. Add the mushrooms, celery, and garlic and continue to sauté for another 3 minutes or until the mushrooms turn golden brown. Then press Cancel to end the Sauté mode. Add the roast, broth, tomatoes, salt, pepper, rosemary, and thyme. 3. Seal the lid, press Manual, and set the cooking time to 30 minutes. When it is done, turn the valve to venting to release the pressure quickly. 4. Add the cauliflower. Seal the lid again, press Manual, and set the timer for 5 minutes. After that, let the pressure release naturally. 5. Take off the lid and shred the meat with two forks. Taste the liquid and add more salt if necessary. Ladle the stew into bowls and garnish with thyme leaves.

Gigante Bean Soup with Celery and Olives

Prep time: 30 minutes | Cook time: 12 minutes | Serves 6 to 8

- 1½ tablespoons table salt, for brining
- 1 pound (454 g) dried gigante beans, picked over and rinsed
- 2 tablespoons extra-virgin olive oil, plus extra for drizzling
- 5 celery ribs, cut into ½-inch pieces, plus ½ cup leaves, minced
- 1 onion, chopped
- ½ teaspoon table salt
- 4 garlic cloves, minced
- 4 cups vegetable or chicken broth
- 4 cups water
- 2 bay leaves
- ½ cup pitted kalamata olives, chopped
- 2 tablespoons minced fresh marjoram or oregano
- Lemon wedges

1. In a large container, dissolve 1½ tablespoons of salt in 2 quarts of cold water. Add the beans and let them soak at room temperature for a minimum of 8 hours, or up to 24 hours. After soaking, drain and rinse the beans thoroughly. 2. Using the highest sauté function on the Instant Pot, heat oil until it shimmers. Add the celery pieces, onion, and ½ teaspoon of salt, and cook until the vegetables are softened, which should take about 5 minutes. Stir in the garlic and cook for another 30 seconds, or until it becomes fragrant. Next, stir in the broth, water, beans, and bay leaves. 3. Lock the lid into place and ensure the pressure release valve is closed. Select the high-pressure cook function and cook for 6 minutes. Once the cooking time is up, turn off the Instant Pot and allow the pressure to release naturally for 15 minutes. After that, perform a quick-release of any remaining pressure. Carefully remove the lid, making sure that the steam escapes away from you. 4. In a bowl, combine celery leaves, olives, and marjoram. Discard the bay leaves. Taste the soup and season it with salt and pepper as needed. Top each serving with the celery-olive mixture and drizzle with extra oil. Serve the soup with lemon wedges on the side.

Garlic Beef Soup

Prep time: 12 minutes | Cook time: 42 minutes | Serves 8

- 10 strips bacon, chopped
- 1 medium white onion, chopped
- Cloves squeezed from 3 heads roasted garlic, or 6 cloves garlic, minced
- 1 to 2 jalapeño peppers, seeded and chopped (optional)
- 2 pounds (907 g) boneless beef chuck roast, cut into 4 equal-sized pieces
- 5 cups beef broth
- 1 cup chopped fresh cilantro, plus more for garnish
- 2 teaspoons fine sea salt
- 1 teaspoon ground black pepper
- For Garnish:
- 1 avocado, peeled, pitted, and diced
- 2 radishes, very thinly sliced
- 2 tablespoons chopped fresh chives

1. Put the bacon in the Instant Pot and select Sauté. Cook, stirring occasionally, for 4 minutes or until the bacon is crispy. Remove the bacon with a slotted spoon, leaving the fat in the pot. Place the bacon on a plate lined with paper towels to drain. 2. Add the onion, garlic, and jalapeños (if using) to the Instant Pot and sauté for 3 minutes or until the onion is soft. Press Cancel to end the Sauté cycle. 3. Add the beef, broth, cilantro, salt, and pepper. Stir to mix well. 4. Seal the lid, press Manual, and set the timer for 35 minutes. After cooking, allow the pressure to release naturally. 5. Remove the lid and shred the beef with two forks. Taste the liquid and adjust the salt if necessary. 6. Ladle the soup into bowls. Garnish with the reserved bacon, avocado, radishes, chives, and additional cilantro.

Broccoli and Bacon Cheese Soup

Prep time: 6 minutes | Cook time: 10 minutes | Serves 6

- 3 tablespoons butter
- 2 stalks celery, diced
- ½ yellow onion, diced
- 3 garlic cloves, minced
- 3½ cups chicken stock
- 4 cups chopped fresh broccoli florets
- 3 ounces (85 g) block-style cream cheese, softened and cubed
- ½ teaspoon ground nutmeg
- ½ teaspoon sea salt
- 1 teaspoon ground black pepper
- 3 cups shredded Cheddar cheese
- ½ cup shredded Monterey Jack cheese
- 2 cups heavy cream
- 4 slices cooked bacon, crumbled
- 1 tablespoon finely chopped chives

1. Choose the Sauté mode on the Instant Pot. Allow the pot to heat up, then add the butter and continue heating until it has completely melted. 2. Incorporate the celery, onions, and garlic into the pot. Keep sautéing for approximately 5 minutes, or until the vegetables have reached a softened state. 3. Pour in the chicken stock and broccoli florets. Increase the heat to bring the liquid to a rolling boil. 4. Secure the lid in place. Switch to Manual mode and set the cooking time to 5 minutes at high pressure. 5. After the cooking cycle is finished, let the pressure release naturally for 10 minutes. Following this, release any remaining pressure manually. 6. Open the lid of the pot and add the cream cheese, nutmeg, sea salt, and black pepper. Stir thoroughly until all ingredients are well combined. 7. Return to Sauté mode and bring the soup back up to a boil. Gradually stir in the Cheddar and Jack cheeses until they have fully melted. Once melted, incorporate the heavy cream and stir well. 8. Use a ladle o distribute the soup into serving bowls. Garnish each bowl with bacon and chives before serving. Enjoy the hot soup!

Chapter 7
Vegetables and Sides

Sautéed Broccoli with Garlic and Almonds

Prep time: 10 minutes | Cook time: 4 minutes | Serves 4 to 6

- 6 cups broccoli florets
- 1 cup water
- 1½ tablespoons olive oil
- 8 garlic cloves, thinly sliced
- 2 shallots, thinly sliced
- ½ teaspoon crushed red pepper flakes
- Grated zest and juice of 1 medium lemon
- ½ teaspoon kosher salt
- Freshly ground black pepper, to taste
- ¼ cup chopped roasted almonds
- ¼ cup finely slivered fresh basil

1. Pour the water into the Instant Pot. Place the broccoli florets in a steamer basket and lower into the pot. 2. Close and secure the lid. Select the Steam setting and set the cooking time for 2 minutes at Low Pressure. Once the timer goes off, use a quick pressure release. Carefully open the lid. 3. Transfer the broccoli to a large bowl filled with cold water and ice. Once cooled, drain the broccoli and pat dry. 4. Select the Sauté mode on the Instant Pot and heat the olive oil. Add the garlic to the pot and sauté for 30 seconds, tossing constantly. Add the shallots and pepper flakes to the pot and sauté for 1 minute. 5. Stir in the cooked broccoli, lemon juice, salt and black pepper. Toss the ingredients together and cook for 1 minute. 6. Transfer the broccoli to a serving platter and sprinkle with the chopped almonds, lemon zest and basil. Serve immediately.

Herbed Parsley Potatoes

Prep time: 10 minutes | Cook time: 5 minutes | Serves 4

- 3 tablespoons margarine, divided
- 2 pounds medium red potatoes (about 2 ounces each), halved lengthwise
- 1 clove garlic, minced
- ½ teaspoon salt
- ½ cup low-sodium chicken broth
- 2 tablespoons chopped fresh parsley

1. Place 1 tablespoon margarine in the inner pot of the Instant Pot and select Sauté. 2. After margarine is melted, add potatoes, garlic, and salt, stirring well. 3. Sauté 4 minutes, stirring frequently. 4. Add chicken broth and stir well. 5. Seal lid, make sure vent is on sealing, then select Manual for 5 minutes on high pressure. 6. When cooking time is up, manually release the pressure. 7. Strain potatoes, toss with remaining 2 tablespoons margarine and chopped parsley, and serve immediately.

Spiced Indian Okra

Prep time: 8 minutes | Cook time: 7 minutes | Serves 6

- 1 pound (454 g) young okra
- 4 tablespoons ghee or avocado oil
- ½ teaspoon cumin seeds
- ¼ teaspoon ground turmeric
- Pinch of ground cinnamon
- ½ medium onion, diced
- 2 cloves garlic, minced
- 2 teaspoons minced fresh ginger
- 1 serrano chile, seeded and ribs removed, minced
- 1 small tomato, diced
- ½ teaspoon sea salt
- ¼ teaspoon cayenne pepper (optional)
- 1 cup vegetable stock or filtered water

1. Rinse and thoroughly dry the okra. Slice it on a diagonal into slices ½ to ¾ inch thick, discarding the stems. 2. Set the Instant Pot to Sauté. Once hot, add the ghee and heat until melted. Stir in the cumin seeds, turmeric, and cinnamon and cook until they are fragrant, about 1 minute. This may cause the cumin seeds to jump and pop. Add the onion and cook, stirring frequently, until soft and translucent, about 3 minutes. Add the garlic, ginger, and serrano chile and sauté for an additional minute. Press Cancel. 3. Stir in the tomato, okra, salt, cayenne (if using), and stock. Secure the lid and set the steam release valve to Sealing. Press the Manual button and set the cook time to 2 minutes. 4. When the Instant Pot beeps, carefully switch the steam release valve to Venting to quick-release the pressure. When fully released, open the lid. Stir gently and allow the okra to rest on the Keep Warm setting for a few minutes before serving.

Assorted Vegetable Mix

Prep time: 20 minutes | Cook time: 2 minutes | Serves 8

- 2 medium parsnips
- 4 medium carrots
- 1 turnip, about 4½ inches diameter
- 1 cup water
- 1 teaspoon salt
- 3 tablespoons sugar
- 2 tablespoons canola or olive oil
- ½ teaspoon salt

1. Clean and peel vegetables. Cut in 1-inch pieces. 2. Place the cup of water and 1 teaspoon salt into the Instant Pot's inner pot with the vegetables. 3. Secure the lid and make sure vent is set to sealing. Press Manual and set for 2 minutes. 4. When cook time is up, release the pressure manually and press Cancel. Drain the water from the inner pot. 5. Press Sauté and stir in sugar, oil, and salt. Cook until sugar is dissolved. Serve.

Sauerkraut and Mushroom Bake

Prep time: 6 minutes | Cook time: 15 minutes | Serves 6

- 1 tablespoon olive oil
- 1 celery rib, diced
- ½ cup chopped leeks
- 2 pounds (907 g) canned sauerkraut, drained
- 6 ounces (170 g) brown mushrooms, sliced
- 1 teaspoon caraway seeds
- 1 teaspoon brown mustard
- 1 bay leaf
- 1 cup dry white wine

1. Press the Sauté button to heat up your Instant Pot. Now, heat the oil and cook celery and leeks until softened. 2. Add the sauerkraut and mushrooms and cook for 2 minutes more. 3. Add the remaining ingredients and stir to combine well. 4. Secure the lid. Choose Manual mode and High Pressure; cook for 10 minutes. Once cooking is complete, use a natural pressure release; carefully remove the lid. Bon appétit!

Brussels Sprouts in Lemon Dressing with Poppy Seeds

Prep time: 10 minutes | Cook time: 2 minutes | Serves 4

- 1 pound (454 g) Brussels sprouts
- 2 tablespoons avocado oil, divided
- 1 cup vegetable broth or chicken bone broth
- 1 tablespoon minced garlic
- ½ teaspoon kosher salt
- Freshly ground black pepper, to taste
- ½ medium lemon
- ½ tablespoon poppy seeds

1. Trim the Brussels sprouts by cutting off the stem ends and removing any loose outer leaves. Cut each in half lengthwise (through the stem). 2. Set the electric pressure cooker to the Sauté/More setting. When the pot is hot, pour in 1 tablespoon of the avocado oil. 3. Add half of the Brussels sprouts to the pot, cut-side down, and let them brown for 3 to 5 minutes without disturbing. Transfer to a bowl and add the remaining tablespoon of avocado oil and the remaining Brussels sprouts to the pot. Hit Cancel and return all of the Brussels sprouts to the pot. 4. Add the broth, garlic, salt, and a few grinds of pepper. Stir to distribute the seasonings. 5. Close and lock the lid of the pressure cooker. Set the valve to sealing. 6. Cook on high pressure for 2 minutes. 7. While the Brussels sprouts are cooking, zest the lemon, then cut it into quarters. 8. When the cooking is complete, hit Cancel and quick release the pressure. 9. Once the pin drops, unlock and remove the lid. 10. Using a slotted spoon, transfer the Brussels sprouts to a serving bowl. Toss with the lemon zest, a squeeze of lemon juice, and the poppy seeds. Serve immediately.

Cabbage and Tempeh with Lemon

Prep time: 8 minutes | Cook time: 10 minutes | Serves 3

- 2 tablespoons sesame oil
- ½ cup chopped scallions
- 2 cups shredded cabbage
- 6 ounces (170 g) tempeh, cubed
- 1 tablespoon coconut aminos
- 1 cup vegetable stock
- 2 garlic cloves, minced
- 1 tablespoon lemon juice
- Salt and pepper, to taste
- ¼ teaspoon paprika
- ¼ cup roughly chopped fresh cilantro

1. Press the Sauté button to heat up your Instant Pot. Heat the sesame oil and sauté the scallions until tender and fragrant. 2. Then, add the cabbage, tempeh, coconut aminos, vegetable stock, garlic, lemon juice, salt, pepper, and paprika. 3. Secure the lid. Choose Manual mode and Low Pressure; cook for 3 minutes. Once cooking is complete, use a quick pressure release; carefully remove the lid. 4. Press the Sauté button to thicken the sauce if desired. Divide between serving bowls, garnish with fresh cilantro, and serve warm. Bon appétit!

Mixed Vegetable Curry

Prep time: 25 minutes | Cook time: 3 minutes | Serves 10

- 16-ounce package baby carrots
- 3 medium potatoes, unpeeled, cubed
- 1 pound fresh or frozen green beans, cut in 2-inch pieces
- 1 medium green pepper, chopped
- 1 medium onion, chopped
- 1–2 cloves garlic, minced
- 15-ounce can garbanzo beans, drained
- 28-ounce can crushed tomatoes
- 3 teaspoons curry powder
- 1½ teaspoons chicken bouillon granules
- 1¾ cups boiling water
- 3 tablespoons minute tapioca

1. Combine carrots, potatoes, green beans, pepper, onion, garlic, garbanzo beans, crushed tomatoes, and curry powder in the Instant Pot. 2. Dissolve bouillon in boiling water, then stir in tapioca. Pour over the contents of the Instant Pot and stir. 3. Secure the lid and make sure vent is set to sealing. Press Manual and set for 3 minutes. 4. When cook time is up, manually release the pressure.

Grilled Corn on the Cob

Prep time: 5 minutes | Cook time: 12 to 15 minutes | Serves 4

- 2 large ears fresh corn
- Olive oil for misting
- Salt, to taste (optional)

1. Shuck corn, remove silks, and wash. 2. Cut or break each ear in half crosswise. 3. Spray corn with olive oil. 4. Air fry at 390°F (199°C) for 12 to 15 minutes or until browned as much as you like. 5. Serve plain or with coarsely ground salt.

Zucchini with Moroccan Spices

Prep time: 10 minutes | Cook time: 6 minutes | Serves 4

- 2 tablespoons avocado oil
- ½ medium onion, diced
- 1 clove garlic, minced
- ¼ teaspoon cayenne pepper
- ¼ teaspoon ground coriander
- ¼ teaspoon ground cumin
- ¼ teaspoon ground ginger
- Pinch of ground cinnamon
- 1 Roma (plum) tomato, diced
- 2 medium zucchini, cut into 1-inch pieces
- ½ tablespoon fresh lemon juice
- ¼ cup bone broth or vegetable stock

1. Set the Instant Pot to Sauté. When hot, add the oil. Add the onion and sauté, stirring frequently, until translucent, about 2 minutes. Add the garlic, cayenne, coriander, cumin, ginger, and cinnamon and cook until fragrant, about 1 minute. Stir in the tomato and zucchini and cook 2 minutes longer. 2. Press Cancel. Add the lemon juice and broth. Secure the lid and set the steam release valve to Sealing. Press the Manual button, adjust the pressure to Low, and set the cook time to 1 minute. 3. When the Instant Pot beeps, carefully switch the steam release valve to Venting to quick-release the pressure. When fully released, open the lid. Stir and serve warm.

Instant Pot Cooked Zucchini Sticks

Prep time: 5 minutes | Cook time: 8 minutes | Serves 2

- 2 zucchinis, trimmed and cut into sticks
- 2 teaspoons olive oil
- ½ teaspoon white pepper
- ½ teaspoon salt
- 1 cup water

1. Place the zucchini sticks in the Instant Pot pan and sprinkle with the olive oil, white pepper and salt. 2. Pour the water and put the trivet in the pot. Place the pan on the trivet. 3. Lock the lid. Select the Manual setting and set the cooking time for 8 minutes at High Pressure. Once the timer goes off, use a quick pressure release. Carefully open the lid. 4. Remove the zucchinis from the pot and serve.

Spiced Cauliflower with Tomatoes

Prep time: 10 minutes | Cook time: 2 minutes | Serves 4 to 6

- 1 medium head cauliflower, cut into bite-size pieces
- 1 (14-ounce / 397-g) can sugar-free diced tomatoes, undrained
- 1 bell pepper, thinly sliced
- 1 (14-ounce / 397-g) can full-fat coconut milk
- ½ to 1 cup water
- 2 tablespoons red curry paste
- 1 teaspoon salt
- 1 teaspoon garlic powder
- ½ teaspoon onion powder
- ½ teaspoon ground ginger
- ¼ teaspoon chili powder
- Freshly ground black pepper, to taste

1. Add all the ingredients, except for the black pepper, to the Instant Pot and stir to combine. 2. Lock the lid. Select the Manual setting and set the cooking time for 2 minutes at High Pressure. Once the timer goes off, use a quick pressure release. Carefully open the lid. 3. Sprinkle the black pepper and stir well. Serve immediately.

Cauliflower Puree with Parmesan

Prep time: 7 minutes | Cook time: 5 minutes | Serves 4

- 1 head cauliflower, cored and cut into large florets
- ½ teaspoon kosher salt
- ½ teaspoon garlic pepper
- 2 tablespoons plain Greek yogurt
- ¾ cup freshly grated Parmesan cheese
- 1 tablespoon unsalted butter or ghee (optional)
- Chopped fresh chives

1. Pour 1 cup of water into the electric pressure cooker and insert a steamer basket or wire rack. 2. Place the cauliflower in the basket. 3. Close and lock the lid of the pressure cooker. Set the valve to sealing. 4. Cook on high pressure for 5 minutes. 5. When the cooking is complete, hit Cancel and quick release the pressure. 6. Once the pin drops, unlock and remove the lid. 7. Remove the cauliflower from the pot and pour out the water. Return the cauliflower to the pot and add the salt, garlic pepper, yogurt, and cheese. Use an immersion blender or potato masher to purée or mash the cauliflower in the pot. 8. Spoon into a serving bowl, and garnish with butter (if using) and chives.

Chanterelle and Cheddar Mushrooms

Prep time: 10 minutes | Cook time: 5 minutes | Serves 4

- 1 tablespoon olive oil
- 2 cloves garlic, minced
- 1 (1-inch) ginger root, grated
- 16 ounces (454 g) Chanterelle mushrooms, brushed clean and sliced
- ½ cup unsweetened tomato purée
- ½ cup water
- 2 tablespoons dry white wine
- 1 teaspoon dried basil
- ½ teaspoon dried thyme
- ½ teaspoon dried dill weed
- ⅓ teaspoon freshly ground black pepper
- Kosher salt, to taste
- 1 cup shredded Cheddar cheese

1. Press the Sauté button on the Instant Pot and heat the olive oil. Add the garlic and grated ginger to the pot and sauté for 1 minute, or until fragrant. Stir in the remaining ingredients, except for the cheese. 2. Lock the lid. Select the Manual mode and set the cooking time for 5 minutes on Low Pressure. When the timer goes off, perform a quick pressure release. Carefully open the lid.. 3. Serve topped with the shredded cheese.

Tomato-infused Spaghetti Squash Noodles

Prep time: 15 minutes | Cook time: 14 to 16 minutes | Serves 4

- 1 medium spaghetti squash
- 1 cup water
- 2 tablespoons olive oil
- 1 small yellow onion, diced
- 6 garlic cloves, minced
- 2 teaspoons crushed red pepper flakes
- 2 teaspoons dried oregano
- 1 cup sliced cherry tomatoes
- 1 teaspoon kosher salt
- ½ teaspoon freshly ground black pepper
- 1 (14.5-ounce / 411-g) can sugar-free crushed tomatoes
- ¼ cup capers
- 1 tablespoon caper brine
- ½ cup sliced olives

1. With a sharp knife, halve the spaghetti squash crosswise. Using a spoon, scoop out the seeds and sticky gunk in the middle of each half. 2. Pour the water into the Instant Pot and place the trivet in the pot with the handles facing up. Arrange the squash halves, cut side facing up, on the trivet. 3. Lock the lid. Select the Manual mode and set the cooking time for 7 minutes on High Pressure. When the timer goes off, use a quick pressure release. Carefully open the lid. 4. Remove the trivet and pour out the water that has collected in the squash cavities. Using the tines of a fork, separate the cooked strands into spaghetti-like pieces and set aside in a bowl. 5. Pour the water out of the pot. Select the Sauté mode and heat the oil. 6. Add the onion to the pot and sauté for 3 minutes. Add the garlic, pepper flakes and oregano to the pot and sauté for 1 minute. 7. Stir in the cherry tomatoes, salt and black pepper and cook for 2 minutes, or until the tomatoes are tender. 8. Pour in the crushed tomatoes, capers, caper brine and olives and bring the mixture to a boil. Continue to cook for 2 to 3 minutes to allow the flavors to meld. 9. Stir in the spaghetti squash noodles and cook for 1 to 2 minutes to warm everything through. 10. Transfer the dish to a serving platter and serve.

Flawless Sweet Potatoes

Prep time: 5 minutes | Cook time: 15 minutes | Serves 4 to 6

- 4–6 medium sweet potatoes
- 1 cup of water

1. Scrub skin of sweet potatoes with a brush until clean. Pour water into inner pot of the Instant Pot. Place steamer basket in the bottom of the inner pot. Place sweet potatoes on top of steamer basket. 2. Secure the lid and turn valve to seal. 3. Select the Manual mode and set to pressure cook on high for 15 minutes. 4. Allow pressure to release naturally (about 10 minutes). 5. Once the pressure valve lowers, remove lid and serve immediately.

Masala Gobi

Prep time: 5 minutes | Cook time: 4 to 5 minutes | Serves 4 to 6

- 1 tablespoon olive oil
- 1 teaspoon cumin seeds
- 1 white onion, diced
- 1 garlic clove, minced
- 1 head cauliflower, chopped
- 1 tablespoon ground coriander
- 1 teaspoon ground cumin
- ½ teaspoon garam masala
- ½ teaspoon salt
- 1 cup water

1. Set the Instant Pot to the Sauté mode and heat the olive oil. Add the cumin seeds to the pot and sauté for 30 seconds, stirring constantly. Add the onion and sauté for 2 to 3 minutes, stirring constantly. Add the garlic and sauté for 30 seconds, stirring frequently. 2. Stir in the remaining ingredients. 3. Lock the lid. Select the Manual mode and set the cooking time for 1 minute on High Pressure. When the timer goes off, perform a quick pressure release. Carefully open the lid. 4. Serve immediately.

Satarash Egg Dish

Prep time: 10 minutes | Cook time: 5 minutes | Serves 4

- 2 tablespoons olive oil
- 1 white onion, chopped
- 2 cloves garlic
- 2 ripe tomatoes, puréed
- 1 green bell pepper, deseeded and sliced
- 1 red bell pepper, deseeded and sliced
- 1 teaspoon paprika
- ½ teaspoon dried oregano
- ½ teaspoon turmeric
- Kosher salt and ground black pepper, to taste
- 1 cup water
- 4 large eggs, lightly whisked

1. Press the Sauté button on the Instant Pot and heat the olive oil. Add the onion and garlic to the pot and sauté for 2 minutes, or until fragrant. Stir in the remaining ingredients, except for the eggs. 2. Lock the lid. Select the Manual mode and set the cooking time for 3 minutes on High Pressure. When the timer goes off, perform a quick pressure release. Carefully open the lid. 3. Fold in the eggs and stir to combine. Lock the lid and let it sit in the residual heat for 5 minutes. Serve warm.

Orange and Dill-infused Beet & Watercress Salad

Prep time: 20 minutes | Cook time: 8 minutes | Serves 4

- 2 pounds (907 g) beets, scrubbed, trimmed, and cut into ¾-inch pieces
- ½ cup water
- 1 teaspoon caraway seeds
- ½ teaspoon table salt
- 1 cup plain Greek yogurt
- 1 small garlic clove, minced to paste
- 5 ounces (142 g) watercress, torn into bite-size pieces
- 1 tablespoon extra-virgin olive oil, divided, plus extra for drizzling
- 1 tablespoon white wine vinegar, divided
- 1 teaspoon grated orange zest plus 2 tablespoons juice
- ¼ cup hazelnuts, toasted, skinned, and chopped
- ¼ cup coarsely chopped fresh dill
- Coarse sea salt

1. Combine beets, water, caraway seeds, and table salt in Instant Pot. Lock lid in place and close pressure release valve. Select high pressure cook function and cook for 8 minutes. Turn off Instant Pot and quick-release pressure. Carefully remove lid, allowing steam to escape away from you. 2. Using slotted spoon, transfer beets to plate; set aside to cool slightly. Combine yogurt, garlic, and 3 tablespoons beet cooking liquid in bowl; discard remaining cooking liquid. In large bowl toss watercress with 2 teaspoons oil and 1 teaspoon vinegar. Season with table salt and pepper to taste. 3. Spread yogurt mixture over surface of serving dish. Arrange watercress on top of yogurt mixture, leaving 1-inch border of yogurt mixture. Add beets to now-empty large bowl and toss with orange zest and juice, remaining 2 teaspoons vinegar, and remaining 1 teaspoon oil. Season with table salt and pepper to taste. Arrange beets on top of watercress mixture. Drizzle with extra oil and sprinkle with hazelnuts, dill, and sea salt. Serve.

Parmesan Zucchini Noodles

Prep time: 5 minutes | Cook time: 5 minutes | Serves 2

- 1 large zucchini, trimmed and spiralized
- 1 tablespoon butter
- 1 garlic clove, diced
- ½ teaspoon chili flakes
- 3 ounces (85 g) Parmesan cheese, grated

1. Set the Instant Pot on the Sauté mode and melt the butter. Add the garlic and chili flakes to the pot. Sauté for 2 minutes, or until fragrant. 2. Stir in the zucchini spirals and sauté for 2 minutes, or until tender. 3. Add the grated Parmesan cheese to the pot and stir well. Continue to cook it for 1 minute, or until the cheese melts. 4. Transfer to a plate and serve immediately

Fiery Cauliflower Florets

Prep time: 5 minutes | Cook time: 7 minutes | Serves 4

- 13 ounces (369 g) cauliflower head
- 1 cup water
- 1 tablespoon coconut cream
- 1 tablespoon avocado oil
- 1 teaspoon ground paprika
- 1 teaspoon ground turmeric
- ½ teaspoon ground cumin
- ½ teaspoon salt

1. Pour the water in the Instant Pot and insert the trivet. 2. In the mixing bowl, stir together the coconut cream, avocado oil, paprika, turmeric, cumin and salt. 3. Carefully brush the cauliflower head with the coconut cream mixture. Sprinkle the remaining coconut cream mixture over the cauliflower. 4. Transfer the cauliflower head onto the trivet. 5. Lock the lid. Select the Manual mode and set the cooking time for 7 minutes at High Pressure. When the timer goes off, use a natural pressure release for 10 minutes, then release any remaining pressure. Carefully open the lid. 6. Serve immediately.

Sweetly Caramelized Onions

Prep time: 10 minutes | Cook time: 35 minutes | Serves 8

- 4 tablespoons margarine
- 6 large Vidalia or other sweet onions, sliced into thin half rings
- 10-ounce can chicken, or vegetable, broth

1. Press Sauté on the Instant Pot. Add in the margarine and let melt. 2. Once the margarine is melted, stir in the onions and sauté for about 5 minutes. Pour in the broth and then press Cancel. 3. Secure the lid and make sure vent is set to sealing. Press Manual and set time for 20 minutes. 4. When cook time is up, release the pressure manually. Remove the lid and press Sauté. Stir the onion mixture for about 10 more minutes, allowing extra liquid to cook off.

Braised Radishes and Sugar Snap Peas with Dukkah Spice

Prep time: 20 minutes | Cook time: 5 minutes | Serves 4

- ¼ cup extra-virgin olive oil, divided
- 1 shallot, sliced thin
- 3 garlic cloves, sliced thin
- 1½ pounds (680 g) radishes, 2 cups greens reserved, radishes trimmed and halved if small or quartered if large
- ½ cup water
- ½ teaspoon table salt
- 8 ounces (227 g) sugar snap peas, strings removed, sliced thin on bias
- 8 ounces (227 g) cremini mushrooms, trimmed and sliced thin
- 2 teaspoons grated lemon zest plus 1 teaspoon juice
- 1 cup plain Greek yogurt
- ½ cup fresh cilantro leaves
- 3 tablespoons dukkah

1. Using highest sauté function, heat 2 tablespoons oil in Instant Pot until shimmering. Add shallot and cook until softened, about 2 minutes. Stir in garlic and cook until fragrant, about 30 seconds. Stir in radishes, water, and salt. Lock lid in place and close pressure release valve. Select high pressure cook function and cook for 1 minute. 2. Turn off Instant Pot and quick-release pressure. Carefully remove lid, allowing steam to escape away from you. Stir in snap peas, cover, and let sit until heated through, about 3 minutes. Add radish greens, mushrooms, lemon zest and juice, and remaining 2 tablespoons oil and gently toss to combine. Season with salt and pepper to taste. 3. Spread ¼ cup yogurt over bottom of 4 individual serving plates. Using slotted spoon, arrange vegetable mixture on top and sprinkle with cilantro and dukkah. Serve.

Chinese Pe-Tsai and Onion Stir-fry

Prep time: 5 minutes | Cook time: 8 minutes | Serves 4

- 2 tablespoons sesame oil
- 1 yellow onion, chopped
- 1 pound (454 g) pe-tsai cabbage, shredded
- ¼ cup rice wine vinegar
- 1 tablespoon coconut aminos
- 1 teaspoon finely minced garlic
- ½ teaspoon salt
- ¼ teaspoon Szechuan pepper

1. Set the Instant Pot on the Sauté mode and heat the sesame oil. Add the onion to the pot and sauté for 5 minutes, or until tender. Stir in the remaining ingredients. 2. Lock the lid. Select the Manual mode and set the cooking time for 3 minutes on High Pressure. When the timer goes off, perform a quick pressure release. Carefully open the lid. 3. Transfer the cabbage mixture to a bowl and serve immediately.

Zucchini Noodles with Sesame and Scallions

Prep time: 10 minutes | Cook time: 3 minutes | Serves 6

- 2 large zucchinis, trimmed and spiralized
- ¼ cup chicken broth
- 1 tablespoon chopped scallions
- 1 tablespoon coconut aminos
- 1 teaspoon sesame oil
- 1 teaspoon sesame seeds
- ¼ teaspoon chili flakes

1. Set the Instant Pot on the Sauté mode. Add the zucchini spirals to the pot and pour in the chicken broth. Sauté for 3 minutes and transfer to the serving bowls. 2. Sprinkle with the scallions, coconut aminos, sesame oil, sesame seeds and chili flakes. Gently stir the zoodles. 3. Serve immediately.

Cabbage with Thyme

Prep time: 10 minutes | Cook time: 5 minutes | Serves 4

- 1 pound (454 g) white cabbage
- 2 tablespoons butter
- 1 teaspoon dried thyme
- ½ teaspoon salt
- 1 cup water

1. Cut the white cabbage on medium size petals and sprinkle with the butter, dried thyme and salt. Place the cabbage petals in the Instant Pot pan. 2. Pour the water and insert the trivet in the Instant Pot. Put the pan on the trivet. 3. Set the lid in place. Select the Manual mode and set the cooking time for 5 minutes on High Pressure. When the timer goes off, do a quick pressure release. Carefully open the lid. 4. Serve immediately.

Easy Cauliflower Gnocch

Prep time: 5 minutes | Cook time: 2 minutes | Serves 4

- 2 cups cauliflower, boiled
- ½ cup almond flour
- 1 tablespoon sesame oil
- 1 teaspoon salt
- 1 cup water

1. In a bowl, mash the cauliflower until puréed. Mix it up with the almond flour, sesame oil and salt. 2. Make the log from the cauliflower dough and cut it into small pieces. 3. Pour the water in the Instant Pot and add the gnocchi. 4. Lock the lid. Select the Manual mode and set the cooking time for 2 minutes on High Pressure. Once the timer goes off, perform a natural pressure release for 5 minutes, then release any remaining pressure. Carefully open the lid. 5. Remove the cooked gnocchi from the water and serve.

Brussels Sprouts with Garlic and Almonds

Prep time: 5 minutes | Cook time: 15 minutes | Serves 4

- 1 pound (454 g) Brussels sprouts
- 1 teaspoon sea salt
- 1 teaspoon garlic powder
- 1 tablespoon butter
- 1 small onion, diced
- 2 cloves garlic, crushed
- 3 strips uncured bacon, cut into ½-inch pieces
- 1 tablespoon extra-fine blanched almond slivers
- ½ cup chicken broth
- 2 tablespoons chopped scallions, for garnish

1. Wash the Brussels sprouts well and discard any old and rotten leaves. Trim the ends off and cut the Brussels sprouts in half vertically. Put any loose leaves with the rest of the Brussels sprouts, sea salt and garlic powder in a large mixing bowl and mix. 2. Turn on the Instant Pot by pressing Sauté and set to More. Insert the inner pot and wait until the panel says "Hot." 3. Add the butter, onion and garlic and sauté for 2 minutes or until the onion is soft. Add the bacon and sauté for 3 minutes or until the bacon starts to shrivel. If there's too much bacon grease, you can spoon out some of it now. You want some bacon grease, but not so much that the Brussels sprouts won't brown. 4. Push the bacon to the side and add half of the Brussels sprouts to brown. Place the Brussels sprouts with their flat sides down on the inner pot. Do not to crowd them and don't mix until the sides turn brown. 5. When most of the sides are browned, take them out, place them in a bowl and set aside. Add the remaining Brussels sprouts to the inner pot to brown the sides. If needed, add more bacon grease back so as not to burn the Brussels sprouts. When they are browned, add the first batch of the browned Brussels sprouts back to the inner pot and add the almonds and the chicken broth and mix while scraping the bottom of the inner pot to loosen up all the bits and pieces. 6. Hit Cancel, then press the Manual button and set the timer for 8 minutes on High Pressure. 7. Close the lid tightly and move the steam release handle to Sealing. When the timer goes off, turn the steam release handle to the Venting position carefully for the steam to escape and the float valve to drop down. Press Cancel. Open the lid. 8. Garnish with the chopped scallions and serve immediately.

Turmeric-infused Green Cabbage Stew

Prep time: 5 minutes | Cook time: 4 minutes | Serves 4

- 2 tablespoons olive oil
- ½ cup sliced yellow onion
- 1 teaspoon crushed garlic
- Sea salt and freshly ground black pepper, to taste
- 1 teaspoon turmeric powder
- 1 serrano pepper, chopped
- 1 pound (454 g) green cabbage, shredded
- 1 celery stalk, chopped
- 2 tablespoons rice wine
- 1 cup roasted vegetable broth

1. Place all of the above ingredients in the Instant Pot. 2. Secure the lid. Choose Manual mode and High Pressure; cook for 4 minutes. Once cooking is complete, use a quick pressure release; carefully remove the lid. 3. Divide between individual bowls and serve warm. Bon appétit!

Asparagus in Creamy Cheese Sauce

Prep time: 5 minutes | Cook time: 1 minute | Serves 4

- 1½ pounds (680 g) fresh asparagus
- 1 cup water
- 2 tablespoons olive oil
- 4 garlic cloves, minced
- Sea salt, to taste
- ¼ teaspoon ground black pepper
- ½ cup shredded Copoundy cheese

1. Pour the water into the Instant Pot and put the steamer basket in the pot. 2. Place the asparagus in the steamer basket. Drizzle the asparagus with the olive oil and sprinkle with the garlic on top. Season with salt and black pepper. 3. Close and secure the lid. Select the Manual mode and set the cooking time for 1 minute at High Pressure. Once cooking is complete, do a quick pressure release. Carefully open the lid. 4. Transfer the asparagus to a platter and served topped with the shredded cheese.

Cauliflower Cheese Macaroni

Prep time: 6 minutes | Cook time: 3 minutes | Serves 6

- 1 cup water
- 1 large cauliflower, chopped into bite-size florets
- 1 cup heavy whipping cream
- ½ cup sour cream
- 1 cup shredded Gruyère or Mozzarella cheese
- 2½ cups shredded sharp Cheddar cheese
- 1 teaspoon ground mustard
- 1 teaspoon ground turmeric
- Sea salt, to taste
- Pinch of cayenne pepper (optional)

1. Pour the water into the Instant Pot. Place a metal steaming basket inside. Put the cauliflower florets in the basket. Secure the lid and set the steam release valve to Sealing. Press the Manual button and set the cook time to 3 minutes. When the Instant Pot beeps, carefully switch the steam release valve to Venting to quick-release the pressure. When fully released, open the lid. 2. Meanwhile, prepare the cheese sauce. In a large skillet, gently bring the cream to a simmer over medium to medium-low heat. Whisk in the sour cream until smooth, then gradually whisk in the Gruyère and 2 cups of the Cheddar until melted. Stir in the ground mustard and turmeric. Taste and adjust the salt. 3. Remove the cauliflower from the pot and toss it in the cheese sauce to coat. Serve warm, topped with the remaining Cheddar and a sprinkling of cayenne (if using).

Italian Foraged Mushrooms

Prep time: 30 minutes | Cook time: 3 minutes | Serves 10

- 2 tablespoons canola oil
- 2 large onions, chopped
- 4 garlic cloves, minced
- 3 large red bell peppers, chopped
- 3 large green bell peppers, chopped
- 12 ounces package oyster mushrooms, cleaned and chopped
- 3 fresh bay leaves
- 10 fresh basil leaves, chopped
- 1 teaspoon salt
- 1½ teaspoons pepper
- 28 ounces can Italian plum tomatoes, crushed or chopped

1. Press Sauté on the Instant Pot and add in the oil. Once the oil is heated, add the onions, garlic, peppers, and mushroom to the oil. Sauté just until mushrooms begin to turn brown. 2. Add remaining ingredients. Stir well. 3. Secure the lid and make sure vent is set to sealing. Press Manual and set time for 3 minutes. 4. When cook time is up, release the pressure manually. Discard bay leaves.

Green Beans, Potatoes, and Basil

Prep time: 20 minutes | Cook time: 10 minutes | Serves 4

- 2 tablespoons extra-virgin olive oil, plus extra for drizzling
- 1 onion, chopped fine
- 2 tablespoons minced fresh oregano or 2 teaspoons dried
- 2 tablespoons tomato paste
- 4 garlic cloves, minced
- 1 (14½-ounce / 411-g) can whole peeled tomatoes, drained with juice reserved, chopped
- 1 cup water
- 1 teaspoon table salt
- ¼ teaspoon pepper
- 1½ pounds (680 g) green beans, trimmed and cut into 2-inch lengths
- 1 pound (454 g) Yukon Gold potatoes, peeled and cut into 1-inch pieces
- 3 tablespoons chopped fresh basil or parsley
- 2 tablespoons toasted pine nuts
- Shaved Parmesan cheese

1. Using highest sauté function, heat oil in Instant Pot until shimmering. Add onion and cook until softened, about 5 minutes. Stir in oregano, tomato paste, and garlic and cook until fragrant, about 30 seconds. Stir in tomatoes and their juice, water, salt, and pepper, then stir in green beans and potatoes. Lock lid in place and close pressure release valve. Select high pressure cook function and cook for 5 minutes. 2. Turn off Instant Pot and quick-release pressure. Carefully remove lid, allowing steam to escape away from you. Season with salt and pepper to taste. Sprinkle individual portions with basil, pine nuts, and Parmesan and drizzle with extra oil. Serve.

Asparagus and Kale Stir-Fry

Prep time: 5 minutes | Cook time: 3 minutes | Serves 4

- 8 ounces (227 g) asparagus, chopped
- 2 cups chopped kale
- 2 bell peppers, chopped
- 1 tablespoon avocado oil
- 1 teaspoon apple cider vinegar
- ½ teaspoon minced ginger
- ½ cup water

1. Pour the water into the Instant Pot. 2. In the Instant Pot pan, stir together the remaining ingredients. 3. Insert the trivet and place the pan on it. 4. Set the lid in place. Select the Manual mode and set the cooking time for 3 minutes on High Pressure. When the timer goes off, perform a quick pressure release. Carefully open the lid. 5. Serve immediately.

Butter-basted Whole Cauliflower

Prep time: 5 minutes | Cook time: 8 minutes | Serves 4

- 1 large cauliflower, rinsed and patted dry
- 1 cup water
- 4 tablespoons melted butter
- 2 cloves garlic, minced
- Pinch of sea salt
- Pinch of fresh ground black pepper
- 1 tablespoon chopped fresh flat leaf parsley, for garnish

1. Pour the water into the Instant Pot and put the trivet in the pot. Place the cauliflower on the trivet. 2. Lock the lid. Select the Manual mode and set the cooking time for 3 minutes at High Pressure. 3. Preheat the oven to 550°F (288°C). Line a baking sheet with parchment paper. 4. In a small bowl, whisk together the butter, garlic, sea salt and black pepper. Set aside. 5. When the timer beeps, use a quick pressure release. Carefully open the lid. 6. Transfer the cauliflower to the lined baking sheet. Dab and dry the surface with a clean kitchen towel. Brush the cauliflower with the garlic butter. 7. Place the baking sheet with the cauliflower in the preheated oven and roast for 5 minutes, or until the cauliflower is golden brown. Drizzle with any remaining garlic butter and sprinkle with the chopped parsley. Serve immediately.

Chapter 8

Desserts

Egg Custard Tarts

Prep time: 10 minutes | Cook time: 20 minutes | Serves 2

- ¼ cup almond flour
- 1 tablespoon coconut oil
- 2 egg yolks
- ¼ cup coconut milk
- 1 tablespoon erythritol
- 1 teaspoon vanilla extract
- 1 cup water, for cooking

1. Make the dough by mixing almond flour and coconut oil together. 2. Place the dough into 2 mini tart molds, pressing it down to form cup shapes. 3. Pour water into the Instant Pot and insert the steamer rack. 4. Position the tart molds on the steamer rack inside the Instant Pot, then close and seal the lid. 5. Cook on Manual mode at High Pressure for 3 minutes, followed by a quick pressure release. 6. Whisk vanilla extract, erythritol, coconut milk, and egg yolks until well blended. 7. Pour this liquid into the tart molds, close the lid again. 8. Cook on Manual mode at High Pressure for 7 minutes. 9. Allow a natural pressure release for an additional 10 minutes before serving.

Pumpkin Pie Pudding

Prep time: 10 minutes | Cook time: 20 minutes | Serves 6

- Nonstick cooking spray
- 2 eggs
- ½ cup heavy (whipping) cream or almond milk (for dairy-free)
- ¾ cup Swerve
- 1 (15-ounce / 425-g) can pumpkin purée
- 1 teaspoon pumpkin pie spice
- 1 teaspoon vanilla extract
- For Serving:
- ½ cup heavy (whipping) cream

1. Ensure the 6-by-3-inch pan is thoroughly greased with cooking spray, reaching all crevices. 2. In a medium bowl, beat the eggs until frothy. Incorporate the cream, Swerve, pumpkin purée, pumpkin pie spice, and vanilla, stirring until well amalgamated. 3. Transfer the mixture to the prepared pan, covering it with either a silicone lid or aluminum foil. 4. Add 2 cups of water to the Instant Pot's inner cooking pot, followed by placing a trivet inside. Position the covered pan on top of the trivet. 5. Secure the lid and select Manual mode, adjusting the pressure to High. Cook for 20 minutes, then allow the pressure to release naturally for 10 minutes before performing a quick-release for any remaining pressure. Unlock the lid. 6. Remove the pan and refrigerate for 6 to 8 hours. 7. To serve, prepare whipped cream by beating heavy cream with a hand mixer until soft peaks form, being careful not to overbeat and turn it into butter. Garnish each pudding with a dollop of the whipped cream before serving.

Fudgy Walnut Brownies

Prep time: 10 minutes | Cook time: 1 hour | Serves 12

- ¾ cup walnut halves and pieces
- ½ cup unsalted butter, melted and cooled
- 4 large eggs
- 1½ teaspoons instant coffee crystals
- 1½ teaspoons vanilla extract
- 1 cup Lakanto Monkfruit Sweetener Golden
- ¼ teaspoon fine sea salt
- ¾ cup almond flour
- ¾ cup natural cocoa powder
- ¾ cup stevia-sweetened chocolate chips

1. Over medium heat in a dry small skillet, toast walnuts, stirring frequently, for approximately five minutes until they turn golden. Then transfer the walnuts to a bowl to cool down. 2. Pour one cup of water into the Instant Pot. Line the bottom of a 7 - by - 3 - inch round cake pan with a circle of parchment paper. Grease the sides of the pan and the parchment paper or coat them with nonstick cooking spray. 3. Put the butter into a medium bowl. Add the eggs one at a time, whisking continuously. After that, whisk in coffee crystals, vanilla, sweetener, and salt. Finally, stir in flour and cocoa powder just until they are combined. Using a rubber spatula, fold in chocolate chips and walnuts. 4. Transfer the batter into the prepared pan and use the spatula to spread it evenly. Cover the pan tightly with aluminum foil. Place the pan on a long - handled silicone steam rack, and while holding the handles of the steam rack, lower it into the Instant Pot. 5. Fasten the lid and set the Pressure Release to Sealing. Choose the Cake, Pressure Cook, or Manual setting and set the cooking time to 45 minutes at high pressure. (Note that the pot will take about ten minutes to reach the required pressure before the cooking program starts.) 6. When the cooking program is finished, let the pressure release naturally for ten minutes, and then move the Pressure Release to Venting to release any remaining steam. Open the pot while wearing heat - resistant mitts, grasp the handles of the steam rack, and lift it out of the pot. Uncover the pan carefully to avoid being scalded by the steam or getting condensation dripped onto the brownies. Let the brownies cool in the pan on a cooling rack for about two hours until they reach room temperature. 7. Run a butter knife around the edge of the pan to ensure that the brownies are not sticking to the sides. Invert the brownies onto the rack, lift off the pan, and peel off the parchment paper. Then invert the brownies onto a serving plate and cut them into twelve wedges. The brownies can be stored in an airtight container in the refrigerator for up to five days or in the freezer for up to four months.

Strawberry Cheesecake

Prep time: 20 minutes | Cook time: 10 minutes | Serves 2

- 1 tablespoon gelatin
- 4 tablespoon water (for gelatin)
- 4 tablespoon cream cheese
- 1 strawberry, chopped
- ¼ cup coconut milk
- 1 tablespoon Swerve

1. Combine the gelatin and water, then allow the mixture to sit for 10 minutes. 2. Meanwhile, pour coconut milk into the Instant Pot. 3. Heat the coconut milk on Sauté mode until it comes to a boil, which should take about 10 minutes. 4. In the meantime, mash the strawberries and mix them with cream cheese. 5. Add this strawberry-cream cheese mixture to the hot coconut milk and stir until smooth. 6. Let the liquid cool for 10 minutes, then add the gelatin. Whisk until the gelatin has completely melted. 7. Finally, pour the cheesecake mixture into the mold and freeze for 3 hours.

Lemon Vanilla Cheesecake

Prep time: 15 minutes | Cook time: 20 minutes | Serves 6

- 2 teaspoons freshly squeezed lemon juice
- 2 teaspoons vanilla extract or almond extract
- ½ cup sour cream, divided, at room temperature
- ½ cup plus 2 teaspoons Swerve
- 8 ounces (227 g) cream cheese, at room temperature
- 2 eggs, at room temperature

1. Pour 2 cups of water into the inner cooking pot of the Instant Pot, then place a trivet (preferably with handles) in the pot. Line the sides of a 6-inch springform pan with parchment paper. 2. In a food processor, put the lemon juice, vanilla, ¼ cup of sour cream, ½ cup of Swerve, and the cream cheese. 3. Blend all the ingredients gently yet thoroughly, scraping down the sides of the bowl whenever necessary. 4. Add the eggs and blend just long enough to incorporate them well, which takes 20 to 30 seconds. By now, the mixture will be pourable. 5. Pour the mixture into the prepared pan. Cover the pan with aluminum foil and place it on the trivet. (If your trivet doesn't have handles, it might be a good idea to use a foil sling to make removing the pan easier.) 6. Lock the lid in place. Select Manual and set the pressure to High. Cook for 20 minutes. Once the cooking is done, let the pressure release naturally. Then unlock the lid. 7. Meanwhile, in a small bowl, combine the remaining ¼ cup of sour cream and 2 teaspoons of Swerve to make the topping. 8. Remove the cheesecake and take off the foil. Spread the topping over the top. Applying the topping while the cheesecake is still hot helps the topping melt into the cheesecake. 9. Place the cheesecake in the refrigerator and refrain from disturbing it. Seriously, leave it alone and let it chill for at least 6 to 8 hours. It won't taste good when hot. 10. When you're ready to serve, open the sides of the pan and peel off the parchment paper. Then slice and serve.

Cocoa Cookies

Prep time: 15 minutes | Cook time: 25 minutes | Serves 4

- ½ cup coconut flour
- 3 tablespoons cream cheese
- 1 teaspoon cocoa powder
- 1 tablespoon erythritol
- ¼ teaspoon baking powder
- 1 teaspoon apple cider vinegar
- 1 tablespoon butter
- 1 cup water, for cooking

1. Make the dough by mixing coconut flour, cream cheese, cocoa powder, erythritol, baking powder, apple cider vinegar, and butter together. Knead the dough thoroughly. 2. Transfer the dough into the baking pan and flatten it into the shape of a cookie. 3. Pour water into the instant pot and insert the steamer rack. 4. Place the pan with the cookie inside the instant pot. Close and seal the lid. 5. Cook the cookie using the Manual (High Pressure) setting for 25 minutes. Perform a quick pressure release. Allow the cookie to cool down well.

Blackberry Crisp

Prep time: 5 minutes | Cook time: 5 minutes | Serves 1

- 10 blackberries
- ½ teaspoon vanilla extract
- 2 tablespoons powdered erythritol
- ⅛ teaspoon xanthan gum
- 1 tablespoon butter
- ¼ cup chopped pecans
- 3 teaspoons almond flour
- ½ teaspoon cinnamon
- 2 teaspoons powdered erythritol
- 1 cup water

1. Put the blackberries, vanilla, erythritol, and xanthan gum into a 4-inch ramekin. Gently stir to ensure that the blackberries are evenly coated. 2. In a small bowl, combine the remaining ingredients. Spread this mixture over the blackberries in the ramekin, and then cover the ramekin with foil. 3. Press the Manual button on the Instant Pot and set the cooking time to 4 minutes. When the timer sounds, perform a quick-release of the pressure. 4. Serve the dessert warm. You can also add a scoop of whipped cream on top if you like.

Lemon and Ricotta Torte

Prep time: 15 minutes | Cook time: 35 minutes | Serves 12

- Cooking spray
- Torte:
- 1⅓ cups Swerve
- ½ cup (1 stick) unsalted butter, softened
- 2 teaspoons lemon or vanilla extract
- 5 large eggs, separated
- 2½ cups blanched almond flour
- 1¼ (10-ounce / 284-g) cups whole-milk ricotta cheese
- ¼ cup lemon juice
- 1 cup cold water
- Lemon Glaze:
- ½ cup (1 stick) unsalted butter
- ¼ cup Swerve
- 2 tablespoons lemon juice
- 2 ounces (57 g) cream cheese (¼ cup)
- Grated lemon zest and lemon slices, for garnish

1. Prepare a baking pan by lining it with parchment paper and spraying it with cooking spray. Afterward, set the prepared pan aside. 2. To make the torte, take the bowl of a stand mixer and place the Swerve, butter, and extract inside. Operate the mixer for 8 to 10 minutes until all the ingredients are thoroughly combined, ensuring you scrape down the sides of the bowl from time to time to incorporate any residue. 3. Next, introduce the egg yolks into the mixer and continue the blending process until a uniform mixture is achieved. Subsequently, add the almond flour and blend until the batter becomes smooth. Then, gently stir in the ricotta and lemon juice until they are evenly distributed. 4. In a separate medium-sized bowl, whisk the egg whites vigorously until stiff peaks are formed. Once the egg whites are ready, incorporate them into the batter, stirring thoroughly. Pour the final batter into the previously prepared baking pan and use a spatula to even out the top surface. 5. Position a trivet at the base of your Instant Pot and pour water into it. Employ a foil sling to carefully lower the baking pan onto the trivet, making sure to tuck in the sides of the sling neatly. 6. Securely seal the lid of the Instant Pot. Press either the Pressure Cook or Manual button and set the timer to 30 minutes. After the cooking cycle is completed, allow the pressure to release naturally. 7. Put the lid in place and lock it. Select the Manual mode and adjust the cooking time to 30 minutes at High Pressure. 8. When the timer sounds, let the pressure release naturally for 10 minutes before carefully opening the lid. 9. Utilize the foil sling to lift the baking pan out of the Instant Pot. Transfer the torte to the refrigerator and let it chill for 40 minutes before applying the glaze. 10. At the same time, prepare the glaze: Place the butter in a large pan and heat it over high heat for approximately 5 minutes until it turns a rich brown color, stirring periodically. Once browned, remove the pan from the heat. While stirring the browned butter, add the Swerve. 11. Gently add the lemon juice and cream cheese to the butter mixture. Allow the glaze to cool for a few minutes until it begins to thicken. 12. Take the chilled torte out of the refrigerator and transfer it to a serving plate. Pour the glaze evenly over the torte, then place it back in the refrigerator for an additional 30 minutes to let the glaze set. 13. Sprinkle the lemon zest over the top of the torte and arrange the lemon slices attractively around the torte on the plate. 14. Finally, serve the torte.

Chipotle Black Bean Brownies

Prep time: 15 minutes | Cook time: 30 minutes | Serves 8

- Nonstick cooking spray
- ½ cup dark chocolate chips, divided
- ¾ cup cooked calypso beans or black beans
- ½ cup extra-virgin olive oil
- 2 large eggs
- ¼ cup unsweetened dark chocolate cocoa powder
- ⅓ cup honey
- 1 teaspoon vanilla extract
- ⅓ cup white wheat flour
- ½ teaspoon chipotle chili powder
- ½ teaspoon ground cinnamon
- ½ teaspoon baking powder
- ½ teaspoon kosher salt

1. Spray a 7-inch Bundt pan using nonstick cooking spray. 2. Put half of the chocolate chips in a small bowl and microwave them for 30 seconds. Stir the chips, and if they have not completely melted, repeat the microwaving process until they are fully melted. 3. In a food processor, combine the beans and oil by blending. Add the melted chocolate chips, eggs, cocoa powder, honey, and vanilla. Blend until the resulting mixture is smooth. 4. In a large bowl, mix the flour, chili powder, cinnamon, baking powder, and salt by whisking. Pour the bean mixture from the food processor into the large bowl and stir with a wooden spoon until the ingredients are thoroughly combined. Stir in the remaining chocolate chips. 5. Pour the batter into the previously prepared Bundt pan. Cover the pan loosely with foil. 6. Pour 1 cup of water into the electric pressure cooker. 7. Place the Bundt pan on the wire rack and lower it into the pressure cooker. 8. Close and lock the lid of the pressure cooker. Set the valve to the sealing position. 9. Cook at high pressure for 30 minutes. 10. When the cooking process is completed, press the Cancel button and perform a quick pressure release. 11. Once the pin drops, unlock the lid and remove it. 12. Carefully transfer the pan to a cooling rack and leave it there for about 10 minutes. Then, invert the cake onto the rack and let it cool completely. 13. Cut the cake into slices and serve.

Tapioca Berry Parfaits

Prep time: 10 minutes | Cook time: 6 minutes | Serves 4

- 2 cups unsweetened almond milk
- ½ cup small pearl tapioca, rinsed and still wet
- 1 teaspoon almond extract
- 1 tablespoon pure maple syrup
- 2 cups berries
- ¼ cup slivered almonds

1. Initiate the process by meticulously pouring the almond milk into the electric pressure cooker. Subsequently, deftly stir in the tapioca and almond extract until they are homogenously blended. 2. Then, securely fasten and lock the lid of the pressure cooker, and concurrently adjust the valve to the sealing state. 3. Set the cooker to High pressure mode and let it cook undisturbed for a duration of 6 minutes. 4. Once the cooking concludes, promptly hit the Cancel button. Allow the pressure to naturally subside for 10 minutes, and thereafter, swiftly release any residual pressure. 5. When the pressure pin descends, carefully unlock and remove the lid, and then transfer the pot to a cooling rack. 6. Stir in the maple syrup with precision and permit the mixture to cool for roughly an hour. 7. In petite glasses, skillfully construct multiple layers of tapioca, berries, and almonds, and then refrigerate for 1 hour. 8. Eventually, serve the dish in its chilled state.

Cocoa Custard

Prep time: 5 minutes | Cook time: 7 minutes | Serves 4

- 2 cups heavy cream (or full-fat coconut milk for dairy-free)
- 4 large egg yolks
- ¼ cup Swerve, or more to taste
- 1 tablespoon plus 1 teaspoon unsweetened cocoa powder, or more to taste
- ½ teaspoon almond extract
- Pinch of fine sea salt
- 1 cup cold water

1. Heat the cream in a pan over medium-high heat for approximately 2 minutes until it becomes hot. 2. Place all the remaining ingredients except the water in a blender and blend until smooth. 3. While the blender is running, slowly pour in the hot cream. Taste and adjust the sweetness to your liking. Add more cocoa powder if desired. 4. Use a spatula to scoop the custard mixture into four ramekins. Cover the ramekins with aluminum foil. 5. Place a trivet in the Instant Pot and pour in the water. Place the ramekins on the trivet. 6. Lock the lid. Select the Manual mode and set the cooking time for 5 minutes at High Pressure. 7. When the timer beeps, use a quick pressure release. Carefully remove the lid. 8. Remove the foil and set the foil aside. Let the custard cool for 15 minutes. Cover the ramekins with the foil again and place in the refrigerator to chill completely, about 2 hours. 9. Serve.

Caramelized Pumpkin Cheesecake

Prep time: 15 minutes | Cook time: 45 minutes | Serves 8

- Crust:
- 1½ cups almond flour
- 4 tablespoons butter, melted
- 1 tablespoon Swerve
- 1 tablespoon granulated erythritol
- ½ teaspoon ground cinnamon
- Cooking spray
- Filling:
- 16 ounces (454 g) cream cheese, softened
- ½ cup granulated erythritol
- 2 eggs
- ¼ cup pumpkin purée
- 3 tablespoons Swerve
- 1 teaspoon vanilla extract
- ¼ teaspoon pumpkin pie spice
- 1½ cups water

1. To make the crust: In a medium bowl, mix together the almond flour, butter, Swerve, erythritol, and cinnamon. Use a fork to press the mixture firmly. 2. Spray the pan with cooking spray and line its bottom with parchment paper. 3. Press the crust evenly into the pan. Work the crust up the sides of the pan, reaching about halfway from the top, ensuring there are no uncovered areas on the bottom. 4. Put the crust in the freezer for 20 minutes while you prepare the filling. 5. To make the filling: In a large bowl, using a hand mixer at medium speed, combine the cream cheese and erythritol. Beat the mixture until the cream cheese becomes light and fluffy, which takes 2 to 3 minutes. 6. Add the eggs, pumpkin purée, Swerve, vanilla, and pumpkin pie spice. Beat until all the ingredients are well incorporated. 7. Take the crust out of the freezer and pour the filling into it. Cover the pan with aluminum foil and place it on the trivet. 8. Pour the water into the pot and carefully lower the trivet into the pot. 9. Put the lid in place. Select the Manual mode and set the cooking time to 45 minutes at High Pressure. When the timer finishes, perform a quick pressure release. Open the lid carefully. 10. Take the trivet and cheesecake out of the pot. Remove the foil from the pan. The center of the cheesecake should still be slightly jiggly. 11. Let the cheesecake cool on the counter for 30 minutes before putting it in the refrigerator to set. Leave the cheesecake in the refrigerator for at least 6 hours before removing the sides and serving.

Cinnamon Roll Cheesecake

Prep time: 15 minutes | Cook time: 35 minutes | Serves 12

- Crust:
- 3½ tablespoons unsalted butter or coconut oil
- 1½ ounces (43 g) unsweetened baking chocolate, chopped
- 1 large egg, beaten
- ⅓ cup Swerve
- 2 teaspoons ground cinnamon
- 1 teaspoon vanilla extract
- ¼ teaspoon fine sea salt
- Filling:
- 4 (8-ounce / 227-g) packages cream cheese, softened
- ¾ cup Swerve
- ½ cup unsweetened almond milk (or hemp milk for nut-free)
- 1 teaspoon vanilla extract
- ¼ teaspoon almond extract (omit for nut-free)
- ¼ teaspoon fine sea salt
- 3 large eggs
- Cinnamon Swirl:
- 6 tablespoons (¾ stick) unsalted butter (or butter flavored coconut oil for dairy-free)
- ½ cup Swerve
- Seeds scraped from ½ vanilla bean (about 8 inches long), or 1 teaspoon vanilla extract
- 1 tablespoon ground cinnamon
- ¼ teaspoon fine sea salt
- 1 cup cold water

1. Line a baking pan with two layers of aluminum foil. 2. To make the crust, melt the butter in a pan over medium-low heat. Slowly incorporate the chocolate and stir until it is melted. Then, stir in the egg, sweetener, cinnamon, vanilla extract, and salt. 3. Transfer the crust mixture to the prepared baking pan and spread it using your hands so that it covers the bottom entirely. 4. For the filling, place the cream cheese, sweetener, milk, extracts, and salt in the bowl of a stand mixer and mix until they are well combined. Add the eggs one by one, and after each addition, mix at low speed just until blended. Then, blend until the filling is smooth. Pour half of the filling over the crust. 5. To make the cinnamon swirl, heat the butter over high heat in a pan until the butter froths and brown flecks appear, stirring from time to time. Stir in the sweetener, vanilla seeds, cinnamon, and salt. Remove from the heat and let it cool slightly. 6. Spoon half of the cinnamon swirl onto the cheesecake filling in the baking pan. Use a knife to cut through the filling several times with the cinnamon swirl for a marbled effect. Add the remaining cheesecake filling and cinnamon swirl on top. Cut through the cheesecake filling with the cinnamon swirl several more times. 7. Put a trivet at the bottom of the Instant Pot and pour in the water. Use a foil sling to lower the baking pan onto the trivet. Cover the cheesecake with 3 large sheets of paper towel to prevent condensation from leaking onto it. Tuck in the sides of the sling. 8. Lock the lid. Select the Manual mode and set the cooking time to 26 minutes at High Pressure. 9. When the timer goes off, use a natural pressure release for 10 minutes. Carefully take off the lid. 10. Use the foil sling to lift the pan out of the Instant Pot. 11. Let the cheesecake cool, then put it in the refrigerator for 4 hours to chill and set completely before slicing and serving.

Almond Butter Blondies

Prep time: 10 minutes | Cook time: 20 minutes | Serves 8

- ½ cup creamy natural almond butter, at room temperature
- 4 large eggs
- ¾ cup Lakanto Monkfruit Sweetener Golden
- 1 teaspoon pure vanilla extract
- ½ teaspoon fine sea salt
- 1¼ cups almond flour
- ¾ cup stevia-sweetened chocolate chips

1. Begin by pouring 1 cup of water into the Instant Pot. Prepare a 7 by 3-inch round cake pan by placing a parchment paper circle at the bottom. Grease the sides of the pan and the parchment with butter or apply a nonstick cooking spray. 2. In a medium bowl, combine the almond butter. Whisk in the eggs one at a time, ensuring each is fully incorporated before adding the next. Then, add the sweetener, vanilla extract, and salt, whisking until smooth. Gently fold in the flour just until combined, followed by the chocolate chips. 3. Transfer the batter into the prepared pan and use a rubber spatula to spread it evenly. Secure the pan tightly with aluminum foil. Place the pan on a long-handled silicone steam rack and carefully lower the rack with the pan into the Instant Pot. 4. Close and lock the lid, setting the Pressure Release valve to Sealing. Select the Cake, Pressure Cook, or Manual setting and set the timer for 40 minutes on high pressure. (Note: The Instant Pot will take roughly 10 minutes to build pressure before cooking begins.) 5. After the cooking cycle completes, allow the pressure to release naturally for 10 minutes, then switch the Pressure Release valve to Venting to release any remaining steam. Using heat-resistant mitts, remove the steam rack from the pot. Carefully uncover the pan, avoiding steam burns and preventing condensation from dripping onto the blondies. Let the blondies cool in the pan on a cooling rack for about 5 minutes. 6. Run a butter knife around the edges of the pan to ensure the blondies are not sticking. Invert the pan onto the cooling rack, lift it off, and peel away the parchment paper. Allow the blondies to cool completely for 15 minutes, then transfer them to a serving plate and cut into eight wedges. Store the blondies in an airtight container in the refrigerator for up to five days or freeze them for up to four months.

Vanilla Poppy Seed Cake

Prep time: 10 minutes | Cook time: 25 minutes | Serves 6

- 1 cup almond flour
- 2 eggs
- ½ cup erythritol
- 2 teaspoons vanilla extract
- 1 teaspoon lemon extract
- 1 tablespoon poppy seeds
- 4 tablespoons melted butter
- ¼ cup heavy cream
- ⅛ cup sour cream
- ½ teaspoon baking powder
- 1 cup water
- ¼ cup powdered erythritol, for garnish

1. Combine the almond flour, eggs, erythritol, vanilla, lemon, and poppy seeds in a large bowl. 2. Incorporate the butter, heavy cream, sour cream, and baking powder into the mixture. 3. Transfer the entire mixture into a 7-inch round cake pan and cover it with foil. 4. Pour water into the Instant Pot and position a steam rack at the bottom. Place the baking pan on the steam rack and secure the lid by clicking it closed. Press the Cake button and then press the Adjust button to reduce the heat setting. Set the cooking time to 25 minutes. 5. Once the timer goes off, allow the pressure to release naturally for 15 minutes, and then perform a quick release for any remaining pressure. Let the cake cool down completely. For serving, sprinkle powdered erythritol on top.

Pumpkin Walnut Cheesecake

Prep time: 15 minutes | Cook time: 50 minutes | Serves 6

- 2 cups walnuts
- 3 tablespoons melted butter
- 1 teaspoon cinnamon
- 16 ounces (454 g) cream cheese, softened
- 1 cup powdered erythritol
- ⅓ cup heavy cream
- ⅔ cup pumpkin purée
- 2 teaspoons pumpkin spice
- 1 teaspoon vanilla extract
- 2 eggs
- 1 cup water

1. Initially, set the oven temperature to 350°F (180°C). Place the walnuts, butter, and cinnamon into a food processor. Operate the food processor in pulse mode until a cohesive ball of dough is formed, and remember to scrape down the interior sides of the processor when required. The resulting dough should have the consistency to hold together in a ball shape. 2. Transfer the dough into a greased 7 - inch springform pan and press it down evenly. Bake the dough in the preheated oven for approximately 10 minutes, or until it begins to develop a brownish hue. Once baked, remove the pan from the oven and set it aside. As the crust is baking, commence preparing the cheesecake filling. 3. Take a large bowl and stir the cream cheese until it attains a completely smooth texture. With the aid of a rubber spatula, incorporate the erythritol, heavy cream, pumpkin purée, pumpkin spice, and vanilla into the cream cheese, ensuring thorough mixing. 4. In a small bowl, use a whisk to beat the eggs until well blended. Gradually add the beaten eggs to the large bowl, using a gentle folding motion to combine all the ingredients until they are just incorporated. 5. Pour the prepared mixture into the baked crust and cover the pan with aluminum foil. Pour water into the Instant Pot and position a steam rack at the bottom of the pot. Carefully place the pan containing the mixture onto the steam rack and then secure the lid of the Instant Pot by clicking it into place. Press the Cake button, followed by the Adjust button, and adjust the heat setting to a higher level. Set the timer for 40 minutes. 6. When the timer sounds, allow the pressure to release naturally. Once the pressure indicator shows that the pressure has dropped, carefully lift the pan out of the Instant Pot and place it on the countertop. Remove the foil from the pan. Allow the cheesecake to cool for an additional hour, after which it should be refrigerated. Serve the cheesecake when it is chilled.

Greek Yogurt Strawberry Pops

Prep time: 5 minutes | Cook time: 0 minutes | Serves 6

- 2 ripe bananas, peeled, cut into ½-inch pieces, and frozen
- ½ cup plain 2 percent Greek yogurt
- 1 cup chopped fresh strawberries

1. Start by placing the bananas and yogurt into a food processor and blend on high for about two minutes until the mixture is largely smooth, allowing a few small pieces to remain. Next, scrape down the sides of the bowl, add the strawberries, and continue blending for an additional minute until the mixture is completely smooth. 2. Pour the smooth mixture evenly into six ice-pop molds. Gently tap each mold on the countertop several times to eliminate any air bubbles, then insert an ice-pop stick into each mold and move them to the freezer. Let the molds freeze solid for at least four hours. 3. When ready to serve, briefly run each mold under cold running water for about five seconds, being careful to keep water out of the molds, and then easily remove the ice pops. Enjoy the ice pops immediately or store them in a ziplock freezer bag in the freezer for up to two months.

Candied Mixed Nuts

Prep time: 5 minutes | Cook time: 15 minutes | Serves 8

- 1 cup pecan halves
- 1 cup chopped walnuts
- ⅓ cup Swerve, or more to taste
- ⅓ cup grass-fed butter
- 1 teaspoon ground cinnamon

1. Begin by preheating your oven to a temperature of 350°F (180°C). At the same time, line a baking sheet with aluminum foil to prepare it for later use. 2. As the oven is heating up, pour ½ cup of filtered water into the inner pot of the Instant Pot. Subsequently, add the pecans, walnuts, Swerve, butter, and cinnamon to the pot. Stir the nut mixture thoroughly. After that, close the lid of the Instant Pot and adjust the pressure valve to the Sealing position. Utilize the Manual mode and set it to cook at High Pressure for a duration of 5 minutes. 3. Once the cooking process is completed, carry out a quick release by carefully moving the pressure valve to the Venting position. Then, strain the nuts. Pour the strained nuts onto the previously prepared baking sheet, spreading them out evenly. Put the baking sheet into the oven and let the nuts bake for a period ranging from 5 to 10 minutes. Keep an eye on them to ensure they don't overcook and become overly crisp. Allow the nuts to cool before serving. You can store any leftovers in the refrigerator or freezer for future consumption.

Chocolate Cake with Walnuts

Prep time: 10 minutes | Cook time: 20 minutes | Serves 6

- 1 cup almond flour
- ⅔ cup Swerve
- ¼ cup unsweetened cocoa powder
- ¼ cup chopped walnuts
- 1 teaspoon baking powder
- 3 eggs
- ⅓ cup heavy (whipping) cream
- ¼ cup coconut oil
- Nonstick cooking spray

1. Place the flour, Swerve, cocoa powder, walnuts, baking powder, eggs, cream, and coconut oil in a large bowl. Use a hand mixer at high speed to combine the ingredients until they are well incorporated and the mixture appears fluffy. This helps to prevent the cake from being too dense. 2. Grease a heatproof pan, such as a 3-cup Bundt pan that fits in the Instant Pot, using cooking spray. Pour the cake batter into the pan and cover it with aluminum foil. 3. Pour 2 cups of water into the inner cooking pot of the Instant Pot, and then place a trivet in the pot. Put the pan on the trivet. 4. Lock the lid of the Instant Pot in place. Select Manual and adjust the pressure to High. Cook for 20 minutes. When the cooking is complete, let the pressure release naturally for 10 minutes, and then quick-release any remaining pressure. 5. Carefully remove the pan and allow it to cool for 15 to 20 minutes. Invert the cake onto a plate. You can serve the cake either hot or at room temperature. If desired, serve it with a dollop of whipped cream.

Pumpkin Pie Spice Pots De Crème

Prep time: 5 minutes | Cook time: 7 minutes | Serves 4

- 2 cups heavy cream (or full-fat coconut milk for dairy-free)
- 4 large egg yolks
- ¼ cup Swerve, or more to taste
- 2 teaspoons pumpkin pie spice
- 1 teaspoon vanilla extract
- Pinch of fine sea salt
- 1 cup cold water

1. Heat the cream in a pan over medium-high heat for approximately 2 minutes until it becomes hot. 2. Put all the remaining ingredients, except the water, in a medium bowl and stir them until the mixture is smooth. 3. Slowly pour the hot cream into the bowl while stirring continuously. Taste the mixture and adjust the sweetness according to your preference. Use a spatula to scoop the mixture into four ramekins. Cover the ramekins with aluminum foil. 4. Place a trivet in the Instant Pot and pour the water into it. Put the ramekins on the trivet. 5. Lock the lid. Select the Manual mode and set the cooking time to 5 minutes at High Pressure. 6. When the timer rings, perform a quick pressure release. Carefully remove the lid. 7. Take off the foil from the ramekins and set it aside. Allow the pots de crème to cool for 15 minutes. Cover the ramekins with the foil once again and place them in the refrigerator to chill completely for about 2 hours. 8. Serve the pots de crème.

Coconut Squares

Prep time: 15 minutes | Cook time: 4 minutes | Serves 2

- ⅓ cup coconut flakes
- 1 tablespoon butter
- 1 egg, beaten
- 1 cup water, for cooking

1. Combine coconut flakes, butter, and an egg together. 2. Subsequently, place the mixture into a square-shaped mold and flatten it thoroughly. 3. Pour water into the instant pot and insert the steamer rack. 4. Put the mold containing the dessert onto the rack. Close and seal the lid. 5. Cook the meal in Manual mode at High Pressure for 4 minutes. Perform a quick pressure release. 6. Allow the cooked dessert to cool slightly and then cut it into squares.

Flourless Chocolate Tortes

Prep time: 7 minutes | Cook time: 10 minutes | Serves 8

- 7 ounces (198 g) unsweetened baking chocolate, finely chopped
- ¾ cup plus 2 tablespoons unsalted butter (or butter-flavored coconut oil for dairy-free)
- 1¼ cups Swerve, or more to taste
- 5 large eggs
- 1 tablespoon coconut flour
- 2 teaspoons ground cinnamon
- Seeds scraped from 1 vanilla bean (about 8 inches long), or 2 teaspoons vanilla extract
- Pinch of fine sea salt

1. Grease eight ramekins. Put the chocolate and butter in a pan and place it over medium heat, stirring until the chocolate melts completely, approximately taking three minutes. 2. Remove the pan from the heat, then add the remaining ingredients and stir until the mixture attains a smooth consistency. Taste the mixture and adjust the sweetness to suit your preference. Pour the batter into the greased ramekins. 3. Place a trivet at the bottom of the Instant Pot and pour one cup of cold water into it. Put four of the ramekins on the trivet. 4. Lock the lid. Select the Manual mode and set the cooking time at High Pressure for seven minutes. 5. When the timer beeps, carry out a quick pressure release. Carefully remove the lid. 6. Use tongs to remove the ramekins. Repeat the procedure with the remaining ramekins. 7. Serve the tortes either warm or chilled.

Glazed Pumpkin Bundt Cake

Prep time: 7 minutes | Cook time: 35 minutes | Serves 12

- Cake:
- 3 cups blanched almond flour
- 1 teaspoon baking soda
- ½ teaspoon fine sea salt
- 2 teaspoons ground cinnamon
- 1 teaspoon ground nutmeg
- 1 teaspoon ginger powder
- ¼ teaspoon ground cloves
- 6 large eggs
- 2 cups pumpkin purée
- 1 cup Swerve
- ¼ cup (½ stick) unsalted butter (or coconut oil for dairy-free), softened
- Glaze:
- 1 cup (2 sticks) unsalted butter (or coconut oil for dairy-free), melted
- ½ cup Swerve

1. In a large bowl, combine the almond flour, baking soda, salt, and spices by stirring. In another large bowl, add the eggs, pumpkin, sweetener, and butter, and stir until the mixture becomes smooth. Pour the wet ingredients into the dry ingredients and mix them thoroughly. 2. Apply grease to a 6-cup Bundt pan. Pour the batter into the prepared pan, and cover it first with a paper towel and then with aluminum foil. 3. Put a trivet at the bottom of the Instant Pot and pour 2 cups of cold water into it. Place the Bundt pan on the trivet. 4. Lock the lid. Select the Manual mode and set the cooking time to 35 minutes at High Pressure. 5. When the timer makes a sound, use a natural pressure release for 10 minutes. Carefully take off the lid. 6. Let the cake cool in the pot for 10 minutes before taking it out. 7. While the cake is cooling, make the glaze: In a small bowl, mix the butter and sweetener together. Spoon the glaze over the warm cake. 8. Allow the cake to cool for 5 minutes before slicing and serving.

Chocolate Chip Banana Cake

Prep time: 15 minutes | Cook time: 25 minutes | Serves 8

- Nonstick cooking spray
- 3 ripe bananas
- ½ cup buttermilk
- 3 tablespoons honey
- 1 teaspoon vanilla extract
- 2 large eggs, lightly beaten
- 3 tablespoons extra-virgin olive oil
- 1½ cups whole wheat pastry flour
- ⅛ teaspoon ground nutmeg
- 1 teaspoon ground cinnamon
- ¼ teaspoon salt
- 1 teaspoon baking soda
- ⅓ cup dark chocolate chips

1. First, spritz a 7-inch Bundt pan with nonstick cooking spray. 2. Then, in a large bowl, mash the bananas thoroughly. Next, add the buttermilk, honey, vanilla, eggs, and olive oil, and stir them together until they are well incorporated. 3. After that, in a medium bowl, combine the flour, nutmeg, cinnamon, salt, and baking soda by whisking. 4. Subsequently, add the flour mixture to the banana mixture and mix them thoroughly. Then, stir in the chocolate chips. Pour the batter into the previously prepared Bundt pan. Cover the pan with foil. 5. Next, pour 1 cup of water into the electric pressure cooker. Place the pan on the wire rack and lower it into the pressure cooker. 6. Subsequently, close and lock the lid of the pressure cooker. Set the valve to the sealing position. 7. Then, cook at high pressure for 25 minutes. 8. Once the cooking is done, press the Cancel button and perform a quick pressure release. 9. After the pin drops, unlock and remove the lid. 10. Carefully transfer the pan to a cooling rack, uncover it, and let it cool for 10 minutes. 11. Subsequently, invert the cake onto the rack and let it cool for about one hour. 12. Finally, slice and serve the cake.

Hearty Crème Brûlée

Prep time: 5 minutes | Cook time: 30 minutes | Serves 4

- 5 egg yolks
- 5 tablespoons powdered erythritol
- 1½ cups heavy cream
- 2 teaspoons vanilla extract
- 2 cups water

1. In a small bowl, utilize a fork to break up the egg yolks. Subsequently, stir in the erythritol. 2. Pour the cream into a small saucepan and position it over medium-low heat. Allow the cream to warm up for 3 to 4 minutes. Subsequently, remove the saucepan from the heat. 3. Temper the egg yolks by slowly adding a small spoonful of the warm cream while continuously whisking. Repeat this step three times to ensure the egg yolks are thoroughly tempered. 4. Gradually add the tempered eggs to the cream, whisking all the while. Then, add the vanilla and whisk once more. 5. Pour the cream mixture into the ramekins, with each ramekin containing ½ cup of liquid. Cover each ramekin with aluminum foil. 6. Insert the trivet into the Instant Pot. Add water to the pot. Carefully place the ramekins on top of the trivet. 7. Close the lid of the Instant Pot. Select the Manual mode and set the cooking time at High Pressure for 11 minutes. 8. When the timer beeps, perform a natural release for 15 minutes. Then, release any remaining pressure and open the lid. 9. Carefully remove a ramekin from the pot. Remove the foil and check if it is done. The custard should be mostly set, with a slightly jiggly center. 10. Place all the ramekins in the refrigerator for 2 hours to chill and set. Serve the custard chilled.

Coconut Almond Cream Cake

Prep time: 10 minutes | Cook time: 40 minutes | Serves 8

- Nonstick cooking spray
- 1 cup almond flour
- ½ cup unsweetened shredded coconut
- ⅓ cup Swerve
- 1 teaspoon baking powder
- 1 teaspoon apple pie spice
- 2 eggs, lightly whisked
- ¼ cup unsalted butter, melted
- ½ cup heavy (whipping) cream

1. Start by applying a coating of cooking spray to a 6-inch round cake pan. 2. In a medium-sized bowl, combine the almond flour, coconut, Swerve, baking powder, and apple pie spice, mixing them thoroughly. 3. Gradually add the eggs to the mixture, followed by the butter and then the cream, ensuring each ingredient is well incorporated before adding the next. 4. Transfer the resulting batter into the greased pan and cover it tightly with aluminum foil. 5. Pour 2 cups of water into the inner pot of the Instant Pot, place a trivet inside, and set the cake pan atop the trivet. 6. Secure the lid of the Instant Pot, select the Manual setting, set the pressure to High, and cook for 40 minutes. After the cooking time ends, allow the pressure to release naturally for 10 minutes before performing a quick release to vent any remaining steam, then carefully unlock the lid. 7. Gently remove the pan from the Instant Pot and let the cake cool for 15 to 20 minutes. Invert the cake onto a serving plate and, if desired, garnish with shredded coconut, almond slices, or a dusting of powdered sweetener before serving.

Nutmeg Cupcakes

Prep time: 5 minutes | Cook time: 30 minutes | Serves 7

- Cake:
- 2 cups blanched almond flour
- 2 tablespoons grass-fed butter, softened
- 2 eggs
- ½ cup unsweetened almond milk
- ½ cup Swerve, or more to taste
- ½ teaspoon ground nutmeg
- ½ teaspoon baking powder
- Frosting:
- 4 ounces (113 g) full-fat cream cheese, softened
- 4 tablespoons grass-fed butter, softened
- 2 cups heavy whipping cream
- 1 teaspoon vanilla extract
- ½ cup Swerve, or more to taste
- 6 tablespoons sugar-free chocolate chips (optional)

1. Pour 1 cup of filtered water into the inner pot of the Instant Pot, and then insert the trivet. In a large bowl, mix together the flour, butter, eggs, almond milk, Swerve, nutmeg, and baking powder. Stir the mixture thoroughly. If necessary, work in batches to transfer the mixture into a well-greased muffin (or egg bites) mold that is compatible with the Instant Pot. 2. Put the molds onto the trivet and cover them loosely with aluminum foil. Close the lid, set the pressure release to Sealing, and select the Manual function. Set the Instant Pot to cook at High Pressure for 30 minutes. 3. While waiting, combine the cream cheese, butter, whipping cream, vanilla, Swerve, and chocolate chips in a large bowl. Use an electric hand mixer to blend until a light and fluffy texture is achieved. Put the frosting in the refrigerator. 4. Once the cupcakes have finished cooking, let the pressure release naturally for approximately 10 minutes. Then, switch the pressure release to Venting. Open the Instant Pot and take out the food. Let it cool, and then evenly top each cupcake with a scoop of frosting.

Traditional Kentucky Butter Cake

Prep time: 5 minutes | Cook time: 35 minutes | Serves 4

- 2 cups almond flour
- ¾ cup granulated erythritol
- 1½ teaspoons baking powder
- 4 eggs
- 1 tablespoon vanilla extract
- ½ cup butter, melted
- Cooking spray
- ½ cup water

1. In a medium bowl, thoroughly mix the almond flour, erythritol, and baking powder by whisking. Whisk vigorously to ensure there are no lumps left. 2. Incorporate the eggs and vanilla into the mixture, whisking until they are evenly distributed. 3. Add the butter and continue whisking until the batter attains a mostly smooth and well-combined texture. 4. Coat the pan with cooking spray and pour the batter into it. Then, tightly cover the pan with aluminum foil. 5. Pour water into the pot. Place the Bundt pan on the trivet and carefully lower it into the pot. 6. Secure the lid in place. Select the Manual mode and set the cooking time to 35 minutes at High Pressure. When the timer finishes, perform a quick pressure release. Open the lid with caution. 7. Take the pan out of the pot. Allow the cake to cool while it is still in the pan before turning it out onto a plate.

Lemon-Ricotta Cheesecake

Prep time: 10 minutes | Cook time: 30 minutes | Serves 6

- Unsalted butter or vegetable oil, for greasing the pan
- 8 ounces (227 g) cream cheese, at room temperature
- ¼ cup plus 1 teaspoon Swerve, plus more as needed
- ⅓ cup full-fat or part-skim ricotta cheese, at room temperature
- Zest of 1 lemon
- Juice of 1 lemon
- ½ teaspoon lemon extract
- 2 eggs, at room temperature
- 2 tablespoons sour cream

1. Thoroughly grease a 6-inch springform pan. It is most easily done by using a silicone basting brush, which allows one to reach all the crevices. Alternatively, you can line the pan's sides with parchment paper. 2. In the bowl of a stand mixer, blend the cream cheese, ¼ cup of Swerve, ricotta, lemon zest, lemon juice, and lemon extract at high speed until a perfectly smooth mixture without any lumps is achieved. 3. Taste the blend to see if the sweetness meets your preference and adjust accordingly if required. 4. Add the eggs, then lower the speed and blend gently until the eggs are just incorporated. Overbeating at this stage can lead to a cracked crust. 5. Pour the mixture into the prepared pan and cover it using either aluminum foil or a silicone lid. 6. Pour 2 cups of water into the inner cooking pot of the Instant Pot, and then place a trivet in the pot. Put the covered pan on the trivet. 7. Lock the lid firmly. Select the Manual option and set the pressure to High. Cook for 30 minutes. After the cooking is completed, let the pressure release naturally. Unlock the lid. 8. Carefully remove the pan from the pot and take off the foil. 9. In a small bowl, mix the sour cream with the remaining 1 teaspoon of Swerve and spread the mixture over the top of the warm cake. 10. Refrigerate the cheesecake for 6 to 8 hours. Do not rush! The cheesecake needs this time to reach its optimal state.

Ultimate Chocolate Cheesecake

Prep time: 10 minutes | Cook time: 50 minutes | Serves 12

- 2 cups pecans
- 2 tablespoons butter
- 16 ounces (454 g) cream cheese, softened
- 1 cup powdered erythritol
- ¼ cup sour cream
- 2 tablespoons cocoa powder
- 2 teaspoons vanilla extract
- 2 cups low-carb chocolate chips
- 1 tablespoon coconut oil
- 2 eggs
- 2 cups water

1. Begin by preheating the oven to 400°F (205°C). Subsequently, place the pecans and butter into a food processor and pulse until a dough-like consistency is achieved. After that, press the mixture into the base of a 7-inch springform pan. Bake the mixture for 10 minutes and then set it aside to cool. 2. While the crust is being baked, in a large bowl, mix the cream cheese, erythritol, sour cream, cocoa powder, and vanilla together using a rubber spatula. Set this mixture aside. 3. In a medium bowl, combine the chocolate chips and coconut oil. Microwave the combination in 20-second increments until the chocolate starts to melt, and then stir until the mixture is smooth. Gently fold this chocolate mixture into the cheesecake mixture. 4. Add the eggs and fold them in gently, taking care not to overmix. Pour the resultant mixture over the cooled pecan crust and cover it with foil. 5. Pour water into the Instant Pot and place a steam rack at the bottom. Put the cheesecake on the steam rack and close the lid by clicking it. Press the Manual button and adjust the time to 40 minutes. When the timer sounds, allow the pressure to release naturally. Carefully remove the cheesecake and let it cool completely. Serve it chilled.

Deconstructed Tiramisu

Prep time: 5 minutes | Cook time: 9 minutes | Serves 4

- 1 cup heavy cream (or full-fat coconut milk for dairy-free)
- 2 large egg yolks
- 2 tablespoons brewed decaf espresso or strong brewed coffee
- 2 tablespoons Swerve, or more to taste
- 1 teaspoon rum extract
- 1 teaspoon unsweetened cocoa powder, or more to taste
- Pinch of fine sea salt
- 1 cup cold water
- 4 teaspoons Swerve, for topping

1. Put the cream in a pan and heat it over medium-high heat until it becomes hot, which usually takes approximately 2 minutes. Stir it occasionally to ensure even heating. 2. Put the egg yolks, coffee, sweetener, rum extract, cocoa powder, and salt into a blender. Blend these ingredients at a high speed until a smooth and consistent mixture is obtained. Ensure there are no lumps left in the mixture. 3. While the blender is running, gradually pour the hot cream into it. Stop the blender after adding all the cream, then taste the mixture. Adjust the sweetness by adding more sweetener if necessary. If a stronger chocolate flavor is desired, add a bit more cocoa powder at this stage. 4. Use a spatula to carefully scoop the prepared mixture into four ramekins. Ensure that the mixture is evenly distributed among the ramekins. Then, cover each ramekin tightly with aluminum foil. 5. Insert a trivet at the bottom of the Instant Pot. Pour in an appropriate amount of water. Place the ramekins on the trivet, ensuring they are stable and won't tip over. 6. Securely lock the lid of the Instant Pot. Go to the control panel and select the Manual mode. Set the cooking time to 7 minutes under High Pressure. Start the cooking process. 7. When the timer indicates that the cooking time is up, perform a quick pressure release to let the pressure out. Do this carefully to avoid any potential splashes. After the pressure is released, carefully remove the lid. 8. Keep the ramekins covered with the aluminum foil and transfer them to the refrigerator. Leave them there for around 2 hours, or until they are completely chilled. This will help the mixture set properly. 9. Take the ramekins out of the refrigerator after chilling. Sprinkle 1 teaspoon of Swerve evenly on top of each tiramisu. Then, place them under the oven broiler. The heat from the broiler will melt the sweetener, creating a nice topping. Keep an eye on the process to prevent burning. 10. After melting the sweetener, put the ramekins back into the fridge. Let the topping cool and set for about 20 minutes. This step is important to ensure the topping solidifies. 11. Once everything is ready, serve the tiramisu. Add some extra decorations if desired, such as chocolate shavings or a dollop of whipped cream on top.

Spiced Pear Applesauce

Prep time: 15 minutes | Cook time: 5 minutes | Makes: 3½ cups

- 1 pound pears, peeled, cored, and sliced
- 2 teaspoons apple pie spice or cinnamon
- Pinch kosher salt
- Juice of ½ small lemon

1. In the electric pressure cooker, mix the apples, pears, apple pie spice, salt, lemon juice, and ¼ cup of water. 2. Close and secure the lid of the pressure cooker. Adjust the valve to the sealing setting. 3. Cook under high pressure for 5 minutes. 4. Once the cooking is done, press the Cancel button and allow the pressure to release in a natural way. 5. After the pin drops, unlock and take off the lid. 6. Use a potato masher to mash the apples and pears until they reach your desired consistency. 7. Serve the dish while it is still warm, or let it cool down to room temperature and then put it in the refrigerator.

Vanilla Crème Brûlée

Prep time: 7 minutes | Cook time: 9 minutes | Serves 4

- 1 cup heavy cream (or full-fat coconut milk for dairy-free)
- 2 large egg yolks
- 2 tablespoons Swerve, or more to taste
- Seeds scraped from
- ½ vanilla bean (about 8 inches long), or 1 teaspoon vanilla extract
- 1 cup cold water
- 4 teaspoons Swerve, for topping

1. Warm the cream in a saucepan over medium-high heat until it becomes hot, approximately 2 minutes. 2. In a blender, combine the egg yolks, Swerve, and vanilla seeds, then blend until the mixture is smooth. 3. While the blender is operating, gradually stream in the heated cream. Taste the mixture and adjust the sweetness to your preference. 4. Using a spatula, evenly distribute the custard into four ramekins. 5. Pour water into the Instant Pot and place a trivet inside. 6. Secure the lid, select Manual mode, and set the pressure to cook for 7 minutes on High Pressure. 7. Once the timer signals, perform a quick pressure release and carefully open the lid. 8. Keep the ramekins covered with foil and refrigerate them for about 2 hours until they are fully chilled. 9. Sprinkle 1 teaspoon of Swerve over the top of each crème brûlée and use the oven broiler to caramelize the sweetener. 10. Allow the topping to cool in the refrigerator for 5 minutes before serving.

Goat Cheese–Stuffed Pears

Prep time: 6 minutes | Cook time: 2 minutes | Serves 4

- 2 ounces goat cheese, at room temperature
- 2 teaspoons pure maple syrup
- 2 ripe, firm pears, halved lengthwise and cored
- 2 tablespoons chopped pistachios, toasted

1. Fill the electric pressure cooker with 1 cup of water and insert a wire rack or trivet into it. 2. In a small bowl, blend the goat cheese and maple syrup together. n3. Scoop the goat cheese mixture into the pear halves from which the cores have been removed. Position the pears on the rack within the pot, with the cut side facing upward. 4. Securely close and lock the lid of the pressure cooker. Set the valve to the sealing state. 5. Cook at high pressure for a duration of 2 minutes. 6. When the cooking process is finished, press the Cancel button and initiate a quick pressure release. 7. Once the pressure indicator pin has dropped, unlock the lid and take it off. 8. With the help of tongs, carefully transfer the pears onto serving plates. 9. Sprinkle pistachios over the pears and serve promptly.

Southern Almond Pie

Prep time: 10 minutes | Cook time: 35 minutes | Serves 12

- 2 cups almond flour
- 1½ cups powdered erythritol
- 1 teaspoon baking powder
- Pinch of salt
- ½ cup sour cream
- 4 tablespoons butter, melted
- 1 egg
- 1 teaspoon vanilla extract
- Cooking spray
- 1½ teaspoons ground cinnamon
- 1½ teaspoons Swerve
- 1 cup water

1. In a spacious mixing bowl, whisk together the almond flour, powdered erythritol, baking powder, and salt. 2. Blend in the sour cream, butter, egg, and vanilla, stirring until the mixture is thoroughly combined; the batter will become exceptionally thick, almost akin to cookie dough. 3. Lightly grease the baking dish with cooking spray and optionally line it with parchment paper for easier removal. 4. Pour the dense batter into the prepared dish and smooth the top using an offset spatula. 5. In a separate small bowl, mix the cinnamon and Swerve, then evenly sprinkle this blend over the batter's surface. 6. Securely cover the dish with aluminum foil, add water to the pot, place the trivet inside, and carefully lower the dish onto the trivet. 7. Close and seal the lid, select Manual mode, set the pressure to High, and cook for 35 minutes; once the timer finishes, perform a quick pressure release and cautiously open the lid. 8. Remove both the trivet and the pie from the pot, take off the foil from the pan—the pie should be firm yet tender with a slightly cracked top. 9. Let the pie cool completely before slicing and serving.

Keto Brownies

Prep time: 15 minutes | Cook time: 15 minutes | Serves 8

- 1 cup coconut flour
- 1 tablespoon cocoa powder
- 1 tablespoon coconut oil
- 1 teaspoon vanilla extract
- 1 teaspoon baking powder
- 1 teaspoon apple cider vinegar
- ⅓ cup butter, melted
- 1 tablespoon erythritol
- 1 cup water, for cooking

1. In the mixing bowl, blend erythritol, melted butter, apple cider vinegar, baking powder, vanilla extract, coconut oil, and coconut flour together. 2. Stir the mixture vigorously until it attains a smooth consistency and transfer it into the baking pan. Use a spatula to even out the surface of the batter. 3. Pour water into the instant pot and insert the steamer rack inside. 4. Position the pan with the brownie batter onto the steamer rack. Close the lid tightly and ensure it is properly sealed. 5. Set the instant pot to Manual mode and cook the brownie at High Pressure for 15 minutes. 6. After that, let the pressure release naturally for 5 minutes. 7. Slice the cooked brownies into bars.

Vanilla Butter Curd

Prep time: 5 minutes | Cook time: 6 hours | Serves 3

- 4 egg yolks, whisked
- 2 tablespoon butter
- 1 tablespoon erythritol
- ½ cup organic almond milk
- 1 teaspoon vanilla extract

1. Switch the instant pot to Sauté mode and when the "Hot" indication appears, add the butter. M2. Melt the butter without bringing it to a boil, and then add the whisked egg yolks, almond milk, and vanilla extract. 3. Add erythritol and stir the mixture with a whisk. 4. Cook the meal on the Low setting for 6 hours.

Chapter 8 Desserts

Lime Muffins

Prep time: 10 minutes | Cook time: 15 minutes | Serves 6

- 1 teaspoon lime zest
- 1 tablespoon lemon juice
- 1 teaspoon baking powder
- 1 cup almond flour
- 2 eggs, beaten
- 1 tablespoon Swerve
- ¼ cup heavy cream
- 1 cup water, for cooking

1. Begin by whisking together the lemon juice, baking powder, almond flour, eggs, Swerve, and heavy cream in a mixing bowl until thoroughly combined. 2. Once the batter reaches a smooth consistency, incorporate the lime zest and stir well. 3. Evenly distribute the batter into the muffin molds. 4. Pour water into the Instant Pot and place the rack inside. 5. Carefully set the filled muffin molds on top of the rack. 6. Securely close and seal the Instant Pot lid. 7. Select the Manual setting, choose High Pressure, and set the timer for 15 minutes. 8. After the cooking time has elapsed, allow the pressure to release naturally.

Daikon and Almond Cake

Prep time: 10 minutes | Cook time: 45 minutes | Serves 12

- 5 eggs, beaten
- ½ cup heavy cream
- 1 cup almond flour
- 1 daikon, diced
- 1 teaspoon ground cinnamon
- 2 tablespoon erythritol
- 1 tablespoon butter, melted
- 1 cup water

1. Begin by whisking together the eggs, heavy cream, almond flour, ground cinnamon, and erythritol in a mixing bowl until thoroughly blended. 2. Once the mixture achieves a smooth consistency, gently fold in the daikon using a spatula to ensure it is evenly distributed. 3. Transfer the batter into the prepared cake pan, spreading it out uniformly. 4. Pour water into the Instant Pot and place the trivet inside. 5. Carefully position the cake pan on top of the trivet within the Instant Pot. 6. Securely close the lid, select the Manual setting, and set the timer for 45 minutes on High Pressure. After the cooking cycle completes, perform a quick pressure release and cautiously open the lid. 7. Remove the cake from the Instant Pot and serve it immediately.

Pecan Pumpkin Pie

Prep time: 5 minutes | Cook time: 40 minutes | Serves 5 to 6

- Base:
- 2 tablespoons grass-fed butter, softened
- 1 cup blanched almond flour
- ½ cup chopped pecans
- Topping:
- ½ cup Swerve, or more to taste
- ⅓ cup heavy whipping cream
- ½ teaspoon ground cinnamon
- ½ teaspoon ginger, finely grated
- ½ teaspoon ground nutmeg
- ½ teaspoon ground cloves
- 1 (14-ounce / 397-g) can organic pumpkin purée
- 1 egg

1. Pour 1 cup of filtered water into the inner pot of the Instant Pot, and then insert the trivet. Use an electric mixer to combine the butter, almond flour, and pecans, mixing thoroughly. Transfer the mixture into a well-greased, Instant Pot-friendly pan, form a crust at the bottom of the pan, and apply a slight coating on the sides, then freeze for 15 minutes. In a large bowl, thoroughly combine the topping ingredients. 2. Take the pan out of the freezer, add the topping evenly, and place the pan onto the trivet. Cover it loosely with aluminum foil. Close the lid, set the pressure release to Sealing, and select the Manual function. Set the Instant Pot to 40 minutes on High Pressure. 3. Once cooked, let the pressure release naturally from the Instant Pot for about 10 minutes, then carefully switch the pressure release to Venting. 4. Open the Instant Pot and remove the pan. Cool in the refrigerator for 4 to 5 hours, serve, and enjoy!

Appendix 1
Instant Pot Cooking Timetable

Dried Beans, Legumes and Lentils

Dried Beans and Legume	Dry (Minutes)	Soaked (Minutes)
Soy beans	25 – 30	20 – 25
Scarlet runner	20 – 25	10 – 15
Pinto beans	25 – 30	20 – 25
Peas	15 – 20	10 – 15
Navy beans	25 – 30	20 – 25
Lima beans	20 – 25	10 – 15
Lentils, split, yellow (moong dal)	15 – 18	N/A
Lentils, split, red	15 – 18	N/A
Lentils, mini, green (brown)	15 – 20	N/A
Lentils, French green	15 – 20	N/A
Kidney white beans	35 – 40	20 – 25
Kidney red beans	25 – 30	20 – 25
Great Northern beans	25 – 30	20 – 25
Pigeon peas	20 – 25	15 – 20
Chickpeas (garbanzo bean chickpeas)	35 – 40	20 – 25
Cannellini beans	35 – 40	20 – 25
Black-eyed peas	20 – 25	10 – 15
Black beans	20 – 25	10 – 15

Fish and Seafood

Fish and Seafood	Fresh (minutes)	Frozen (minutes)
Shrimp or Prawn	1 to 2	2 to 3
Seafood soup or stock	6 to 7	7 to 9
Mussels	2 to 3	4 to 6
Lobster	3 to 4	4 to 6
Fish, whole (snapper, trout, etc.)	5 to 6	7 to 10
Fish steak	3 to 4	4 to 6
Fish fillet,	2 to 3	3 to 4
Crab	3 to 4	5 to 6

Fruits

Fruits	Fresh (in Minutes)	Dried (in Minutes)
Raisins	N/A	4 to 5
Prunes	2 to 3	4 to 5
Pears, whole	3 to 4	4 to 6
Pears, slices or halves	2 to 3	4 to 5
Peaches	2 to 3	4 to 5
Apricots, whole or halves	2 to 3	3 to 4
Apples, whole	3 to 4	4 to 6
Apples, in slices or pieces	2 to 3	3 to 4

Meat

Meat and Cuts	Cooking Time (minutes)	Meat and Cuts	Cooking Time (minutes)
Veal, roast	35 to 45	Duck, with bones, cut up	10 to 12
Veal, chops	5 to 8	Cornish Hen, whole	10 to 15
Turkey, drumsticks (leg)	15 to 20	Chicken, whole	20 to 25
Turkey, breast, whole, with bones	25 to 30	Chicken, legs, drumsticks, or thighs	10 to 15
Turkey, breast, boneless	15 to 20	Chicken, with bones, cut up	10 to 15
Quail, whole	8 to 10	Chicken, breasts	8 to 10
Pork, ribs	20 to 25	Beef, stew	15 to 20
Pork, loin roast	55 to 60	Beef, shanks	25 to 30
Pork, butt roast	45 to 50	Beef, ribs	25 to 30
Pheasant	20 to 25	Beef, steak, pot roast, round, rump, brisket or blade, small chunks, chuck,	25 to 30
Lamb, stew meat	10 to 15		
Lamb, leg	35 to 45	Beef, pot roast, steak, rump, round, chuck, blade or brisket, large	35 to 40
Lamb, cubes,	10 t0 15		
Ham slice	9 to 12	Beef, ox-tail	40 to 50
Ham picnic shoulder	25 to 30	Beef, meatball	10 to 15
Duck, whole	25 to 30	Beef, dressed	20 to 25

Appendix 2

INDEX

A

Ahi Tuna and Cherry Tomato Salad ··············· 51
Albóndigas Sinaloenses ·············· 21
Almond Butter Blondies ·············· 93
Ann's Italian Hunter Chicken ·············· 35
Apple Cider Pecan Chicken ·············· 39
Aromatic Monkfish Stew ·············· 44
Asparagus and Kale Stir-Fry ·············· 86
Asparagus in Creamy Cheese Sauce ·············· 85
Assorted Vegetable Mix ·············· 79
Avocado and Serrano Chile Soup ·············· 75
Avocado Super Green Power Bowl ·············· 12

B

Bacon Broccoli Soup ·············· 69
Bacon Curry Soup ·············· 74
Bacon Lettuce and Tomato Chicken Salad ·············· 33
Bacon Spinach Eggs ·············· 15
Bacon-Wrapped Egg Cups ·············· 10
Bacon, Leek, and Cauliflower Soup ·············· 68
Baked Eggs with Parmesan ·············· 8
Basic Nutritional Values ·············· 26
Bavarian Beef ·············· 28
BBQ Pulled Chicken ·············· 36
BBQ Ribs and Broccoli Slaw ·············· 24
Beef and Eggplant Tagine ·············· 67
Beef and Mushroom Stew ·············· 75
Beef and Sausage Medley ·············· 21
Beef Brisket with Cabbage ·············· 18
Beef Cheeseburger Pie ·············· 22
Beef Meatball Minestrone ·············· 71
Beef Ribs with Radishes ·············· 21
Bite-sized Chocolate Chip Muffins ·············· 10
Blackberry Baked Brie ·············· 56
Blackberry Crisp ·············· 90
Blackberry Vanilla Delight Cake ·············· 16
Blade Pork with Sauerkraut ·············· 22
Blue Cheese Mushroom Soup ·············· 69
Boiled Peanuts ·············· 57

Bone Broth Brisket with Tomatoes ·············· 27
Braised Radishes and Sugar Snap Peas with Dukkah Spice 84
Braised Striped Bass with Zucchini and Tomatoes ·············· 45
Breakfast Casserole with Sausage and Cauliflower ·············· 12
Broccoli and Bacon Cheese Soup ·············· 77
Broccoli and Cabbage Slaw ·············· 62
Broccoli and Red Feta Soup ·············· 69
Broccoli Cheddar Egg Muffins ·············· 10
Broccoli Cheddar Soup ·············· 70
Broccoli in Garlic-Herb & Cheese Sauce ·············· 60
Brussels Sprouts in Lemon Dressing with Poppy Seeds 80
Brussels Sprouts with Garlic and Almonds ·············· 85
Buffalo Chicken Meatballs ·············· 56
Buffalo Chicken Soup ·············· 65
Butter-basted Whole Cauliflower ·············· 87
Buttercup Squash Soup ·············· 67
Butternut Squash Soup ·············· 68

C

Cabbage and Pork Soup ·············· 71
Cabbage and Tempeh with Lemon ·············· 80
Cabbage Roll Soup ·············· 73
Cabbage with Thyme ·············· 84
Cajun Cod Fillet ·············· 49
Candied Mixed Nuts ·············· 95
Caramelized Pumpkin Cheesecake ·············· 92
Carnitas Burrito Bowls ·············· 23
Casablanca-Style Chicken ·············· 34
Cauliflower Cheese Macaroni ·············· 86
Cauliflower Fritters with Cheese ·············· 56
Cauliflower Puree with Parmesan ·············· 81
Cayenne Cod ·············· 45
Chanterelle and Cheddar Mushrooms ·············· 82
Cheese Stuffed Bell Peppers ·············· 55
Cheese Zucchini Tots ·············· 60
Cheesesteak Stuffed Peppers ·············· 28
Cheesy Broccoli Dip ·············· 62
Cheesy Cauliflower Bites ·············· 59
Cheesy Mushroom Baked Chicken ·············· 35

Cheesy Pancetta & Pizza Dip	61
Cheesy Vegetable Casserole	9
Chicken and Asparagus Soup	73
Chicken and Green Cabbage Meatballs	39
Chicken and Kale Soup	67
Chicken Brunswick Stew	71
Chicken Cabbage Salad	62
Chicken Celery Salad with Mayo	62
Chicken Meatball Thai Yellow Curry	40
Chicken Noodle Soup	64
Chicken Poblano Pepper Soup	70
Chicken Stuffed with Bruschetta and Cheese	39
Chicken Vegetable Soup	70
Chicken with Lemon, Fingerling Potatoes & Olives	34
Chicken Zucchini Soup	64
Chile Verde Pulled Pork with Tomatillos	18
Chili and Turmeric Haddock	43
Chili Pork Loin	18
Chinese Pe-Tsai and Onion Stir-fry	84
Chinese Spare Ribs	56
Chipotle Black Bean Brownies	91
Chocolate Cake with Walnuts	95
Chocolate Chip Banana Cake	96
Chocolate Chip Fluffy Pancake	11
Chunky Fish Soup with Tomatoes	51
Cider-Herb Pork Tenderloin	20
Cilantro Pork	25
Cinnamon Roll Cheesecake	93
Classic Cinnamon Swirl Coffee Cake	9
Classic Hard-boiled Eggs	8
Cocoa Cookies	90
Cocoa Custard	92
Coconut Almond Cream Cake	97
Coconut Cajun Shrimp	58
Coconut Milk-Braised Squid	45
Coconut Squares	95
Cod with Warm Tabbouleh Salad	52
Colby Pepper Cheese Dip	58
Cranberry Almond Creamy Grits	8
Creamy Chicken Wild Rice Soup	64
Creamy Coconut Chicken Curry	31
Creamy Kale Omelet	16
Creamy Onion and Spinach	58
Creamy Pork Liver	20
Creamy Soft Scrambled Eggs	13
Creamy Spinach Dish	59
Creamy Sweet Potato Soup	75
Crispy Brussels Sprouts with Bacon	57

Crispy Parmesan Chicken	38
Crispy Parmesan Zucchini Fries	62
Crunchy Blueberry Almond Cereal	7
Cuban Pork Shoulder	27
Curried Chicken Soup	73

D

Daikon and Almond Cake	101
Deconstructed Tiramisu	99
Delicate Poached Eggs	13
Delicious Roasted Garlic Bulbs	61
Dijon-Glazed Turkey	37
Dill Salmon Cakes	48
Divan-Style Broccoli Chicken	37

E

Easy Cauliflower Gnocch	85
Easy Chicken Masala	39
Easy Pot Roast and Vegetables	27
Easy Southern Brunswick Stew	70
Egg Custard Tarts	89
Egg Meatloaf	28
Egg-Stuffed Bell Peppers	14
Escabèche-Style Chicken	35
Fast Spring Kale Appetizer	54

F

Feta-Topped Chicken Thighs	38
Fiery Baked Feta Foil Packets	61
Fiery Cauliflower Florets	83
Filipino Pork Loin	24
Fish Bake with Veggies	44
Fish Packets with Pesto and Cheese	49
Fish Tagine	43
Flawless Sweet Potatoes	82
Flourless Chocolate Tortes	96
Foil-Pack Haddock with Spinach	52
Foil-Packet Salmon	46
French Dip Chuck Roast	19
French Market Soup	73
Fried Cheese Shell Chicken Tacos	32
Fudgy Walnut Brownies	89

G

Garam Masala Fish	44
Garlic Beef Soup	77
Garlic Butter Italian Sausages	28
Garlic Herb Butter	59

Garlic Tuna Casserole ⋯⋯⋯⋯⋯⋯⋯⋯⋯⋯⋯⋯⋯⋯⋯ 51
Garlic-Infused Rotisserie Chicken⋯⋯⋯⋯⋯⋯⋯ 40
Garlicky Chicken Soup ⋯⋯⋯⋯⋯⋯⋯⋯⋯⋯⋯⋯⋯ 74
Gigante Bean Soup with Celery and Olives ⋯⋯⋯⋯ 76
Glazed Pumpkin Bundt Cake ⋯⋯⋯⋯⋯⋯⋯⋯⋯⋯ 96
Goat Cheese–Stuffed Pears ⋯⋯⋯⋯⋯⋯⋯⋯⋯⋯ 100
Golden Bacon Sticks ⋯⋯⋯⋯⋯⋯⋯⋯⋯⋯⋯⋯⋯⋯ 29
Greek Yogurt Strawberry Pops ⋯⋯⋯⋯⋯⋯⋯⋯⋯ 94
Greek-Style Chicken ⋯⋯⋯⋯⋯⋯⋯⋯⋯⋯⋯⋯⋯⋯ 36
Green Beans, Potatoes, and Basil ⋯⋯⋯⋯⋯⋯⋯⋯ 86
Green Chile Corn Chowder ⋯⋯⋯⋯⋯⋯⋯⋯⋯⋯⋯ 74
Grilled Corn on the Cob ⋯⋯⋯⋯⋯⋯⋯⋯⋯⋯⋯⋯ 81
Ground Turkey Lettuce Cups ⋯⋯⋯⋯⋯⋯⋯⋯⋯⋯ 55

H

Haddock and Veggie Foil Packets ⋯⋯⋯⋯⋯⋯⋯⋯ 43
Halibut Stew with Bacon and Cheese ⋯⋯⋯⋯⋯⋯ 48
Ham and Baked Egg Delight ⋯⋯⋯⋯⋯⋯⋯⋯⋯⋯ 15
Hearty Crème Brûlée ⋯⋯⋯⋯⋯⋯⋯⋯⋯⋯⋯⋯⋯⋯ 97
Hearty Hamburger and Lentil Stew ⋯⋯⋯⋯⋯⋯⋯ 72
Hearty Porcupine Meatballs ⋯⋯⋯⋯⋯⋯⋯⋯⋯⋯ 58
Herb-Crusted Cod Steaks ⋯⋯⋯⋯⋯⋯⋯⋯⋯⋯⋯ 50
Herb-Infused Sausage Balls ⋯⋯⋯⋯⋯⋯⋯⋯⋯⋯ 61
Herb-Infused Shrimp ⋯⋯⋯⋯⋯⋯⋯⋯⋯⋯⋯⋯⋯ 60
Herbed Parsley Potatoes ⋯⋯⋯⋯⋯⋯⋯⋯⋯⋯⋯⋯ 79
Herbed Pork Roast with Asparagus ⋯⋯⋯⋯⋯⋯⋯ 26
Hot and Sour Soup ⋯⋯⋯⋯⋯⋯⋯⋯⋯⋯⋯⋯⋯⋯⋯ 72

I

Instant Pot Cooked Zucchini Sticks ⋯⋯⋯⋯⋯⋯⋯ 81
Instant Pot Perfect Boiled Eggs ⋯⋯⋯⋯⋯⋯⋯⋯⋯ 16
Instantly Good Beef Stew ⋯⋯⋯⋯⋯⋯⋯⋯⋯⋯⋯⋯ 66
Italian Foraged Mushrooms ⋯⋯⋯⋯⋯⋯⋯⋯⋯⋯ 86

J

Jalapeño Cream Chicken Dip ⋯⋯⋯⋯⋯⋯⋯⋯⋯⋯ 58
Jalapeño Poppers with Bacon ⋯⋯⋯⋯⋯⋯⋯⋯⋯⋯ 55

K

Kale Curry Soup ⋯⋯⋯⋯⋯⋯⋯⋯⋯⋯⋯⋯⋯⋯⋯⋯ 69
Keto Brownies ⋯⋯⋯⋯⋯⋯⋯⋯⋯⋯⋯⋯⋯⋯⋯⋯ 100
Korean Short Rib Lettuce Wraps ⋯⋯⋯⋯⋯⋯⋯⋯ 27

L

Lamb Koobideh ⋯⋯⋯⋯⋯⋯⋯⋯⋯⋯⋯⋯⋯⋯⋯⋯ 25
Lamb Sirloin Masala ⋯⋯⋯⋯⋯⋯⋯⋯⋯⋯⋯⋯⋯⋯ 26
Layered Seven Dip ⋯⋯⋯⋯⋯⋯⋯⋯⋯⋯⋯⋯⋯⋯⋯ 54
Lemon and Ricotta Torte ⋯⋯⋯⋯⋯⋯⋯⋯⋯⋯⋯⋯ 91

Lemon Butter Mahi Mahi ⋯⋯⋯⋯⋯⋯⋯⋯⋯⋯⋯⋯ 52
Lemon Salmon with Tomatoes ⋯⋯⋯⋯⋯⋯⋯⋯⋯⋯ 46
Lemon Shrimp Skewers ⋯⋯⋯⋯⋯⋯⋯⋯⋯⋯⋯⋯ 44
Lemon Vanilla Cheesecake ⋯⋯⋯⋯⋯⋯⋯⋯⋯⋯⋯ 90
Lemon-Flavored Artichokes ⋯⋯⋯⋯⋯⋯⋯⋯⋯⋯⋯ 59
Lemon-Ricotta Cheesecake ⋯⋯⋯⋯⋯⋯⋯⋯⋯⋯⋯ 98
Light and Fluffy Vanilla Pancakes ⋯⋯⋯⋯⋯⋯⋯⋯ 8
Lime Muffins ⋯⋯⋯⋯⋯⋯⋯⋯⋯⋯⋯⋯⋯⋯⋯⋯⋯ 101
Louisiana Shrimp Gumbo ⋯⋯⋯⋯⋯⋯⋯⋯⋯⋯⋯⋯ 48

M

Mackerel and Broccoli Casserole ⋯⋯⋯⋯⋯⋯⋯⋯ 50
Mahi-Mahi Fillets with Peppers ⋯⋯⋯⋯⋯⋯⋯⋯⋯ 45
Masala Gobi ⋯⋯⋯⋯⋯⋯⋯⋯⋯⋯⋯⋯⋯⋯⋯⋯⋯⋯ 82
Mascarpone Tilapia with Nutmeg ⋯⋯⋯⋯⋯⋯⋯⋯ 46
Mediterranean Salmon with Whole-Wheat Couscous ⋯ 47
Mexican-Style Chicken Carnitas ⋯⋯⋯⋯⋯⋯⋯⋯⋯ 36
Mississippi Pork Butt Roast ⋯⋯⋯⋯⋯⋯⋯⋯⋯⋯⋯ 19
Mixed Greens Chicken Salad ⋯⋯⋯⋯⋯⋯⋯⋯⋯⋯ 34
Mixed Vegetable Curry ⋯⋯⋯⋯⋯⋯⋯⋯⋯⋯⋯⋯⋯ 80
Morning Crunch Cereal ⋯⋯⋯⋯⋯⋯⋯⋯⋯⋯⋯⋯⋯ 14
Moroccan Lamb Stew ⋯⋯⋯⋯⋯⋯⋯⋯⋯⋯⋯⋯⋯⋯ 18
Moroccan-Spiced Chicken Tagine ⋯⋯⋯⋯⋯⋯⋯⋯ 36
Mushroom and Bacon Quiche Lorraine ⋯⋯⋯⋯⋯ 13
Mushroom and Tomato Braised Chicken ⋯⋯⋯⋯⋯ 37
Mushrooms Filled with Cheese ⋯⋯⋯⋯⋯⋯⋯⋯⋯ 57

N

Nancy's Vegetable Beef Soup ⋯⋯⋯⋯⋯⋯⋯⋯⋯⋯ 76
Nutmeg Cupcakes ⋯⋯⋯⋯⋯⋯⋯⋯⋯⋯⋯⋯⋯⋯⋯ 97
Nutmeg-Infused Creamy Chicken ⋯⋯⋯⋯⋯⋯⋯⋯ 35
Nutty Cauliflower Porridge ⋯⋯⋯⋯⋯⋯⋯⋯⋯⋯⋯⋯ 7
Nutty Slow-Cooked Granola ⋯⋯⋯⋯⋯⋯⋯⋯⋯⋯⋯ 12

O

Orange and Dill-infused Beet & Watercress Salad ⋯⋯ 83
Osso Buco with Gremolata ⋯⋯⋯⋯⋯⋯⋯⋯⋯⋯⋯ 25

P

Parmesan Chicken Balls with Chives ⋯⋯⋯⋯⋯⋯⋯ 54
Parmesan Zucchini Noodles ⋯⋯⋯⋯⋯⋯⋯⋯⋯⋯⋯ 83
Pecan Pumpkin Pie ⋯⋯⋯⋯⋯⋯⋯⋯⋯⋯⋯⋯⋯⋯ 101
Pecan Walnut Crunch Granola ⋯⋯⋯⋯⋯⋯⋯⋯⋯⋯ 12
Peppers, Kale, and Feta Greek Frittata ⋯⋯⋯⋯⋯⋯ 11
Perch Fillets with Red Curry ⋯⋯⋯⋯⋯⋯⋯⋯⋯⋯ 50
Poblano-Spiced Chicken ⋯⋯⋯⋯⋯⋯⋯⋯⋯⋯⋯⋯ 40
Pork Breakfast Patties ⋯⋯⋯⋯⋯⋯⋯⋯⋯⋯⋯⋯⋯⋯ 8
Pork Chops in Creamy Mushroom Gravy ⋯⋯⋯⋯⋯ 19

Pork Meatballs with Thyme · 22
Pork Quill Egg Molds · 15
Pork Steaks with Pico de Gallo · 23
Pork Taco Casserole · 24
Pot Roast with Gravy and Vegetables · 19
Potato and Bacon Gratin · 10
Potato Shredded Omelet · 14
Provençal Chicken Soup · 65
Pulled Chicken · 37
Pumpkin Mini Mug Muffin · 15
Pumpkin Pie Pudding · 89
Pumpkin Pie Spice Pots De Crème · 95
Pumpkin Walnut Cheesecake · 94

Q

Quick Popcorn · 62
Quick Speedy Chicken Cacciatore · 33
Quick Steak Tacos · 20
Quinoa and Turkey with Unstuffed Bell Peppers · 32

R

Rosemary Baked Haddock · 43
Rosemary Catfish · 47
Rosemary Lamb Chops · 20

S

Salade Niçoise with Oil-Packed Tuna · 50
Salmon with Dill Butter · 48
Satarash Egg Dish · 83
Sauerkraut and Mushroom Bake · 80
Sautéed Broccoli with Garlic and Almonds · 79
Savory Garlic Meatballs · 60
Savory Italian Tomatillos · 60
Shepherd's Pie with Cauliflower-Carrot Mash · 29
Shredded Pork Hash · 13
Shrimp and Asparagus Risotto · 49
Shrimp and Bok Choy Salad Boats · 59
Shrimp Louie Salad with Thousand Island Dressing · 46
Shrimp Zoodle Alfredo · 51
Sicilian Fish Stew · 74
Smoked Salmon Asparagus Quiche Bites · 14
Smoked Salmon Coddled Egg Toasts · 9
Southern Almond Pie · 100
Southwest Avocado Frittata · 7
Spanish-Style Turkey Meatball Soup · 68
Spiced Cauliflower with Tomatoes · 81
Spiced Chicken Soup with Squash and Chickpeas · 66
Spiced Indian Okra · 79

Spiced Pear Applesauce · 99
Spiced Rub Whole Chicken · 32
Spicy Crack Chicken Breasts · 38
Spicy Kung Pao Chicken · 34
Spicy Mexican Beef Morning Chili · 7
Spicy Sausage and Chicken Stew · 65
Strawberry Cheesecake · 90
Strawberry Nut Millet Breakfast Bowl · 11
Sweet Candied Pecans · 57
Sweetly Caramelized Onions · 84
Swiss Chard and Chicken Soup · 67

T

Tapioca Berry Parfaits · 92
Texas-Style BBQ Chicken and Cabbage Slaw · 31
Tilapia Fillets with Arugula · 52
Tomato Paprika Chicken · 32
Tomato-Braised Chicken Legs · 39
Tomato-infused Spaghetti Squash Noodles · 82
Traditional Chicken Salad · 33
Traditional Kentucky Butter Cake · 98
Triple Cheese Quiche · 16
Trout Casserole · 48
Tuna Stuffed Poblano Peppers · 49
Tuna-Stuffed Deviled Eggs · 61
Turkey Tetrazzini · 38
Turmeric Pork Loin · 25
Turmeric Salmon · 47
Turmeric-infused Green Cabbage Stew · 85

U

Ultimate Chocolate Cheesecake · 98
Unstuffed Cabbage Soup · 66

V

Vanilla Butter Curd · 100
Vanilla Crème Brûlée · 99
Vanilla Poppy Seed Cake · 94
Vegetable and Cheese Frittata · 13
Venison and Tomato Stew · 76

W

Whole Chicken with Herbs and Lemon · 31
Wine-Braised Chicken · 41

Z

Zucchini Noodles with Sesame and Scallions · 84
Zucchini with Moroccan Spices · 81

Made in United States
North Haven, CT
15 April 2025